To the memory of Carl McGee, former Western Regional Director, who dedicated his life to the Little Leaguers of America and to: Tom Boyle—The Sage; Al Milham, Marcel Van Geren, Jim Chavez, Tony Monteleone, Jim Gerstenslager—The Heart; Merle Sanders—The Voice; Russ Tinsley—The Eyes; Bill Beebe, Ernie Lewis, Leo Mullen—The Will of Little League. To Creighton Hale—The Protector; Luke LaPorta, Al Herback, Al Price—The Spirit; Steve Keener—The Navigator, and to the hundreds of unheralded volunteers whose love has made Little League a safe haven and America a better place. Finally, to my very own coach, my dad.

A special thanks to Tommy and Jo Lasorda and Mike Scioscia. To the Dodger and Angel major league organizations that have helped Little League and the young boys and girls of America be all they can be. It is only through their mutual allegiance that baseball will remain America's national pastime.

A special thanks to Michael Josephson for allowing me to use his quote, "There is no victory without honor," in Chapter 15.

# Acknowledgments

Many thanks to my children, Vinnie, Kaycee and Michael, my sister Elaine, brothers Jon and Michael, and my wife, Gayle, whose wisdom kept me focused. Special thanks to my mom. Thanks also to Tommy Lasorda and his wife, Jo, and Mike Scioscia who helped make this book all it could be. To Lawrence Robinson who helped edit it, John Monteleone, my agent, and Dean Miller and everyone at Sports Publishing for all their advice and support.

# Life Lessons From Little League: Revisited

## A GUIDE FOR PARENTS AND COACHES

### Vincent M. Fortanasce, M.D.

COMMENTARY BY

TOMMY LASORDA

HALL OF FAMER,
SENIOR VICE PRESIDENT AND
FORMER MANAGER OF THE L.A. DODGERS

FOREWORD BY

MIKE SCIOSCIA

MANAGER OF THE 2002
WORLD CHAMPION ANGELS

SP
SPORTS
PUBLISHING
L.L.C.

www.SportsPublishingLLC.com

ISBN: 1-58261-909-3

Front cover photo courtesy of Al Herback and Al Price
Back cover photos courtesy of author

Publishers: Peter L. Bannon and Joseph J. Bannon Sr.
Senior managing editor: Susan M. Moyer
Acquisitions editor: Noah Adams Amstadter
Developmental editor: Dean Miller
Art director: K. Jeffrey Higgerson
Book design: Jennifer L. Polson
Cover design: Kenneth J. O'Brien
Photo editor: Erin Linden-Levy
Vice president of sales and marketing: Kevin King
Media and promotions managers:
    Nick Obradovich (regional)
    Randy Fouts (national)
    Maurey Williamson (print)

Printed in the United States

Sports Publishing L.L.C.
804 North Neil Street
Champaign, IL 61820

Phone: 1-877-424-2665
Fax: 217-363-2073
Web site: www.SportsPublishingLLC.com

# Contents

# Cleats in the Clay

Last night did I have a vision, or just one of my dreams?
Like an eagle, I hovered over a baseball diamond it seems.
A Little League field of manicured red clay.
A haven, a refuge, for young girls and boys to play!

In the crimson clay three distinct sets of footprints I saw,
Each set composed of one big pair and one cleated small.
Each pair set out from home plate to make three separate trails,
Two sets I saw falter but the third set prevails

The prevailing big 'n' small footprints seem to be having fun
Steadfast side by side, traveled toward the setting sun
I swooped down to see that the little cleated pair grew
Till at the horizon, I could not distinguish between the two.

Then I looked at the two faltering pair, the big footprints faded and vanished,
Leaving the little cleated pair alone, sad, tearful, and banished.
One little cleated pair began to wander aimlessly abandoned I could tell,
The third cleated pair burdened left deep rents in the clay then stumbled n' fell.

That morning my dream took meaning in the Little League Land
As I watched the Dads and children march hand in hand
One dad's face beamed joyfully in the rising sun
Encouraging, good try, nice swing, hey that's my son!

Then a Cherub child's face turned from glee to gloom,
One moment he felt cherished, the next abandoned, he felt doom.
As his dad left, yes vanished, not even saying good-bye,
To do something important, yes, I could see the child cry!

Some dads stayed as the Ump bellowed "Play Ball."
"Come on son, win! Be the best, make me ten feet tall.
"Fulfill my dreams, be all that I was not!
"You must do it son, though you're just a tot!"

Gently their coach said, "Have fun, you'll all do fine."

Then for the first time, I saw on each child a sign.

It said: "Dad don't leave me, dad don't burden me, don't make me stumble n' fall.

"Dad accept me, dad love me, and please, please watch me play ball!"

—Dr. Vincent Fortanasce

# Foreword

BY MIKE SCIOSCIA

MANAGER OF THE 2002 WORLD CHAMPION ANGELS

SOMEONE ONCE ASKED ME what words of wisdom I would have for my pitcher if he was facing Barry Bonds with the bases loaded and the World Series on the line. My answer was, "I'd say nothing other than 'Good luck.'" You see, at a moment of pressure like that, if my pitcher doesn't have the wisdom and the confidence already, then I haven't done my job as a coach. The same I believe is true of parenting.

I often get parents asking me questions such as: "What do I need to tell my child to make him a winner, to prepare him for the Major Leagues?"

First, I say there is nothing you can tell him, you must show him.

Second, prepare your child for life now by remembering that the best ethic is the work ethic; nothing great comes easy. It is not being the best but always trying your best that separates a child with confidence from one without it.

Third, teaching your child to play fairly with honesty is the only way to win. The clever or dishonest way is always the wrong way. That is, unfortunately, often the hardest lesson for fathers to learn.

Winning is fleeting and losing is never fatal. It is OK to lose. Learning to deal with failure is a fact of life. If I gave up every time I lost I wouldn't be manager of the Angels. It is because I never stop trying that I never stop believing in myself or in my team. That helps my team's confidence and has led to success. Similarly, if you never give up on your child, no matter the errors, no matter the strikeouts, if you offer unwavering acceptance and always see the positive in the fact that your child is trying, it will build his or her confidence and you will have a contented and happy child. It is the smile, the pat of reassurance and your presence that will see a child through the rest of his life. That is the legacy you want them to have. It is the legacy my mom and dad left me. Failure is only an opportunity to begin again more wisely. Nothing is impossible for a child who is loved. The surest way to ruining your child's chance for success is to judge them according to winning or losing or preparing them for the majors at twelve.

When you pray for your child don't ask for God to give him a light load but rather a strong back. Finally, remember God's help is hope. Always encourage your child's dreams and hopes but make sure they are your child's dreams, not yours.

My father taught me first to do what I must do then to try to do all I can do. If you can pass that on to your children, you'll soon see them do the impossible. All a child needs is guidance from his parents and coaches along with, as Dr. Vince says, your acceptance and positive attitude. If you want to know how to achieve this, well just read *Life Lessons From Little League: Revisited*. Dr. Fortanasce, Tommy Lasorda, Tommy John, Rod Dedeaux, Orel Hershiser, Dr. Frank Job (the Tommy John doctor) Micky Hagert and many Little League greats such as Luke LaPorta, Jim Chavez, Tony Monteleone, Mike Legg, Tom Boyle, Al Herback and Al Price will guide you through the best ways to make your child's Little League experience a winning one, regardless of the score at the end of a game.

Little League is above all about having fun. When in doubt about how to best teach your child, start with a smile. If you make your children laugh they will always want more. They will want to be around you and they will want to be like you. You will have a companion and a friend forever. It all starts at Little League's field of dreams.

Play ball!

# Introduction

## Why Read This Book?

*"No man can possibly know what life means, what the world means, what anything means until he has a child and loves it. And then the whole universe changes and nothing will again seem exactly as it seemed before."*

—Lafcadio Hearn (author)

**IT WAS PARENTS' NIGHT** at my seven-year-old's grammar school, three days after Father's Day. I was late again. "Tardy," is my middle name. I quickly grabbed my stethoscope and threw it around my neck, hoping anyone who noticed me walking in late would understand my lame excuse: I'm a busy doctor. To my dismay, not only were all the other fathers already there, sitting at their children's desks, but my son's desk was in the front row. I stumbled in and the desk gave a groan as I sat down, announcing my late arrival.

The father at the back of the room was reading a letter from his son entitled, "My Best Friend."

"My best friend tucks me in and tells me fun stories every night," he read. "My best friend is my dad." The line was greeted with an enthusiastic burst of applause. Mr. Clark shone with such pride his face could have lit up a moonless night.

Ms. Tuner, the teacher, directed her gentle voice at me. "Well Dr. Fortanasce, it's so nice to have you join us. I'm sure your duties at the hospital kept you."

I nodded humbly and tried to hide my golf shoes that I hadn't had time to change yet.

"We are reading some of the letters that the children wrote for father's day," she went on. "Would you like to share yours?"

I looked down at the desk and saw Vinnie's letter, written in his endearing, crooked print. My best friend can't wait to see me at night, it read. My best friend catches ball with me. My best friend is my dog, Ziggy.

The silence was deafening, broken only by the clank of my stethoscope as it hit the floor.

What would your child write? What would you like your child to write?

*Life Lessons From Little League: Revisited* is written by me: a psychiatrist, neurologist, ethicist, little league coach and often less than perfect parent, along with Major League and Little League greats such as Tommy Lasorda, Mike Scioscia, Orel Hershiser, Tommy John and the official international Little League coaches Al Herback and Al Price. I've compiled these life lessons of successful parenting and coaching, often learned the hard way, so that your child's journey through Little League can be as enjoyable and rewarding as possible.

Among the topics covered are new findings in the neurological and psychological development of children. Topics include the development of emotional IQ, (more important to success than verbal and mathematic IQ), brain maturation in children and teens (why your child may not listen to you, why children need dreams), the Ying and Yang of coaching (six-year-olds vs. six-teen-year-olds, boys vs. girls—they are not the same). We also look at parental development (have you matured?), violence in sports (the violent person on the field may be you—how to prepare yourself), why the spirit of the game should take precedence over the rules, and "Affuenza," the infection passed to children by over-indulgent parents. There is also a section on umpiring (umpires have feelings too) by Mike Legg and Tim Ward as well as the Four Simple Bases for successful parenting and coaching (they are foolproof) and the Four Reasons parents and coaches don't use them.

> *"This book is better than back-to-back World Series Championships. It's a perfect game plan for you and your child. It's about the real game, the field of life. Believe me, you only get one chance to do it right. You wouldn't send your child out on the field without a good glove. Mom and Dad, you need to be equipped too.* **Life Lessons from Little League** *will help you give your child the game to succeed in life."*
>
> —**Tommy Lasorda**

# 1

## WHOSE DREAM IS IT ANYWAY?

*"Every journey begins with a first step and a dream."*

—Tom Boyle

KENNY LOOKED UP AT HIS MOTHER as she poured his orange juice into a mug with a picture of Eminem on the side. His huge smile could have brightened the darkest of rooms. "Mom, Mom!" he yelled at her.

"What is it?" she asked.

"I know what I want to be when I grow up! I want to be like Sammy Sosa!" His eyes sparkled like fireflies over the desert.

His mother sighed. "He's not another rapper, is he?"

"No, Mom, he's the greatest baseball player ever! I'm gonna be just like him." He spoke his words with the absolute certainty that only a child can manage when talking about his dreams. "Can I get a baseball and a poster of him? I'll clean my room every day. Every day, forever. I promise."

Kenny's mom, a successful accountant, sighed again and, in the cold tone only a disillusioned parent can ever seem to manage, said, "No. Stop daydreaming. You've never even played baseball before, how can you be the greatest player? Now finish your breakfast and practice your math and maybe you'll get a good job someday."

The twinkle in Kenny's eye dimmed and his smile turned to a frown. "It's only study and hard work that will help you make something of your life," his mother said. "It's a degree you need, not a poster!"

A single tear tracked slowly down Kenny's cheek. In a few thoughtless words, both Kenny and his dream had been crushed.

## Dreams

Dreams are important to children. They're inspirational. They may be childhood dreams—to be a major league baseball player, a rock star or an astronaut—but children read about these people, they see them on TV or in the movies, and they are excited by the possibilities. It's what they talk about at school with their friends. These dreams, however unlikely they may seem, provide a child with motivation and direction. The longest journey begins with a single step, and for a child that first step is often an unlikely dream. Nurture that dream and it will bring pleasure, purpose, and a spirit of determination to your child. Success in life isn't measured simply by a diploma or a college degree but by the degree of happiness in life.

Childhood dreams change with age, of course, just as boys hate girls at age eight but think of little else by age 18. The concept of a dream, a goal, is one of the most important motivating forces to develop in a child. Just remember never to crush your child's dream with adult practicalities.

## What Today Is a Dream, May Tomorrow Be a Reality

Peter dreamed of being a ball player like the great Cal Ripken. The reality was that Peter didn't have the speed of a rabbit but that of a tortoise, and as for his eye-hand coordination, well let's just say it was doubtful he would ever win a Gold Glove award. However, his parents were always supportive of his dreams. They took him to see Ripken play. They helped Peter pin a giant poster of Ripken on his bedroom wall and encouraged him to work hard on his game. Peter was focused and happy. He had his dream, and it was of someone who never gave up.

Ten years later, of course, Peter's dreamed changed. He now wanted to be a doctor. He went after that dream with the same zeal that he had pursued his dream of being a baseball player. He graduated medical school at the top of his class. His parents taught him as a child to follow his dream. They taught him that he could do whatever he set his mind to do. And Peter did just that.

Too many parents crush childhood dreams with adult realities. In doing so they crush a child's hope and motivation, they stamp out the impossible, starry-eyed fantasies that make childhood so special. Give me a child with dreams and imagination, and I'll give you a young man or woman with determination and an adult who'll be a success.

# 2

# THE DREAM CATCHER

*"All our dreams can come true if we have*
*the courage to pursue them."*

—**Walt Disney**

**THE PHONE STARTLED ME OUT OF A DEEP SLEEP.** Rubbing my eyes I stretched over to pick it up. "Hello?"

"Hi, Uncle Vin? It's me, Mark. I didn't want to wake you too early. It's 8:15 in the morning there, isn't it? We just had a son at 5:15! What a feeling it is! I can't begin to describe it. When I held him in my arms and gazed into his eyes, for the first time I realized what life is all about!"

I checked the clock next to my bed. It was 2:35 a.m., California time. My nephew used to be a good ballplayer as a child, but he never did have any sense of time.

"I've already gotten him a glove, bat and ball," he went on. "I just can't wait to get him out of the nursery and onto the ball field." Mark was never low on enthusiasm. I wondered if he was going to ask me for a letter of recommendation for college. The ecstasy in Mark's voice, the joy, the hope—I knew Mark was imagining the very same thing I had when my first son, Vinny, had been born. As soon as I realized it was a boy, I had started dreaming of tossing the ball to him and having him toss it back—the beginning of bonding, that invisible magnetic force that forms an inseparable link between parent and child, which often occurs later for fathers than for mothers. In America, the true relationship between father and son often starts with base-ball. The ball field becomes their first common ground. Baseball is a time for sharing and building memories, for fathers—and now mothers—to impart their knowledge to their child. Baseball is more than a ball being tossed to and fro—it is love and acceptance being passed back and forth. Poems are written about the game, books and films are centered on it. "If you build it, he will come," the movie *Field of Dreams* claimed, and every young ballplay-er in the country understood. The gleeful squeals of a child, the warmth and pride that kindles in the heart. . . . Oh, this is the dream of every dad who ever played Little League baseball. I have seen it in the children—a spark in their smiles, an ember that glows and grows as we parents nurture it into a steady flame of strength and resiliency. Every father knows the feeling. My dad once told me, "You never know the meaning of life, of love—of any-thing—until you have a child and play ball with him!"

Yes, I knew what my nephew was feeling and dreaming. I also knew, as you do, that once Thomas James, my new great nephew, came home from the nursery, Mark's life would change in ways he could not imagine. Sleepless nights, soggy diapers, endless feedings—and the quivering chin accompanied by the tiny whimper that ends as soon as you pick him up, only to be re-ignited the very instant he is put down. For the time being, though, Mark was on cloud nine. His feet would collide with the earth soon enough. As I congratulated him and hung up, I put my arms behind my head and slowly closed my eyes. Oh, yes! How I had looked forward, as Mark does today, to being out there with my son. . . .

# *Not the Best, Not the Worst— Just the Reality*

### *If Only I Could Change One Day of My Life*

It seems like only yesterday that little Vinny held my thumb as I led him onto the Little League diamond, my diamond of dreams. His baseball cap was skewed sideways and his glove dragged by his side, but he had a skip in his step and a sparkle in his eyes. I cannot even describe the jumble of feelings I had. I positioned him like a little treasure at third base and walked over to first. I was sure I could see a little burning ember of contentment emanating from his smile.

Little League tryouts would be in two weeks. I would train my son just the way my dad had trained me. I could not believe it. Vinny stood there with a grin and pounded his tiny fist into the glove as he had seen me do so many times. I threw the first ball and watched it bounce toward him. Riveting his eyes on the white sphere as it tumbled forward, he snagged it just at the precise moment, pulled it out of his glove and threw a perfect strike.

Oh God, if this is not heaven, what is? I thought. In the recesses of my brain I heard the major league loudspeaker at Dodger Stadium: "And in the stands today is Dr. Fortanasce, out to see his all-star son playing third base . . ." I heard the chatter and cheers of the fans. I could see Tommy Lasorda penciling him in: Vinny, cleanup batter. I looked back at my son; I could have sworn that was a flame I now saw radiating from his chest.

My next toss was a little harder. Vinny scooped it up again, but this time threw it ten feet wide.

I retrieved the ball and approached my son with a frown of concern. I explained how to throw the ball straight and what the consequences were of a bad throw in Little League. A bad throw was an error, I told him, which was bad, very bad. It would let a man on base, and a potential run to be scored. Going back to first base, I increased the speed of my next throw, giving Vinny a one-bouncer. The ball careened first off the heel of his glove, then off his chest. Without a whimper, he picked it up and threw it—again, ten feet off target. Vinny smiled and pounded his glove, waiting for my next toss. I shook my head no and walked over to third again to instruct him on the art of catching a one-bouncer, and the importance of preventing a ball from getting by you. "If you do, it's an error, AN ERROR." As I walked back across the field again, I remember thinking that I'd have to increase the number of practices if he ever wanted to be ready.

Another toss. Vinny picked it off as I had told him to, but instead of throwing the ball, he just held it. "Vinny, throw the ball," I yelled. He merely looked at me and shook his head no.

"Vinny, throw the ball," I yelled a little louder. Then I noticed his face. The sparkle was gone. The flame had not just dwindled, it had died.

"Dad," he said, "let's go. I don't want to make errors."

Fatherly (and a little annoyed), I stomped over to third base. "Vinny, you will never be a good ball player if you don't practice."

"Daddy, I want to go home."

"Listen, son," I quickly retorted. "Life is not always a game. We are going to play for at least another ten minutes, until you get it right. Tryouts are only two weeks away."

Walking back to first, I suddenly realized I could no longer hear the announcer broadcasting my name. My grin had turned grim. Well, I thought, it is time for Vinny to learn discipline. Just what has his mother been doing all these years with him? Ten minutes of play and already he wants to quit. Kids these days have it too easy, too good.

I reached back and flung the next ball to Vinny. He simply stood there and let the ball, all of one foot to his left, go right by him.

"Vinny," I blared loudly enough to be heard across the ball field, "what's wrong with you?"

In answer, my son started to giggle and dance about like a marionette being pulled by strings.

"Stop acting stupid," I said angrily. This remark, however, only induced more puppet activity. As I briskly passed Vinny to fetch the ball, I saw my dreams melting down into pools of disappointment.

As soon as I arrived home the next day, I found Vinny, patted him on the back and suggested we go out to play. He said he could not find his glove. I told him where it was and would wait for him at the door. When I didn't hear him coming, I went to look for him. I found him standing in front of the TV, watching the same show I had just told him to turn off. Disappointment—no, hurt—overwhelmed me. My son did not want to play with his own father. He did not care for me. He did not really care about getting ready for tryouts. He had no discipline! How could this have happened? How did it happen to me of all people? I'm a doctor! Besides, all children love baseball and all children love playing with their mom or dad!

Need I really explain?

When Vinny was ten, he turned to me out of the blue one day and said, "Dad, remember when you told me about not making errors?"

"Yeah."

"Well, I thought if I did, someone would get hurt real bad. I was afraid if I played, you would get hurt."

He then gave me a crooked little smile and shot out the door to go play, while I stood there with my mouth hanging open. About eight years later, when I was helping him select a college, he gave me that same crooked smile and said, "You know, Dad, preparing for college is a lot like preparing for Little League. I wanted you to accept me for what I was then, and be proud of me—but I was so afraid of disappointing you. It seems I've got the same problem now."

My eyes filled with tears as I realized that Vinny's puppet routine had really been a strong, albeit nonverbal message: "Dad, please like me. Please smile. Look, look, I'm a puppet, here to entertain you." He had been trying his best, but his best was not good enough for me. My dream of playing ball with my son back in his Little League days was not marred due to a lack of his discipline, but because my tone and expressions clearly told him I was withdrawing my acceptance and love. He had no idea what "preparing for tryouts" meant—all he wanted was to have a good time with his dad. He did not want to hurt me by making an "error."

Each of my children has had a different nonverbal way of giving me the same message. My daughter, Kaycee, would become stubborn and deliberately make the same mistake over and over whenever she felt she was not getting a favorable response from me. Michael, though, was the most difficult of all. One moment he would act as if he was too exhausted to even stumble down the baseline; ten minutes later, he would be magically restored to life. Fortunately, I took his pulse during one of those episodes, found it was 180 and took him in for some tests. We discovered that Michael had W.P.W. (Wolff Parkinson White Syndrome), a cardiac arrhythmia that can be fatal—and has been so to several basketball and football stars. Luckily, a new catheter surgery cured the problem. Of course, it also cured what I thought was a nonverbal communication. After the surgery, Michael developed another pattern of behavior that told me loud and clear, "Hey, Dad, lighten up!" He began to twitch his neck and grimace, occasionally letting out a little cheep, like a bird. Being a neurologist, I immediately recognized this as Tourette's syndrome, a neurological disorder characterized by sudden uncontrollable mannerisms, such as twitching, or tics associated with unusual vocalizations. I was not going to make the same mistake twice, so I quickly brought Michael in to see my partner, Charlie, a pediatric neurologist. Luckily, it was not Tourette's syndrome at all, just a nervous habit that went away when *I* changed *my* behavior!

I eventually found out that I was not alone. My interactions with Vinny, Kaycee and Michael turned out to be mild compared with some of the things I saw. Tellingly, it was not the disinterested fathers, but the dedicated ones who tried hardest with their children and had often been baseball aficionados all their lives, who seemed to have the hardest time. Those dads with the biggest dreams had the biggest problems. Even more tellingly, moms rarely had the same difficulties, I noted.

## *I Was Not Alone: Why Won't They Listen?*

Two days after my first dream turned sour with Vinny, I witnessed another dad practicing with his son. "Damn it! Get in front of the ball! Where's your head?"

Finally, the boy just stood still with the ball and refused to throw it—just like Vinny. His father let loose with some bleep, bleep, bleeps and turned his back on his son. Seeing his chance, the boy threw the ball and hit his dad right on the buttocks. To give you a hint of what happened next, the little guy ended up on his tiptoes, holding the same part of his anatomy his father had just fielded the ball with. How could something so potentially wonderful become such a nightmare? I wondered. How does a father with such good intentions turn into a near child abuser?

## *A Solution*

Tri, one of my closest friends, and I coached our first team together. His son Patrick was such an obedient child—until Tri tried to teach him to play, that is. Suddenly dutiful little Patrick would turn into a stone-faced zombie, standing like a rock, staring straight ahead with no expression or response as Tri attempted to talk to him—only to wind up talking to himself. "Why won't he listen? Why won't he try?" Why, why, why indeed! After two practices, Vinny was placed as third baseman and Patrick at shortstop. At the start of the practice, Vinny and Patrick looked and acted just like our sons but, as the practice progressed, a distressing metamorphosis occurred. Vinny evolved from an attentive ballplayer into a giggling puppet, while Patrick, a skilful shortstop, degenerated into a mummified zombie. When we asked them what was wrong, they said, "Nothing." Did they want to play? "Oh, sure," they said with the enthusiasm of a child waiting to have an enema.

Their mothers soon became concerned at how their sons dragged themselves to the ball field. I remember the day it all came to a head, just as I remember September 11 and the planes crashing into the World Trade Center. Vinny and I had just gotten home from practice. I was in the bedroom changing my shoes when my wife walked in. "Vinny told me he doesn't like baseball. He doesn't want to play. I think you are the reason he doesn't like it. If you can't change how you treat him, I am going to pull him out."

"Pull him out? Pull him out! Pull him out!" The words reverberated in my head. This was far beyond a personal crisis—it was more like the end of the world! I could not imagine living without a boy in Little League. Yes, I know it sounds stupid. Imagine me, a doctor who deals with life-and-death situations every day not knowing that life is more than baseball. But deep down I cherished my dream. I was no different to my nephew Mark. No, I was worse. I actually put a glove in his crib at the hospital. The nurses thought it was a cute gesture, but I was serious about raising a champion. My wife's ultimatum made me feel as if I were facing Armageddon, but it also forced me to make a decision. Necessity is the mother of invention, after all.

Deep down I knew my wife was right, because I could see so clearly what Tri was doing wrong. Good Lord, you would have thought he was talking to a professional ballplayer out there. He never applauded Patrick's successes, only reinforced his mistakes. Yet, with my son and the other boys, Tri was a model of patience, positive attitude and support. I, too, had nothing but praise and patience for the rest of my team, but was doing exactly the same thing with my son as Tri was with Patrick. Looking back now I realize I had been living with a myth—well, actually, several myths.

# *The Myths*

### *Fairy Tales Don't Always Come True . . .*

The first myth is that every child will naturally love baseball. This reality only exists in the mind of the parent. Children will like baseball if they get their mom and dad's approval or, later, as they grow, if they are very talented at it and get approval from their friends. Initially, however, parental and coach endorsement is the pivotal issue. Every child will love baseball if his parents love and approve him while he is playing it. My frowns, dissatisfaction and lectures did not give Vinny the idea that I approved of or liked him. Children see their own self-worth through how we see them. Remember "we smile, they smile." When we frown, they think they are bad.

The second myth is that our children will love playing ball with us, which is the flip side of the coin to myth number one. Our kids will enjoy something and want to do it again if they feel they are pleasing us. The same principle continues throughout our lives. Love between a wife and a husband dwindles once one feels the other disapproves or doesn't respect them. Your child will continue to love playing baseball with you as long as you continue to show your love and respect for him.

The third myth is that children always tell the truth. For the most part, they do—but not if they feel they will be punished for it or get into trouble. I can still remember my three children—their faces smeared with icing and their fingers covered with crumbs—swearing in unison, "No, we didn't touch the birthday cake, Dad." Children naturally tell us what they think we want to hear in order to avoid trouble, and trouble was written all over my face.

Parents and coaches must learn to look at the nonverbal messages that tell the real story. Suddenly being unable to find his glove, for instance, and getting distracted by the TV were real messages from Vinny—I was just not "listening" to what he was showing me. Each child has his or her own unique type of nonverbal communication or expression of anxiety or anger. One child I knew would stick her tongue in her cheek when she was angry. I frequently asked her if she was chewing gum or eating but she would always say no. Years later, when she was in high school, I learned she did this tongue-in-cheek routine whenever she got angry. It had started when she first stuck her tongue out at her dad and promptly received a spanking. To protect herself she had developed this disguise technique, which satisfied her need to express herself and, at the same time, allowed her to avoid punishment. Some of the more frequent mannerisms children bring to our neurology clinic are tics, head twitching, forcefully closing their eyes or clucking their tongues. Often these are just nonverbal ways of communicating their tension.

> *"Treat your child like a treasure and they'll treasure you."*
>
> — Tommy Lasorda

The final myth is that a parent is the best teacher for his or her child. This may be true but only if the parent does not have unrealistic expectations or conflicts in his or her own life. Unreasonable expectations begin with you, the parents and your unrealistic dreams. As Tommy Lasorda once told me, "Unrealistic dreams are OK for children but NOT for adults." Children do not start out sharing their parents' dreams and will never grow to share them unless treated with respect, love and honor, whether they make mistakes or not. Children have minds of their own; most often their only expectation of baseball is to have fun. They will react positively if they get their parents' and coaches' approval. One good rule of thumb is to try to deal with what you perceive as faults in your child as gently as you deal with your own, as gently as you wanted your parents to treat you; another is to do something to make your child smile when you are upset with him, and then go back to the task.

## *"Give a Little, Get a Lot"*
### *Jim Gerstenslager, Western Regional Director*

If your dreams of playing ball with your child are rapidly turning into a Stephen King nightmare, step back and take a little reality check.

First, recognize the difference between what you think is the problem and what the problem really is. I thought my problem with Vinny was his attitude, but it was actually my "anticipatory anxiety." I knew the tryouts were coming up, Vinny did not—even if he had, he would have had no concept of what they meant to me. I had gone through 27 years of school always preparing for the next test. My anxious mind said, "What if Vinny isn't ready for the big test? Why, this will be just the beginning of a long line of failure. In fact, he'd be a failure the rest of his life. He will never learn discipline. He will never amount to anything."

Yes, these were *my* problems. Vinny's problem was seeing my frown and hearing my tone of voice, which told him I did not approve of him. Vinny did not want to disappoint me—he wanted to stop playing so he would not hurt me anymore and maybe do something else so we could be friends again, maybe even have fun together.

> *"If you teach your child anything, teach him or her to smile. I've learned that when I smile it pleases my friends and confuses my enemies."*
>
> — Tommy Lasorda

Second, recognize your child's expectations to have fun and make you laugh. Children really do want to make us happy, so go ahead—have fun, roll in the grass, play games. Enjoy the moment. Before you can hope to teach your child anything, he must learn to like you. If you are having fun, you will be fun to be with; if you are always serious and disapproving, you will be the last person he wants to be around. When you have fun together, your child will soon want to be like you, because you love and accept him and want to be with him. Once you have his love he will do anything you say if it is within his capabilities. Remember, just because a child is genetically yours does not mean he will love or want to be with you. You must earn that love—and that, Mom and Dad, takes time together having fun.

Several studies have shown that parents who nurture childhood dreams have children who are happier and have a greater sense of control over their destiny. Talent, character, and a good sense of right and wrong are important. However, without a dream, without hope and motivation, a child is like a fish on dry land, a batter in a canoe, a pitcher on roller blades.

If your child has no goal, no hero, no dream to follow, what do you do?

1. Look at yourself, what's your dream? If the answer is "I don't have one," this may be your problem. Get a dream and let your child have dreams.

2. If you feel that you are nurturing a childhood dream but your child still seems to lack enthusiasm, ask yourself, "Is it my dream, or my child's?" Too many moms and dads are confused by the difference!

3. Inspire your child. After all, a good parent is an example, a great parent is an inspiration. Be an inspiration, a parent who nurtures dreams and hope.

---

### FROM TOMMY LASORDA'S DUGOUT
#### HALL OF FAMER, FORMER MANAGER OF THE L.A. DODGERS

*Child rearing is like flying a kite. You must run gently at first, until the kite begins to soar on its own. Then you slowly play out the string so it can go higher and higher. Once up, changing winds may make it necessary to reel it in closer for a while, or let it out even more. The same goes for children. Never worry about the severity of the wind, because a child, like a kite, flies highest when he goes against the current.*

*If you treat your child right you will know it by the warmth of his smile, the sparkle in his eyes, the glow of his face and the skip in his stride. Next week, when Dr. Vince's nephew Mark's feet have touched the ground again, I think maybe I'll call him and tell him about kite flying!*

---

## Where Are They Now?

Patrick, Tri's son, who was a fine player one moment and a zombie the next, graduated from UCLA and is now a certified accountant. When he thinks back to his Little League days, he smiles and says, "Ah, the Angels." He does not recall his zombie routine—he only remembers the first double play he made at shortstop.

Vinny the puppet enjoyed sports so much he became a tennis and golf teacher and is now completing his master's in psychology with the dream of becoming a sports psychologist. I could have used his help.

# SECTION 1

## THE DIAMOND TO SUCCESSFUL PARENTING

THERE ARE THOSE WHO THINK but never act (the dreamers).

There are those who act without ever thinking (the troublemakers).

There are those few who think and then act (the leaders).

The question is: are children born into one of the categories (nature) or are they taught to be in one (nurture)?

If you believe it is determined by his genetic makeup (nature), then see the latest neurological data that shows a child's I.Q. can be greatly influenced by his environment. (See chapter on Emotional Intelligence).

If you believe it is determined by how you bring him up, then you are right. It is clearly how you nurture your child that is the secret formula for success. In order to reach this goal and to prepare your child for life you need to follow only four basic principals, what I call the four bases of the Diamond to Successful Parenting.

The four bases are:

1st—Communication

2nd—Presence

3rd—Attitude

Home—Acceptance

Every parent wants the same thing for his or her children: for them to be a success, a winner in life: a Garret Anderson, a Barry Bonds, a Sammy Sosa, an Eric Gagne or a Mike Piazza Orel Hershiser. But none of these people were born the way we remember them. Qualities such as confidence, self-esteem, the "right stuff" are not genetically inherited, they are carved out bit by bit, chiseled like a statue from a slab of marble. A child's ability and his brain capacity can be increased by certain mental and physical experiences. Parental influence is essential for a child's success.

Baseball has four bases. Getting around them all brings you to your goal: home with your child. Remember the difference between success and happiness:

Success is getting what you want.

Happiness is liking what you get.

A parent can not protect a child from life, only prepare him or her for it. That preparation can be learned on the Little League field. A recent survey reported a child is twice as likely to finish high school, four times as likely to go to college and 98 percent less likely to be in trouble with the law if they are involved in sports.

# 3

# COMMUNICATION: NOT SO SIMPLE

*"Know who is listening."*

—Al Herback and Al Price
Official Little League Coaches

**IT WAS THE FINAL INNING** and we were down by only two runs. The league championship hung in the balance. It was 1st place or no place. I knew it and so did my little players. I stared into their faces and saw beads of perspiration trickle over their determined brows. "The Yankees are vulnerable, not invincible." I began. "Victory is ours. It just depends on your will to win, your tenacity. Now, are there any questions?"

To my dismay they all looked uncertain. Then Jake blurted out, "My dad's from Tenacity but he says Tennessee."

Getting to first base begins with communication. Communication is the bridge that brings a child and parent together. The word "communication" in Latin means "to come as one to come together." There are two basic steps to communicating: talking and listening. It stands to reason, therefore, that before you can teach, you must communicate. Some parents and coaches forget that a child does not hear nor understand the same as we do.

# *Go Home*

Slowly and cautiously, Mindy approached the chalk-outlined batter's box for the first time. "Hit the ball, Mindy," her dad encouraged. A bright little white sphere, the baseball sat on the tee like a light bulb on top of a lamppost. Mindy reared back with the bat and swung. A sharp resonant crack split the morning air as the ball darted and bounced toward Patrick, the second baseman. Patrick bent to scoop up the ball, but it bounced right through his legs into the outfield. Mindy's little legs carried her all the way to second as the right fielder picked up the ball and flung it over Patrick's head into left field. Parents jumped to their feet in jubilation. Mindy's coach began to shout orders, while the opposing coach barked and groaned at his fielders. Mindy's coach waved her to third base. The little gal had never roused so much adulation and excitement from her coaches and the parents. She ran with all the power her little legs could muster and all the determination in her thumping heart. A giant grin of satisfaction crossed her face as she looked into the roaring crowd. Suddenly, as she reached third base, her coach crouched low and with intensity and excitement of the moment bellowed, "Go home, go home!" Mindy suddenly stopped. Tears welled up in her eyes as she looked at the excited parents urging her to run home; with a bowed head she began her trek toward the parking lot.

"Time!" the umpire called. All the grown-ups were confused by Mindy's actions. Was she hurt? Had she pulled a muscle? Was she frightened by the crowd? Did she have to go to the bathroom? No! Just when she thought she was doing everything right, she was told to go home. They did not need her anymore. Her little heart was broken.

Realizing what happened conjured up all sorts of sighs and empathy from the parents but, being adults—the magicians of logic—they soon forgot the heartwarming episode and began arguing the rules of the game. Was she out for going out of the base pads, as the opposing coach argued, or should the rules be dispensed with since this was an unusual situation?

What do you think?

We adults take so much for granted concerning the use of language. Nothing demonstrates more the developmental gap between Little Leaguers and their parents and coaches than the understanding of language. The apparent misinterpretation of words often sails over the head of these little people, just as it sometimes sails over our heads. The word strike, for example, means something very different to a union member than to a ballplayer, just as tickertape may indicate a parade to a politician but something completely different to a heart doctor.

# *Round or Flat?*

While watching a rerun of a baseball game on TV, my son Vinny turned to his four-year-old brother Michael and said, "I bet you that candy bar that Sammy Sosa scores a home run."

Michael weighed it up for a moment, then nodded. "OK, I bet he doesn't."

Sosa stepped up to the plate and sure enough sent the ball over center field and into the bleachers. As Michael went to hand over the candy bar, Vinny admitted, "I cheated. I saw him hit the home run on the news earlier."

Michael quickly replied, "So did I, but I never thought he could do it again."

For a child under seven, time and space are often one-dimensional. Two separate events, although remembered, are often not connected in the child's mind. That's why, when instructing a child, we must repeat, repeat and repeat. Practice makes perfect. It is not that they are not listening, it's that their "computer" has not yet been programmed to connect events yet. Hence the reason why any car trip is punctuated by the question "Are we there yet?" every five minutes or so.

After a Little League game, I took Michael out for pizza. While we were eating I asked him if he thought the world was round or flat. "It's round and flat," he said with great certainty.

"That's impossible, Michael," I replied. "It can't be both. It must be either round or flat." Michael shook his head and pointed to our pizza.

Depth perception, volume and many spatial relations are concepts that adults take for granted, but a child's neural circuits together with their under-developed sight, hearing and brain senses make them see and interpret things differently. In fact, children under nine years of age simply don't see or recognize things as adults do, so we must take that into account when communicating with them. Parents and coaches should recognize and account for the differences in understanding and communication between adults and children. Say what you mean and mean what you say.

> *"Even with Major Leaguers, you must never leave anything to question. Tell them, then show them and then ask them to show you. You'll be surprised at times what you said and what they saw you say."*
>
> — Tommy Lasorda

## *Like Da Wind*

Stevie, a pleasant, dimple-chinned six-year-old with big brown eyes, strode confidently up to the plate. As I delicately set the ball on the tee, I reminded him, "How are you going to run, Stevie?"

"Like da wind, Coach!"

Wacko! The ball bounced straight to the pitcher. Stevie took off like a shot toward first base. The ball, juggled by the pitcher, was now in his hands and ready to be tossed to first. Stevie, racing down the first base pad, was no more than two steps from the bag. Parents and coaches screamed words of encouragement. "Run, Stevie, run!" Suddenly, just when it appeared that Stevie had the ball beaten by five paces, he put on the brakes and almost came to an abrupt stop, no more than one foot from the bag. He stepped on the base, but not before the ump bellowed, "You're out!"

I took Stevie aside and again reminded him that he could run past first base, he did not have to stop on it. He took this well as I had a big smile on my face and I gave him a little pat on the back.

When Stevie came up again, we had a man on first and second. I asked him, "How are you going to run?"

With a smile on his face, he said in his most determined voice, "Like da wind, Coach."

Then I asked, "Are you going to stop at first base?"

"No, sir, Coach!"

Blam! The ball clunked off the tee to the shortstop. The fans cheered as Stevie ran like there was no tomorrow, right toward the bag, never missing a step.

Three men on base. Attention quickly moved to Charlie. I patted him on the back. "The bases are loaded, Charlie. You know what to do." I looked at third base—there was Jennifer. Second base, Ryan. First base—no one. "Where's Stevie?" I asked.

Everyone stood up. The first base coach remembered him whizzing by. He was nowhere to be found. Wait! There was a little boy with a yellow Angel's uniform running out to the tennis courts in a direct line from home plate. Needless to say, the game was delayed and Stevie retrieved, fully exhausted. If it were not for the fence, who knows where he'd be today! Even I marveled. What Stevie lacked in skill, he made up for in effort.

Coaches and parents often forget the importance our words have on these youngsters. To us, they are just suggestions; to the child, they are commands to be dutifully followed. Stevie ran his little heart out, keeping his promise not to stop, but to go right past first base . . . forever.

## *The Bionic Base Runner*

Vinny, in his first game, was on first base. I crouched low to whisper that he must really turn it on, as the team needed this run. He must dig deep and run his hardest. Vinny's mind went into overdrive. "You bet, Coach," he said firmly.

Patrick hit a towering drive just over second base. Vinny took off like no tomorrow—but in slow motion. His knees pumped high, his fists thrust back and forth, but there was barely any movement. His tiny pet box turtle could have beaten him to second base.

As fortune would have it, the ball went past the charging center fielder. I screamed, I pleaded, I begged on my knees for Vinny to run, but all it resulted in was him pumping and thrusting his hands and feet even more. No! I thought as he began rounding second and going for third. He will be out by an hour! I covered my face in anguish as my son strutted slowly toward third base. Miracle of miracles, the center fielder threw the ball over the second base player's head, into the left field bleachers. As Vinny reached third, I exploded with all the pent-up emotion of a bull being goaded by a red flag. "What are you doing?" I yelled.

"I was using my bionics, like Steve Austin." Steve Austin, played by Lee Majors, was TV's *Six Million Dollar Man*, Vinny's hero. When the character turned on his bionics, he was shown in slow motion to emphasize the effort.

Children's minds interpret things literally and concretely, yet their reality is a collage of fact and fantasy. Like Vinny, they can easily confuse a television hero with their own performance on the field. They are miracles of imagination—dutiful and wanting to please; volatile yet resilient.

## *Mean What You Say:*
### *Communication is 10 percent words,*
### *30 percent tone of voice, 60 percent body language*

Jose was playing shortstop. The bases were loaded with two outs. He knew this was an important play. The batter hit a hard grounder right to him. Just as he got himself in front of the ball it took a bad hop and went over his glove and through his legs. Two runs scored. His coach, seeing him disheartened, shouted, "Great try, Jose, that's getting in front of it."

What a supportive coach. Those few words of encouragement should have made Jose feel a little better about missing the ball. Reassurance is not what Jose heard, though—not when you add what I call process, or the way the words were delivered.

"Great try," the coach repeated, in a sarcastic and sharp tone of voice. He kicked the dirt and shook his head disapprovingly, a look of disgust on his face. What Jose heard of course was that the coach was angry with him. He was bad and had done something wrong even though he had tried his best. Sarcasm hurts. It scares children and leaves scars.

Do you remember the very first communication between you and your infant? It was visual: you smiled and the baby smiled. Next came tone of voice—you made a loud or angry sound and the baby jumped or cried. You spoke softly or gently and he or she cooed and smiled. Although verbal communication, or the actual words used, becomes increasingly important to children between the ages of six and nine, much of what they learn continues to come from nonverbal communication of gestures, facial expressions, actions and habits. When I was a boy in Little League, for example, my dad would tilt his hat back on his head when he was truly upset and say, "Jiminy Crickets." I dreaded it. It made me feel the same way I did when shocked by an unexpected clap of thunder. Obviously my dread came from his tone of voice, not his words. So...

*Communication Lesson #1:* Always make sure your tone of voice and facial expressions are consistent with the meaning of your words; otherwise, children become confused and scared. Kids whose parents communicate inconsistently, their words differing from their expressions, have difficulty trusting their parents and even their friends and teachers (and later in life their wives or husbands). Remember, little boys and girls have a hard enough time processing words without having to decipher the "real" message.

> *"It's not what you say, it's how you say it that matters.*
> *Say what you mean and mean what you say!"*
>
> — Tommy Lasorda

*Communication Lesson #2:* Never underestimate the imagination of a child. Eddy refused to get up to bat when I told him the bases were full. No matter how I pleaded and cajoled, I could not get him up to the tee. Finally, I had to substitute another player to bat for him. The next day his parents explained that he had overheard me describe how I always choked when I had to get up with the bases full. Eddy did not want to choke and die! Always spell things out verbally, not only in practice but during the game as well.

*Communication Lesson #3:* Spelling things out does not mean literally spelling each word; it means repeating and repeating and repeating and repeating . . . and never assuming that the children know the basics. My first-year players, for example, never remembered where first, second, third and home were until their fifth or sixth game—after I had run each one of them over all the bases, first through home, at least two or three times each practice and at least twice a game. That brings us to . . .

***Communication Lesson #4:*** Never assume children—or their parents for that matter—fully understand a word, especially one with several meanings. Remember, many areas, like California and New York, are multicultural.

I will never forget Mrs. Miller. Her little boy was up at bat. When he missed the ball, I advised him to choke up. He kept the same grip and missed the ball again. I had to tell him several more times, "Choke up, choke up," before he would change his grip on the bat. He finally did, but not before his mother came sailing out of the stands to yell at me that her son was scared enough, I did not have to continually remind him he was choking, or messing up!

> *"When you teach a child how to hit, you do not throw curveballs at him; you pitch the balls straight, right down the middle. Your words also need to be straight and say exactly what you mean."*
>
> — **Tommy Lasorda**

Sarcasm, cynicism and double meanings merely confuse children at first, but eventually they lead to mistrust and, finally, to imitation. Many parents think their children "suddenly" turn into teenage monsters, when in fact the parents themselves have been priming them for years to talk back in the same language they have been listening to. As a psychiatrist I see it all the time—parents criticizing their children for habits the children learned from them. Like father like son—like mother, like daughter—rings true not only at home but on the ball field as well. I must admit that after years of self-analysis, I never say "Jiminy Crickets!" like my father did. Instead I say, "Shoot the ugly moose!"—and all three of my children hear the same clap of thunder.

Whatever you say, if you say it in a sincere, warm tone of voice, your message will be understood and your children will appreciate it. And if you don't, I assure you, you will reap the consequences!

---

**FROM LASORDA'S DUGOUT**

*The Wizard says:*

*I've been told the secret of my success is my ability to communicate, but the truth is I don't say much more than most. The difference is how I say it. That goes for other managers like Mike Scioscia, Joe Torre and Dusty Baker. The message gets across because the players know we really care. Tell your children what to do with your heart and soul. They'll listen.*

---

## *Where Are They Now?*

Mindy the mighty base runner who "went home" got her degree in economics and is, ironically enough, now a home ec teacher.

Stevie "Like Da Wind" never stopped running. He went on to be a long-distance runner in college (really, no kidding!) and now he is running for political office.

---

*"Parents and coaches remember: people don't care how much you know until they know how much you care."*

—**Al Herback and Al Price**
**Official Little League Coaches**

# 4

# PRESENCE: THE GIFT

*"No one gets home without being at second. There is no presence like being there."*

—-Mike Scioscia

*"Some say it's a good team that makes good parental attendance. I say it's parents' attendance that makes a good team."*

—Jim Gerstenslager
**Western Regional Director**

**ONE AFTERNOON,** I overheard my seven-year-old daughter, Kaycee, talking to my youngest son, Michael, about time. "You see, Mike," she said, with an authority beyond her tender years, "the past was yesterday, like when we went to play Little League with daddy. And the future is tomorrow when we're supposed to go to see Aunt Elaine. But today is a gift. That's why it's called the present."

My mouth dropped open when I heard her say this. I guess I had never quite thought of time in those terms. Time means something different in the adult world: there's no time to watch our child's Little League game, there's no time to look into her eyes, to see her smile. And most worryingly, there's no time for the child to look into his parents' eyes and see just how important he is to them.

It seems that only when our children have grown up that we finally realize just how important our approval is to them when they're very young.
Their worlds revolve around the approval shown them by their parents. It
means everything to them. By the time they're teenagers, of course, that has
changed completely. Their parents are now nothing more than constant
streams of embarrassment and restrictions, and they will do anything to
avoid us. So, as parents, we have only a small window, a small precious gift
of the present, to experience the adoration and influence over our children's
lives. That time for fathers is generally when their children are between five
and 12 years old and for moms maybe a little longer, from birth to about 14.

## *The Present and Your Child— They are Both Gifts*

I'll never forget Frankie. He was a seven-year-old in his first Little League
season. His parents would always arrive early at the baseball field before each
game but then drive off and leave him. They never once stayed to watch him
play, which always made me feel sorry for him. I always thought that he
could be a much better player if only his parents would stick around and
cheer him on. I knew that his dad must love him, because I would frequently see them around town, with Frankie leading his father around by the hand.
I just couldn't understand why he never stayed for the games.

I usually had Frankie bat low down in the order partly because he wasn't
one of the better players and partly because I made an effort to reward those
parents who stayed to support their kids. I feel more than a little chagrin now
for admitting that. Anyway, before one particular game, Frankie came up to
me and asked if he could bat earlier. I was a little puzzled and asked him why.
"Well," he said, "for the first time today, my dad will be able to see me play."

I looked up to see his mother in the bleachers but not his father. He must
be on his way, I thought, and decided to have Frankie bat at the top of the
order. He played superbly. He had never scored a home run before but managed two in this game. He played tremendous effort and enthusiasm and for
the first time seemed to really enjoy himself. At the end of the game, Frankie
had scored the winning runs and I went over to his mom to congratulate her.

"Frankie wanted to bat first because his dad was going to see him for the first time," I said. "But I don't see his dad anywhere."

His mother choked back a tear and said, "His dad died last week. The reason why he didn't ever stay for the games was because he was blind. Frankie thinks that now his dad is in Heaven he can see and he'll finally be able to watch him play."

I felt a mixture of emotions: guilty that I had presumed his father hadn't really cared and amazed that the idea of his father's presence drove Frankie on to play so very well.

I think the same thing is true of other children whose parents come to games. In fact, I once did a survey and found that my pitcher gave up fewer hits when his parents were watching him than when they were not. Similarly, my batters scored more hits and the fielders registered fewer errors when their parents were there to watch them. Studies conducted at institutions such as Yale in the '70s and '80s discovered that when asked what was the most important thing that they remember about their experiences with Little League and school plays, children answered that it was either their parents' attendance or their lack of attendance. They never talked about the game, they never talked about winning teams or great plays. The thing that 88 percent of them chose as the most important memory was their mom and dad's attendance, or lack thereof.

A parent of one of my players sent his children to the best schools, gave them every privilege that money can buy, then was stunned when his son turned round years later and accused him of being a failure as a parent. Of all the Little League games his son played from the age of four, his father had attended only five. That's how his son had judged him.

## *A Child Always Remembers the Glass Half Full, not Half Empty*

A child's memory is different from an adult's. For us, the present becomes the past, like a continuous stream of video images; for a child it appears more like a series of random snapshots. These snapshots are mainly of two types of memories. Firstly, they are the exceedingly joyful ones, such as opening a birthday present or playing baseball on a beautiful summer's evening. The second type of memories that are unfortunately remembered more frequently are the painful ones, the memories of sorrowful experiences.

This system of retrieving painful events has a purpose in survival terms— it maintains memories that prevent a child from being harmed again. A child bitten by a dog will often avoid pets as an adult. A child injured by a baseball or deliberately left out of a game by a coach bent on winning become memories, or snapshots, that will affect whether the child views the game with fondness or disdain when he grows up.

When most people are asked to think back to their childhood, they will often first remember the time they bumped their head, cut their finger or were taken to the hospital. A parent disappearing from the bleachers when his child badly wants him to be present will be stored in that child's memory as a snapshot.

So remember, unless you're there, unless you're present for your child, you'll be creating sad, lonely memories for him or her. The bad memories of a parent not being there at a game far outweigh the good memories your child will have of his parent.

# Al and Al's Coaches Corner

### Being There

A parent's first step toward making his or her child a success is simply to be present at games. Just being there for the child is so important. Indeed, self-esteem for a child is based on three overriding factors:

- Parental approval.
- His/her own innate talent.
- Peer approval.

Parental approval is most highly sought by pre-teens. The time a parent spends with a child tells the child that he's good, he's valuable, that he's worth your time. At this age, coach, a sitter, or a teacher are weak substitutes for a parent. Your presence is essential.

Children don't understand that you need to work, and will often interpret your absence as meaning that work is more important to you than they are. Years down the road all they'll remember about the games is whether Mom and Dad were there to watch them.

When you're not present, you are communicating a very clear message to your child, whether you intend to or not. You're telling your child he's not worth it. Of course parents are busy and their evenings and weekends are stretched thin between work and family commitments, but there's always time for those who really want to find it. When any of my employees tell me they have to leave work early for a child's sporting event, I never think twice about letting them go. After all, anybody who has the sense to put their family first is going to have an equally healthy attitude toward their job. These are people whom I can trust and rely on, these are people I know have their priorities right. And I know from experience that most other employers feel exactly the same way.

Remember: the most important ingredient to a child's success is the parents' presence. The present truly is a gift, never forget it and always remember that once it's gone, you don't ever get a second chance.

## FROM MANAGER MIKE SCIOSCIA'S DUGOUT

*Some parents think their job is over when they get their child to the field on time. But getting there is just the beginning. It is only the start of a bonding process with your child that can only be achieved by you becoming involved in the game, not simply sitting in the bleachers talking on a cell phone.*

## FROM OREL HERSHISER
### CY YOUNG WINNER, LA DODGERS

*When people ask me about what I remember most about my baseball career, they are usually surprised to hear me say it's not the 1988 season when we won the World Series and I was voted MVP, but rather a fond memory of playing baseball as a child. Specifically it was seeing my mom and dad sitting in the bleachers watching me. This image gave me such a sense of contentment that it's never left me. Their presence made me feel important.*

*The other question people like to ask is what gave me the confidence to keep my composure when the bases were loaded and I was up to bat and the World Series was on the line. Again, they expect me to say the great coaches I've worked with or the physical trainers or my teammates. While they were all certainly very important and influential, nothing compared to the confidence instilled within me by my parents' presence at every game, whether things went well or badly. What a gift! Thanks, Mom and Dad.*

### FROM LASORDA'S DUGOUT

*After my induction into the Major League Hall of Fame, as I was recounting to reporters the events of my life that had taken me to that point, I came to a startling realization. "Now that you have arrived at the pinnacle of baseball success," asked one reporter, "you must be finally be happy?" As I thought about the question, I realized that success was not a place but the road it took to get to that place. More specifically, it was the people who were present along that road: the players, the fans and my loving family, especially my wife Jo. Her presence was an ongoing process and the happiest times were those moments it took to get to my ultimate goal: the games, the sharing of victory and defeat with my wife and kids. Too many parents forget about the present and only think of the future and, in so doing, miss the opportunity to be present for their kids. Don't miss it. Believe me, when you're my age you'll not remember the car you drove or the money you made, but you will remember the great times you had with your family. Or maybe not. It's up to you.*

*Now, Dr. Vince, let's get the kids to third base.*

# 5

# ATTITUDE:
# THE DECISION

*"Positive against all the odds. It's a decision, your decision."*

—Tom Boyle
**Former Western Little League Director, "The Guru"**

**ATTITUDE IS THIRD BASE.**

A fundamental principle in Little League is being positive. While this may seem a little too fundamental to bother stating, when you look at baseball, you realize being positive is no simple task.

First, 50 percent of the teams on any day lose.

Second, mistakes are called errors.

Third, there will be at least three errors for each out made in T-ball. In the farm system, you can expect one error to every out. Even in the minors, the players average one error to every two outs at the beginning of the season.

To complicate matters, the umpire is usually a parent or a high school student, 12 to 15 years of age, who often will please no one with his or her umpiring. As one can imagine, baseball is a regular paradise for anyone discontented. Frustrated parents too intimidated to yell at their bosses and spouses can find it a great outlet. Here they can attack the umpires, berate the managers and coaches and demean all the players on the other side with impunity. Some can go the full nine yards and criticize their own children's teammates—and even their own children:

"How much did they pay you, ump?"

"Where did you learn to play baseball?"

"My son never was any good at sports—or school."

"Johnny stinks, get him out of the infield."

"Why is he playing first base? We will never win with him in there."

Yes, these cruel and demeaning remarks are said right in front of the children. And yes, baseball is filled with errors, misjudgments, miscalls and mistakes. Just imagine your child getting 67 percent of all his test questions in school wrong and only 33 percent correct. Well, in baseball, if he gets on base once for every three times at bat, he is considered a very good batter.

# *Look At What Lies Within, Not Without*

It had to happen eventually, I guess. I finally arrived early for a Little League game. To be honest, it was due to the fact that I had misread the schedule: the game started at 10 a.m. not 9 a.m. Happy to be an hour early rather than an hour late, I settled into the bleachers to watch the Little League game, Orioles versus Braves, that was finishing up on the field that my son's team would soon be taking.

I sat back and took a small bite out of the doughnut I had bought with me. I would have taken a big bite, but I was on a diet. Before I could swallow it I watched Patrick of the Cardinals get in front of a ball hit to him at second base. It hit his glove bounced right out. He then bobbled it and kicked it. By the time he finally got it in his hand the base runner had already passed the bag. But that did not stop Patrick from heaving the ball as hard as he could over the first baseman's head into the stands.

The couch stomped out of the dugout knocking over several bats and kicking the dirt, yelling: "If you can't catch the ball, don't throw it." Patrick's face turned a Cardinal red as his shoulders slumped.

As the next Padres batter got up I looked at each Cardinal's face. Written across the fearful frown of each Cardinal fielder was written, "Please, God, don't let the next ball be hit to me."

The next inning the Cardinals' Ryan hit an identical grounder to the Padres' second baseman. He too bobbled it, kicked it, and threw the ball even farther into the stands. I waited for the Padres coach's reaction. He said, "That's getting in front of it. Good arm. Next time we'll get him." When the next batter got up you could see across each Padres' face a sign saying: "Please Lord, let the next ball be hit to me."

That evening, I reflected on the game I had watched. What was the difference in each? In both games an error had been made, yet when one team was handed a lemon, they had turned sour; the other team had just made lemonade.

*"There is nothing either good or bad, but thinking makes it so."*

— Tom Boyle,
**Former Western Little League Director**

*"Errors are only opportunities in work clothes."*

—Luke La Porta,
**Former Chairman of the Board of
International Little League**

One coach saw an error, the other an opportunity. One made an event presented to him into a disaster. The other made it an opportunity to reward effort. The first coach filled his team with fear and taught them that errors are fatal. The other saw a child's honest effort and accentuated the positive. Where one had used his key to lock out success, the other made the decision to use it to open the door to success.

It is our attitude, our decision to either reward effort or highlight errors that makes the difference between our child's eventual success and failure. Some parents are masters at taking an average child and instilling him with self-confidence. Others can take the most talented child and scare the confidence out of him. Of course, children make errors but twenty years from now will it really matter? Well, it only will if you make it painful enough. The smiles on the faces of the Padres after the game told the whole story. Yes, they'd be back. It was clear to me which team would improve as the season went on and which would not. If you want your team to improve, accentuate the positive.

# *The Tony Principle*

> *"The good coach sees the doughnut,*
> *the bad sees only the hole."*
>
> —Tommy Lasorda

The first rule of being positive is to eliminate the negative. That reminds me of a play I will never forget. The Major League record for errors from one player is three in one inning, but whatever the major leaguers can do, Little Leaguers can do better.

Tony, a very enthusiastic and energetic Little Leaguer, was on the pitcher's mound. Clank! The ball, hit off the tee, went straight to him. It bounced into his glove and bounced right out. Error number one.

Tony quickly picked the ball up and threw it fiercely to first base. Instead of going toward the first baseman's glove, though, the ball hit the corner of the bag causing it to bounce right back toward Tony. Error number two.

As he ran to pick it up, Tony took his eye off the ball to look at the runner. The ball went right through his legs. Error number three.

Tony turned around to retrieve the ball that was now sitting on the pitcher's mound and threw it toward second base. A perfect throw—if the second baseman had been King Kong, twenty feet tall. Error number four.

The ball bounced out into centerfield. The center fielder finally retrieved it and tossed it home just as the batter rounded third base and headed for the plate. Yes, Tony, in his enthusiasm was right there blocking off his own catcher on home plate. The ball rolled into home—in and out of Tony's shiny glove once again. Error number five.

Unbelievable? Absolutely! Did it really happen? Oh, yes! So how did I react to this incredible performance of five errors in one play by the same player? Phenomenal! I was hoarse from screaming, delirious from all the commotion. "What effort, what enthusiasm! I am sure that one play could go into the *Guinness Book of Records*!" I and everyone else marveled at Tony's effort and cheered our heads off. Tony, well he smiled, shrugged his shoulders and enthusiastically awaited the next batter.

Sure, I could have made any number of negative remarks—the list that comes readily to mind is almost endless. I could have benched him for the rest of the season; I could have burned his glove, put him on waivers. That would certainly have made the play into a disaster Tony would never forget. Would it have made the game more fun? Would it have made Tony feel better? Would it have been a good, growth experience? The answers are obvious.

You can always find the positive if you look hard enough. We cheered Tony's effort, we cheered his enthusiasm, and we cheered his energy and alertness.

## *Beyond Simple "Errors"*

Then there was Freddy. Freddy was on second base; no one was on first. "Yo, Freddy, remember: if the ball is hit to third, you do not have to run to third," I, the third base coach, called to him. Freddy gave me a confident thumbs-up sign; he had heard and understood what I said. Freddy also remembered that in the last game, he had run to third base and gotten tagged out. Whack! The ball was hit to third. I quickly glanced to see if Freddy was coming. Thank God he was not.

Oh, no—Freddy was running to first! He got there safe.

"What a slide," I yelled to him as he was called out. "Freddy, good listening. I am proud you did not go to third, just like I told you. That slide was great. After the game we will go over running the bases again." I said all this with a big grin. Luckily, I was in my seventh year of coaching by then. If this had happened during my first, my response might have been dramatically different, possibly causing a bleeding ulcer for one of us and a brain hemorrhage for the other. Unharmed, Freddy continued to play and often was the first child at practice.

Anthony was at third base. "Yo, Anthony! Remember, you have to tag the runner if the ball is thrown to you. Stepping on the bag is not enough."

"Got it, Coach. Tag." Boom! The ball was hit to the pitcher. The man from second, disregarding his coach's pleas to stay there, was off in top gear toward third. Anthony, catching the ball from the pitcher, was standing in front of the bag. The collision was inevitable. But no, Anthony jumped out of the way and let the opponent arrive safely at third base—then he tagged him with the ball.

I yelled, "Great catch from the pitcher, Anthony, and great tag. Next time, let's tag him before he reaches the bag."

"Okay, Coach." Anthony smiled, content with himself. The positive is always there; sometimes in Little League you just need a little creative thinking to find it.

Ryan, a lanky, agile child, was at bat. The ball was on the tee. He positioned his bat right on it as I had taught him. He brought the bat back to the ready position and swung with all the first-grade muscle he could muster. The tee landed about two feet in front of the plate. "Great swing, Ryan."

The umpire set up the tee again. I hollered instructions: "Keep your eye on the ball." Ryan fixed his eye on the ball and swung. He missed everything. "That's keeping your eye on the ball," I said. The ball was set up again. He swung and missed. After ten times, the infield began to get restless. The second baseman was building a dirt mound. The outfield, distracted by cheers from the majors in the opposite field was, consequently, facing the wrong direction altogether.

"Those were practice swings, Ryan. Now, show them how far you can hit the ball." After two more swings, Ryan hit a nice drive just past third base. He arrived on first base with a big smile. Later, I am told, he said to the first-base coach, "I didn't realize I was practicing until the coach reminded me."

Yes, the creative genius is there in all of us—it just takes an opportunity like Little League to bring it out.

> *"The longer I live the more I realize the importance of attitude. Attitude is more important than money, education, success, or what others say or do. It is what makes or breaks a person and a society. We have a choice every day about our attitude. It can be sour or it can be sweet; it can be optimistic or not. I am certain that life is 10 percent what happens and 90 percent how we handle it. As a coach or manager in Little League, you gotta eliminate the negative, accentuate the positive, always be affirmative."*
>
> — Tommy Lasorda

## Andy's Story

Andy was a slightly built, gentle little fellow. His dad had decided he should forgo Little League after his first two years were spent playing the bench. Mr. Clemmon was discouraged, because despite all his efforts Andy never seemed to progress farther than the dugout. He felt Andy's lack of physical stature would probably doom him to continual failure, making the Little League experience less than beneficial, to say the least. After listening to Mr. Clemmon talk about the boy's plight, I persuaded him to have Andy play for me. Why? I guess because I love an underdog—he reminds me of me!

Initially, it appeared that Andy's dad was dead right. Everything the child did seemed a chore to him. His throw was not hard enough to break a window pane, even if he could make a direct hit; his swing was so slow, a spider could have spun a web before he connected—or missed—the ball. One day, out of desperate inspiration, I told Andy he was one of the fastest base runners on the team. Suddenly, his face changed—his whole body seemed to straighten out a little more. Hey, I thought, give him a pat on the back and behind this thin little figure stands one determined young man.

After learning the basics and gaining a modicum of confidence, Andy decided he wanted to be, of all things, the catcher. Yes, the catcher—the guy who stood where the would-be football and hockey players get to be. You know, the guy who stands there in front of home plate just daring you to cross his path. I tried to counsel Andy, but his heart was set. I decided to give him the chance—besides, his parents had already bought him a catcher's glove.

As he crouched behind the plate, our pitcher, Tony, threw fireballs to him. Andy's eyes watered from the force; after several innings, he gingerly removed his glove from his hand as one takes off a Band-aid from a wound. I asked if he would like to play another position, but he answered unequivocally, "No. I can do it."

As time went on, this child who could barely swing a bat, went on to become one of the best catchers in the league and by far the best base runner. His secret no doubt was his parents and his older brother who gave him unconditional support and praise. My part had just been to give him the atmosphere to grow and the feeling that someone believed in him. Andy played with more than his body for me—he played with all his heart.

## *Parents: You Have One Chance*

Parents and other significant adults are the most influential forces in a child's life from infancy to age 12. After that peer—siblings, close friends, acquaintances, etc.—take over as being the most important sources of positive or negative feedback. Actual abilities or talents are important throughout development but are often not appreciated until the teen years or later. Sometimes they are not fully appreciated until the child has left the influence of his or her family.

You have only to listen to one teenager's opinion of another, or one sibling's appraisal by his brother or sister to recognize how rare a child would have to be to evolve a good self-image on the basis of praise from peers. If positive self-appraisal is not formed by the early teens, the child will have a serious problem. This makes the formative years of T-ball and farm, minor and major Little League so precious and is the reason why parents and guardians (such as coaches) are so important.

Prior to age six, children are often very protected. They live in their own world with their parents, isolated from the harsh realities of competition and expectations. At six, their minds are filled with pleasantries like wanting to wear a bright yellow uniform. They enter first grade, Little League and soccer and somehow their doting, docile parents suddenly undergo a scary change or metamorphosis, like a spaniel being enveloped by rabies. One moment the parents are themselves, cheerful and loving, the next they are filled with emotions their children cannot understand. Based on their short life experience, kids often categorize these parental reactions in the only two classifications they are familiar with: approval ("My mommy or daddy likes me, I am good") and disapproval ("My mommy or dad does not like me, I am bad"). Approval, of course, brings repetition of the behavior. "What a poop!" said with a cheery voice brings—hopefully—a repeated performance on the potty. On the other hand, a deep, angry voice—"What did you do to my vase?"—brings trepidation, tears, a quivering chin and—hopefully—avoidance of that behavior.

Well, here comes T-ball and we, as adults, know the only way to become more proficient at the game is to practice. Practice of course takes repetition. Repetition is fostered by parental approval, which promotes continued effort. How can we exude continuous approval, though, when most six-year-old children are lucky to catch a ball dropped into their glove or throw a ball within ten feet of their 45-feet-away target? They are going to make a lot of mistakes; if every time they make one they get a negative response, we can hardly call this a positive experience. We have to find a way, therefore, to make these "errors" (which is what they are called in baseball) into something positive.

## AL AND AL'S COACHING CORNER

*Al Herback and Al Price*

*Official Little League Coaches*

The need for children to learn "how to lose" is more important than "how to win."

Attitude is a decision.

Those with the ability to see the good enable their children to see the good in themselves.

Those who have their effort rewarded rather than the results, learn to value the work ethic.

Those who are treated as valued and precious begin to feel they can be effective.

Those that feel they can change their world, do and never give up.

Being positive is not easy. It takes ingenuity and a decision. A decision to have a positive attitude.

## FROM LASORDA'S DUGOUT

*Anyone can deal with winning, but it takes a special person to deal with defeat. Some players lose their confidence with a single error; others just shake it off and learn from the experience. I believe there is more to learn from losing. It reminds me of a story about an old donkey my dad told me as a kid:*

*One day a farmer's donkey fell down into a well. The animal cried piteously for hours as the farmer tried to figure out what to do. Finally, he decided the animal was old and the well needed to be covered up anyway; it just wasn't worth it to try and pull the donkey out.*

*He invited all his neighbors to come over and help him. They all grabbed a shovel and began to throw dirt into the well. At first the donkey realized what was happening and cried horribly. Then, to everyone's amazement, he quieted down. A few shovel loads later, the farmer finally looked down the well. He was astonished at what he saw. With each shovel of dirt that hit his back, the donkey was doing something amazing. He would shake it off and take a step up. As the farmer's neighbors continued to shovel dirt on top of the animal, he would shake it off and take a step up. Pretty soon, everyone was amazed as the donkey stepped up over the edge of the well and happily trotted off!*

*Remember the Wizard's motto: Life is going to shovel dirt on you, all kinds of dirt; the trick is to shake it off and take a step up and never, never, never give up.*

*Each of our troubles is a steppingstone. We can get out of the deepest problems just by not stopping, never giving up. Shake it off and take a step up! Remember the five simple rules to be happy:*

*1. Forgive and forget.*
*2. Free your mind from worries—most never happen.*
*3. Live simply and appreciate all you have.*
*4. Give more.*
*5. Expect less.*
*6. Believe me, Tommy Lasorda.*

## *Where Are They Now?*

A few years later, Tony was elected to the all-stars team for three years in a row. He is now the first-string pitcher for his college team, a lefty with the potential to become a major leaguer. He has no recollection whatsoever of making those five errors in one play, because no one ever ground them into his memory. I hope he isn't reading this.

Andy, whose arms were so frail they could barely support the weight of the bat and whose father was prepared to take him out of competitive sports because he was too small, is now 25 years old and six feet tall. He is by no stretch of the imagination frail. However, what will see him through life is not the size of his body or the size of his talent, but his character. He'll be graduating from USC as a physician's assistant this year. Whenever I run into him at the hospital he always smiles his big smile and calls me "Coach."

Now the fourth and final base that invites your child to round home with confidence.

# 6

# ACCEPTANCE: THE SECRET

*"All children need is their parents' acceptance to make it home."*

—Aunt Elaine

## *Marty's Mom*

**IT WAS 1956** but it could be any day in the 21st Century. Some things never change, like the feelings we have before a trip to the dentist or the doctor or the anticipation we feel on a Sunday night before returning to work or school after the weekend. It was bad then and it still is now. That is how I feel when I think of Marty and his parents.

Marty was a teammate on my Little League team—yep, even I played Little League as a kid and even then the parents were no different to how they are today. Marty was one of those talented kids: he was fast, a good bat, with a great arm and coordinated to boot. I liked Marty, but mostly I felt sorry for him. It seems like only yesterday that I had to walk around the brand new 1956 Cadillac Marty's parents used to park right in front of the entrance to the Little League field. They had money and weren't afraid to show it. Marty's mom always wore bright, electric yellow and white dresses. The only thing louder than her clothing was her voice. Even amid the din and chatter of the crowded bleachers, her voice used to ring out loud and clear. It wasn't the sound of a foghorn on a distant ship but more like the blaring of an ambulance siren.

"Marty! Hit a home run!" she yelled as her son got up to bat. The bases were loaded and Marty seemed to try to ignore her pleas as he looked intently at the pitch. I can still see the ball fly off his bat, cut through the air and careen off the left field fence. Three runs batted home and Marty was safely on second.

By the top of the sixth and final inning, we were still down two runs with two men on and two out. Marty was up. He had the same look of steely determination as he faced the Johnson Plumber's pitcher. (In those days, the teams were named after their sponsors). As the pitcher wound up, the siren erupted again. "Marty! Don't disappoint me again! This time hit a home run, Marty!"

To be honest, I don't remember what happened, whether we won or lost, if Marty hit a home run or not. But I do remember Marty's expression as his mother bellowed those words.

Marty went on to the best high school and then the best college his parents could afford but soon dropped out. I heard he got into drugs. He had so much going for him but never his parents' acceptance. No matter what he did, he could always have done it better. His mother's expectations were so high, no young child could ever fulfill them. So Marty did the only thing he could. He quit.

> *"Yes, we can hinder or help our children; the choice is ours."*
>
> —Mike Legg, Former Western Little League Director

Some parents think that if a child is not how they think he or she should be, they are unacceptable. They forget a child has his or her own personality and own feelings. Accept your children for what they are, not what you think they should be.

> *"Use what talent you have; the woods would be silent if no birds sang except those that sang best."*

# *Heather's Hobble*

Heather was born with a hip problem that caused her to hobble when she walked. She was so awkward, clumsy and afraid that she might get hurt playing baseball that no coach drafted her into their team until the Little League president asked me if I'd take her on. Somewhat reluctantly, I agreed. What I quickly realized, however, was that what Heather lacked in talent she more than made up for in heart. She approached every game, every at bat with huge determination. She failed time and time again, but her enthusiasm never wavered and she always tried her hardest, cheered on by her parents who always rewarded her effort with plenty of hugs and words of encouragement. By midseason, her attitude had become a source of inspiration to the whole team.

When I asked her father why Heather seemed so well adjusted despite her lack of natural talent, he smiled and said, "While I can't change the color of my daughter's eyes, I certainly can change the sparkle in them. She's what God gave me and I treat her as a gift."

Heather never noticed her hobble and neither did her parents. They loved her and accepted her without condition. They did the three things that tell a child she is accepted:

They supported her effort.

They validated her real accomplishments.

They affirmed her worth.

Heather had everything stacked against her from a physical standpoint, but everything in her favor from a parental one. Her parents made the difference.

# *"Build Bridges Not Walls"*
### *Creighton Hale, Former CEO, International Little League*

How can we help rather than hinder? Marty's mother could have affirmed Marty's effort since few players put in as much work as he did. She could have validated his accomplishments when he batted three runs in and given him a high-five. And then, if there was criticism, she could have given it to him at that time. "The next time you're at bat in that situation, wait for your pitch. You have a great swing!"

Such opportunities also help to build a bond between parent and child. When your child is down, he will feel he can turn to you, the parent, for advice. Why? Because no matter the problem, he knows he will be accepted.

Acceptance is present in every parent. It takes no education, no extraordinary genetic talent, just common sense and diligence. If a parent accepts himself and is content with his child, his acceptance is reflected in the child and the child is self-satisfied. The child does not have to fulfill the parent's need, does not have to win to gain acceptance, but only has to try.

Usually, a parent's lack of acceptance is due to a misguided concept of him- or herself. If parents do not accept their child and miss the opportunity to praise their efforts and accomplishments, a child will grow up not recognizing their own talent or believing in themselves.

> *"It's better to do something imperfectly,*
> *than to do nothing perfectly."*
>
> **—Tom Boyle, Former Western Little League Director**

It is important to give children permission to see your weaknesses as a parent or coach, to see you as human. This allows them and yourself the freedom to not handle all emotions perfectly. In other words, teach them that when you yell or are angry it may be due to your own frustration or failure. Yelling hurtful comments never helps a situation but is sometimes unavoidable because of our mood, current stress level or our need to be perfect.

If you teach your child in advance that "I'm sorry, sometimes I take my bad mood out on you," you teach them what we call emotional intelligence and allow them to admit their faults. This is a way we can be an example and role model.

# *A Coach's Dilemma*

Coaches need to recognize parents who do not accept their children. Coaches need to provide perspective to parents who think their child is ready to win the World Series having only just picked up a bat. A coach might think that it's the parents' problem and they shouldn't interfere. However, it's a problem that affects children and, as a coach, you can be more objective and can provide the positive feedback they need. Try to intervene as close to the offending event as possible. Be kind but be firm. The parents will thank you for it. To Marty's mother, you might say, "Are you satisfied with your son? If not, why not? He is the best in the league and he is having fun on the baseball field."

Coaches must demand parental acceptance of their children, recognition of their talent and effort, so that their children can be placed in a position where they can succeed. Timely development and parental support is crucial for a child's self-acceptance, self-confidence, and self-esteem. A child needs to believe in himself if he is to achieve.

## FROM THE DESK OF DR. GAYLE FORTANASCE

*Accepting children without condition allows them to love themselves, see goodness in themselves, and gives them confidence no matter what their talent. Before a parent can feel acceptance for his child, he must be able to accept himself.*

*A child's self-acceptance and self-confidence depends upon parents and coaches:*

1. *Accepting a child's ability.*
2. *Recognizing his age. It is better for a child to be a big fish in a little pond.*
3. *Always supporting a child's effort.*
4. *Validating a child's true accomplishments, no matter how small.*
5. *Affirming their belief in a child's inherent worth to them.*

*6. Always empowering children to feel they have the answers within them-selves.*

*Acceptance is so simple. It begins with the parents and coaches and is absorbed by the child.*

## *Where Are They Now?*

Heather went on to be a physical therapist. Now she helps others help themselves. I hear she is inspirational and the sparkle is still there.

Marty grew up to be everything his parents wanted: a lawyer at the best firm in the state. Sadly, he was unable to sufficiently please his boss fast enough for what was "expected." When told he would not be asked to be a partner, he went back to his office and ended his life with a single bullet. No one could figure out why. He had it all—except, of course, self-acceptance. He depended on others to accept him and when they did not, he couldn't bear it. His life was successful in all the outward ways, but the price for that status was unbearable. I only wish his parents—especially his dad—had taken Little League's learning more to heart: there is more to success than winning.

# SECTION 2

## EXPECTATIONS

*"Oh expectations, how you cloud my vision. Why when I see so clearly what I must do, I do just the opposite?"*

**—Coach Vince Fortanasce**

**IT SEEMS SO CLEAR** what is needed to nurture your child to be all they can be, so why don't parents use the four bases to success? The answer is because, like me, parents have unconscious expectations.

"One comes in contact with one's true self through one's children," the old adage goes, and sometimes this can be really scary. We teach our children to be who are they are by being who we are—and then we often deny our own part in the process: "Where the hell did he learn to say that?! It must have been from one of those foul-mouthed children at school."

We all have adult expectations of our children. Those expectations come from a combination of whom we think they should be and whom we think we are or we should be. Most parents fall into one of four categories of expectation. I call the first the "overachiever" parent: "My child is representative of what I am. How dare he let his genetic lineage of excellence down! He can do better than that and I will prove it!" This is often typical of the "guys in charge," such as those who own businesses or lawyers or senior executives and foreman. Also in this category are the "fantasy life" parents who imagine themselves the mothers or fathers of a famous or exceptional child. It is good to have dreams, mom and dad, but make sure they are grounded in reality!

The second type is the "Know-it-all-blame-it-all" parent: "My child must be what I imagine I am but am not." This category could be any one of us but is closely allied with category one. Unfortunately, parents in this category most often do not recognize their own attitudes. These moms, dads and coaches are the saddest of all and since they cannot accept themselves, they cannot accept their child. Even more unfortunately, these "Blame-it-all" parents find a million excuses and rationalizations for why their child did not shine today—and blame it on whomever is closest. This is usually their own child or the coach.

The third category is the "unfulfilled" or "I coulda" parent: "My child represents what I always wanted but did not have the opportunity to be. He will not be a laborer like his father; I will make him a million-dollar bonus baby." This is typical of many of us.

Oh—a fourth category also exists: for the perfect parent. If you think you are one of these, the chances are you fall into the second category.

In my experience, the parents in one and three are generally easy to work with. God help the child of a "Blame-it-all" parent, though, and the coaches who have to deal with them! Many of us are a combination of all three types—in fact I believe we all have a little of each within us. The trick is to figure out which one best fits you and then try not to let it get in your children's way.

## FROM LASORDA'S DUGOUT

*Many people ask me, what makes a great coach? I tell them it's the same thing that makes a great parent: knowing oneself. I always remember the quote: "God, give me the serenity to accept the things which cannot be changed; give me the courage to change the things that must be changed; and the wisdom to know the difference."*

*We in the Major Leagues have help learning who we are. We just have to pick up the newspaper and turn to the sports pages. It usually makes our big heads shrink quickly. As a parent or coach, listen to your children, they'll tell you who you are. But you've got to really listen with your heart and mind and soul!*

# 7

# THE "OVERACHIEVER" PARENT: UNDERACHIEVING CHILD

*"You cannot change the child that life gives you—you can change only what you expect from that child."*

—*Orel Hershiser*

**THE OTHER DAY,** I was listening to one of my friends talk to his "4.0 child"—a child with a perfect A grade average. At any gathering of my friends, who are mostly physicians and other professionals, the only allowable number is 4.0, the only allowable letter A. The bragging has gone so far lately that last night I was informed that one of my friend's children had "better than a 4.0 average"—better than perfect. "I have always been shooting for that myself," I said. "If I could not make it, maybe my child will."

As you can see, I entered this social game of "Let's play how great our genetic heritage is" very carefully. The rules are: I let you have your fantasies, you let me have mine. "Huh! Your child has better than a 4.0 average," I tried to say with admiration.

Openly challenging an outrageous exaggeration, you see, is against the social rules in my peer group. In fact, it would be considered offensive, and would probably result in my being ostracized by my peers. Of course, I could have brought the conversation to an even more ludicrous level by pushing the question, but being my own self-confident person, I decided to change the playing field instead—especially since I could not play in their ball park when it came to my kids' grades. I therefore turned the conversation toward something even better and more important than grades—baseball.

"Well," I said, "my daughter has just returned from the All-Star Games. You know, she plays shortstop and pitcher—and sometimes both positions at once." I wanted to say, "And went four for three with one intentional walk," because that, too, is better than perfect.

"Why, that's wonderful," exclaimed the mother of the 4.0-plus daughter in a condescending tone. "Each child does have her own place, doesn't she?"

Now what did she mean by that remark? I thought. Rather than challenge it and find out, I decided just to call it a draw and move on. Besides, she knew, as I did, that what we were touting was nothing but wind.

However harmless this type of social interaction is, it becomes dangerous when we forget that friendly oneupmanship is just a social game and nothing more. The reality of our children—who they really are, and what stage of development they are at—may be (and probably is) very different from our bragging. We must accept our children as they are. When we actually expect our children to live up to these glorified images that we have created in our minds and social intercourse, we take on the traits of the Overachiever parent, whose hallmark words are always superlatives: always wonderful, gorgeous, marvelous, the best. Fortunately, Overachiever parents are easy to recognize by the uneasy competitive, or nauseated feeling you get from not being able to tolerate their bull. They are the ones who tend to name drop the fine schools they went to—Harvard, Yale, Vassar, or Brown. Overachievers often have trouble relating to the concept of what they are, because, after all, they cannot help it if their child is so intelligent or talented. The truth is, children of elementary school age seldom really care about grades, or talent, or intelligence. They are more interested in learning new skills, making friends, learning language, and a host of other wonders the world has to offer. To put it in simple terms, only an Overachiever parent would think an A in second-grade spelling is important.

I will never forget a conversation I had at the La Jolla Beach and Tennis Club one summer. I listened intently as one of the parents described his young son. "He's incredible. You have to see him perform, you won't believe his talent. He is so advanced for his age, really. He's unbelievable."

To find out what this Overachiever parent was really saying, use the old psychiatrist trick of substituting I for he, me for him, and my for his: "I'm incredible. You have to see me perform, you won't believe my talent. I am so advanced for my age, really. I'm unbelievable."

The next time you talk about your child, make sure you're not talking about your expectations.

# *Reality Grounding for Overachiever Parents*

Let's face it: 99.9 percent of our children will never live up to our imagined perfection. If they were to try, 99.9 percent would most likely fail. Those who come close, or continue to try against all odds, often pay a high price for questing after what they eventually realize was never their goal in the first place, but their mother's or father's. In striving for the success their parents demand, these children gradually accumulate the signs of stress. In their twenties and thirties, for example, they develop chronic headaches or stomach problems—diarrhea, constipation, sour stomach. In their forties and fifties, they graduate to stomach ulcers, hypertension, panic attacks, and depression. No matter what they attain, they have learned, it will not be enough; they will have to strive for more. They can never accept themselves, because their parents never accepted them for who they truly are.

All this starts with us, the dads and moms, when we begin to seriously expect our children to be "better than perfect"—with a higher than 4.0 grade point average, or a four-for-three batting average. All this can stop with us, too, just by realizing that we do not have to be perfect, and neither do our children. We need to encourage them to be all they can be by accepting them and rewarding their efforts. Even if they fail or bring home a C-average report card, they deserve a reward for their effort. Yes, it is that simple. Remember, the sure road to failure begins when you try to please everyone.

# 8

# THE "BLAME-IT-ALL-KNOW-IT-ALL" PARENT: BEWARE, IS IT YOU?

*"Some people are alone because they build walls instead of bridges."*

—Luke LaPorta

**I TOOK A LONG, DEEP BREATH** and let the warm spring air cleanse my lungs. It was the first practice of the Little League season, my seventh and probably last year managing T-ball. I closed my eyes to listen to the innocent chatter of the players. The chirping of the sparrows seemed to complement their gleeful squeals, interspersed with the deeper warm tones of the moms and dads. Suddenly, my oneness with nature was interrupted.

"Dr. Fortanasce, I presume?" I opened my eyes and blinked against the sun.

"I am Bradley Burnham, father of Brandon." Before me stood a fortyish, mildly plump gentleman with a starched white shirt, bow tie, and, yes, black and white high-top sneakers.

"I have heard you have an excellent reputation. That is why I elected to have my son Brandon on your team." Well, I thought, he has good taste in coaches, if not in clothes.

"I understand from my wife, Marian, that you expect parental participation," Mr. Burnham enunciated in a British accent, "so I have been practicing with Brandon, and I assure you, he will be more than a credit to your organization. In fact, Brandon said to me just now on the way to the field, 'Dad, I will be the best.'"

"Thank you, Mr. Burnham." As I extended my hand in friendship, I felt a slight tug in my gut.

"Okay, lads," I called to my team. (I had spoken to Mr. Burnham for only one minute, and he had already rubbed off on me.) "All the first-time players out to the field."

Mr. Burnham took this command literally and went out to the field with his son. As I began my introductory directions, I noticed him order several of the children off the shortstop position he had deemed his son's terrain.

I started by throwing soft ground balls to each child to assess his abilities. Brandon very mechanically got in front of his ball and bobbled it. When he finally caught it, he threw it awkwardly in the direction of first base. He immediately cringed, his shoulders sagging. His father openly criticized his catch and throw as "…inadequate and, quite frankly, inferior to your potential." My stomached churned once again. The child had cringed before his father ever spoke! My own rating, according to my motor-skill experience, was that Brandon had average capability and possibly good potential.

I next ordered the children in for batting practice. Mr. Burnham was again right on me, explaining how he had played professional soccer, and how his son would, with proper coaching, follow in his footsteps. He quickly appraised me of the foul experience he had previously had with an inadequate manager who neither took advantage of, nor developed, his Brandon's exceptional potential. The volume of friendly background chatter seemed to mute and the sun to dim as I realized my season with Mr. Burnham had just begun. My mentor in psychiatric training had once said, "Pay attention to your gut feelings, Vince." All of ten minutes had gone by with Mr. Burnham, and my gut was screaming out loud and clear—trouble! I popped two Rolaids.

By the third practice, Mr. Burnham had berated the condition of the field when his son missed a ground ball, blamed the other children for disturbing his son's concentration, and made a number of remarks about the "bloody manners" of his son's teammates. By game time, Mr. Burnham had already decided that the coaching staff favored other children and was not recognizing his son's talent. Unfortunately, Brandon was the one who took the brunt of his father's unfulfilled expectations; Mr. Burnham openly railed at the little tyke, yelling and chastising him. He added a new meaning to the phrase "child abuse." He may not have been hitting and scarring the boy's skin, but he was making deep rents in his psyche. Although there were many incidents with Mr. Burnham over the course of the season, one I will always remember occurred in the second game.

We were short an umpire, so Mr. Burnham had volunteered to take second base. By coincidence, his son just happened to be playing second base as well. The batter hit a soft pop fly to second. Trembling, Brandon positioned himself to catch it. I remember praying he would, because I so feared his father's reaction. The ball seemed to take forever to come down. When it did, it careened off the tip of Brandon's glove and glanced off his chin. Stunned, Brandon turned and cried, holding his hands over his face. Time was quickly called. With tears streaming down his pink cheeks, Brandon reached out toward his dad to be comforted. Horrified, Mr. Burnham literally pushed him away and loudly reprimanded him for crying in front of everyone. I heard a collective gasp from the watching adults, who were obviously as startled as I at Mr. Burnham's reaction. I had to intervene and take Brandon off the field. As he sobbed deeply on the bench, I sat down next to him and placed a fatherly arm over his tiny heaving shoulders. He immediately threw my arm off, then yelled at me for placing him in a position where the sun made it impossible for him to catch the ball.

Meanwhile, a fight had ensued on the field. Mr. Burnham had called the batter out due to the infield-fly rule. No once could convince him there must be someone on base to call the infield-fly rule.

## Hallmarks of the "B-I-A-K-I-A" Parent

Mr. Burnham and his son demonstrate three essentials of the Blame-It-All parent: blame-blame-blame, or "That is not me; I did not do it; You did it!" In psychological terms, this is called 1) denial, 2) suppression, and 3) projection.

Denial is typified by the words, "That is not me." Mr. Burnham refused to recognize, and in fact actively denied, the truth: his son was an average player, and he, the father, was an average-talent (to be generous) adult.

Suppression is typified by the "I did not do it" claim. Mr. Burnham suppressed his own desires by refusing to distinguish between his needs and those of his son. He had to have his son succeed at all costs due to his own perceived shortcomings. His continual criticisms were meant to tell everyone that it was his son (not him) who wanted to be "the best"; it was his son (not him), therefore, who was letting everyone down.

"You did it" indicates projection. Mr. Burnham projected—that is, blamed—any shortcoming or mistake on everything and everyone else: the condition of the field, the sun, the coaches, the other players.

Mr. Burnham had never accepted himself, and therefore could never accept his son. This is so typical of a Blame-It-All parent. It was obvious to me and anyone else who saw him run, for example, that he would have had a hard time bowling, much less being a soccer star. The Blame-It-All's characteristics of denial and projection often lead to frequent confrontations with coaches, umpires, and other parents. Blame-It-All parents use manipulation and dissension to force their distortion of truth or reality onto others, who will not simply accept it, as their child must. Unfortunately, their ultimate opportunity for manipulation comes when they turn manager, which, just as unfortunately, they often do—as did Mr. Burnham. The hallmarks of their teams are winning at all costs; favoritism; berating officials, opposing teams, and coaches; projecting any shortcomings onto others, and using the rules against others while, at the same time, constantly breaking them to their own advantage. Eventually the vice president and president of the league get badgered by a majority of the team's parents, who complain that the coach is not playing some of the children.

The characteristic words used by Blame-It-All parents are similar to the ones used by Overachiever parents, whose children are "the best," "excellent," "exceptional"; the Blame-It-All's child is all those, but with the qualified blame.

"My son is the best, but his manager stinks."

"My son is a great hitter, but did not get on base all year because of the coach."

# *Dealing with the Mr. Burnhams*

These parents are true pains in the butts, believe me! Unfortunately, since we all have a little of each type of parent in us, not every Blame-It-All parent sticks out as much as Mr. Burnham.

How does one deal with this type of dad or mom? With great difficulty, I am afraid. I have, however, developed a three-step approach. First, I acknowledge the parent's good intentions: "Mr. Burnham, it is so clear that you love your child. Your interest in his ball playing tells me that."

Second, I confront his behavior. "Criticizing your son, or blaming others, though, does not solve the problem of his missing the ball."

Third, I offer a positive alternative. "Since you are so concerned, try to always see the bright side of what he does, like getting in front of the ball. If you cannot think of anything positive to say, let someone else comment on his game."

When all coaxing fails, though (and it often does), I find it best to end the relationship. I have three ways of doing that, too.

In the first method, I just let him have it. "Mr. Burnham, you are an overstuffed *^%@##* -head who knows *#@** about baseball. If you do not like how I coach, I will arrange another coach to take your *&%##*!"

My second technique is to kill him with cynicism. "Mr. Burnham, I am only a board-certified neurologist, not a professional T-ball coach. What you need is a psychiatrist."

The third way is to try diplomacy. "Mr. Burnham, I realize you are dissatisfied with your son's progress. I try my best, but I feel you need more than I can give you and your son. Therefore, I will recommend to the league president that he be placed on another team."

The first and second ways, of course, will make you feel a lot better—but the third will solve the problem for you just as well, without worsening the situation for all. Some people are alone because they build walls instead of bridges. Be a bridge builder. Do not accept the unacceptable.

## *Where Are They Now?*

Mr. Burnham's son, Brandon, turned out to be an independent boy. Luckily, he was sent to a private school out of the country and was, he later told me, greatly influenced by a teacher who reminded him of me. "Sort of pudgy around the middle and not too smart," he joked. Brandon still remembers that time I put my arm around him. It made him feel cared for. That surprised me. It is amazing how differently a child and an adult remember the same life event.

# 9

# THE "UNFULFILLED" PARENT: I COULDA BEEN A CONTENDER

*"We cannot live our children's lives,*
*and they cannot heal our childhood wounds."*

—Jim Chavez, DA Washington Little League

**HARRIS RARELY SMILED.** I had never seen such determination in a ten-year-old. His dad, the struggling owner of a small gas station, was always there in his uniform with grease under his fingernails and sweat on his brow—a hardworking, good man. This dad was always practicing with his son, always demanding that he try harder, be better. Harris was definitely talented. The consistency in his pitching and hitting showed hours and hours of practice. His dad, well, he was a good parent—maybe too good. Everything seemed to be life or death to him, as if every pitch his son threw or every swing he took determined the outcome of not only his life, but of the world.

We were playing the Dodgers one day, and Harris was pitching. As he skipped out toward the mound, he was full of enthusiasm, pounding his glove and grinning at the second baseman. I heard his dad yell out, "Remember, Harris, we have to beat the Dodgers today." His dad then proceeded to comment on every pitch Harris made. Despite this, Harris did fine for three innings; in the fourth, though, they started hitting him. His dad's strained demeanor began to crack, and he became openly critical.

"Throw harder."

"Kick that leg up."

"Spring off the mound."

"What's wrong with you?"

He was barking orders at his own son the way a drill sergeant would bark at his troops. A Russian general in frozen Siberia would have had more mercy in his voice.

The bases were loaded. Harris wound up and threw a fast ball down the center of the plate. The determined Dodger slugged it right up the middle to center field. As two runs were scored, I looked at the mound. Harris lay there cringing in pain, crying and holding his arm. His dad did not notice, because he had buried his head in his hands, as if he were watching his gas station and all his possessions go up in smoke. I ran out to help Harris. His elbow was mildly tender, but I could find no other problem. I picked him up gently and walked off the field. He whimpered, "No, I have to pitch or my dad will be hurt."

Harris's arm was not truly injured, and we both knew it. What he really feared was letting his dad down. Harris recognized how much his pitching—and pitching well—meant to his father.

## *"I Coulda Been a Contender"*

Some parents, after 30 to 40 years of their lives, come to the sudden realization that their fantasies and self-expectations have not been met: "If I had only bought that home ten years ago…it's worth a fortune now;" "My brother, he was the quiet one, but smart. He got a good education. He is knocking down the big bucks now, and I don't mean the type with antlers."

I am sure you have heard these laments, if not said them yourself. Each one of us has been struck sometime in our lives by our own self-reflection. When we look at ourselves as we really are, the true meaning of life becomes apparent, seemingly at that moment. Some call it the "time of wisdom."

This sudden parental insight (or hindsight) into all those lost opportunities is probably the most frequent single cause of conflict between good-intentioned parents and their children. The children are unaware of their parents' trials and tribulations; they are untouched by such cruel realities of life as money, prestige and power. They enter the Little League field as Harris did, with bright, wondrous, smiling faces, ready to have a good time. They come to be a part of the great American pastime of baseball. Their gloves reach from their belt buckles to their socks, their uniforms seem somehow built around them like a sack on a stick, and their glistening grins are innocent. They seem so perfectly in contact with nature. Are they aware of what their first stride to home plate means to their parents? More important, do their parents even realize what it means to them? Probably not. I am certain Harris's dad did not recognize what he was doing to his son, nor how he had erased the smile from his little boy's face.

## *Listen to What They Do*

Tucker's dad was an old army sergeant. If he was not, he sure could have fooled me. Tucker played shortstop. He was good, possibly the best shortstop in the league. His dad had an awful lot invested in his son. Talented as he was, though, Tucker did not walk with his head erect and his chest puffed out like the king of the roost. He stood round-shouldered, as if defeated. There was a stumble in his step, a slip to his skip, and a hitch to his hop. He acted as if he carried the world on his little shoulders. Tucker, you see, had a problem: as coordinated as he was, he always seemed to twist his ankle, only to enjoy a miraculous cure several plays later. The twisted ankles occurred whenever he missed a ball—especially if it was on a play his dad considered important. After many such instances, his mother confirmed my suspicions. Why was he so accident prone? By now, it was obvious to us all: Tucker had learned his dad would not yell at him when he was hurt. He had learned he could avoid reprimand through injury.

Did Tucker's father realize what he was teaching his son? Again, as with Harris's dad, probably not, yet both boys were giving their fathers strong warnings. Children at this age, though truthful, continue to communicate some of their most important messages in nonverbal form. We must learn to "hear" what they are saying with their bodies and faces. We must also learn to step back and distinguish our own needs from theirs. Children do not need to be perfect; they need to be content. They do not need to produce under pressure; they need to be encouraged in a positive direction. They do not need angry, biting sarcasm; they need discipline combined with positive reinforcement and praise for appropriate behavior. If we do what causes contentment, we will always see the results in our children, especially through nonverbal signs. They will have a glide in their stride, and a small skip to their step.

## *Sammy and the Tigers' Coach*

The Tigers' coach had some angry words with his team. If I had not known who he was talking to, I would have expected Steinbrenner's Yankees to come running out of the dugout. Instead, a small group of six-, seven- and eight-year-olds walked out with stunted steps, slumped heads, and drooping shoulders; several had tears in their eyes. The Tigers' first baseman threw a practice grounder to the second baseman; it went through the little guy's legs. The coach bellowed, "Get your head in the game, Sammy. Get in front of it. What are you afraid of, the ball hitting you?"

Sammy looked into the dirt. The first man up plunked a grounder right to—who else—Sammy. The ball, not hit very hard, took a bad bounce and hit Sammy in the stomach. Sammy picked the ball up and threw out the runner. His coach barked out, "About time you stopped something." Sammy's face reddened. He sat down on second base and began to cry, holding his stomach.

Being the only doctor on the field, I ran out and asked where it hurt. Sammy pointed to his heart. There was no mark. The ball used for T-ball is very light and generally will not cause injury, even if it hits a child in the head.

Sammy cried out, "I can't play anymore, Coach. Can I go home now?"

As I walked the child off, the coach scoffed, "This kid is a crybaby. He has to learn to take some punishment. Do you think you give up just because you're hit? I can't understand these kids."

Sammy was the coach's son.

A coach who does not understand children is like a schoolteacher who does not know the subject he is expected to teach. Understanding baseball at the T-ball, farm, minor, or major levels is not enough. The coach must also understand the physical, mental, psychological, and moral development of children. These are not seasoned veterans or professionals; they are small children with wholesome hearts and impressionable minds, who respond well to the affirmative and are easily crushed by the negative. If I had taped what some of my fellow coaches and team parents said during the course of the season and played it back to them a year later, most would be horrified. Parents need to nurture their children with warm, positive regard and acceptance, for these are the tools that will make them have the right stuff, and be contented, self-reliant, and successful later in life.

### FROM JIM GERSTENSLAGER
#### WESTERN LITTLE LEAGUE DIRECTOR

*My nine guidelines to being a little league parent are:*

1. *Remember to have fun with your child.*
2. *Don't be an ump from the bleachers.*
3. *Always be positive.*
4. *Accept your children for who they are.*
5. *Never compare your child to others.*
6. *Keep your expectations realistic.*
7. *Be on time for practice and games.*
8. *Make safety a priority.*
9. *Emphasize sportsmanship and effort over winning.*

# *Where Are They Now?*

Tucker Cox, the most talented fielder in the league, dropped out of sports in his senior year of high school. His dad, the infamous Coach Cox, still cannot understand why.

I saw Sammy, the boy who cried when hit by a soft grounder and pointed to his heart to show where it hurt, as a patient when he was a teenager. He was having tension headaches. His mother noticed he got them every time he had an important exam coming up. I had no doubt that his father-coach, who had labeled him a crybaby, was intensely involved, trying his best to help and teach Sammy. Unfortunately, he expected too much from the boy, both in Little League and in his teen years. Despite his good intentions, he managed only to crush rather than nurture him.

# 10

# COACHES' EXPECTATIONS: ROOT OF ALL EVIL

*"Many go through life running from something that is not after them."*

—Dr. Edwin Todd,
My mentor

## *The Headlines*

**I STRODE FROM THE DUGOUT TO THE MOUND,** tipped my cap back, and motioned to the infielders. They quickly gathered around me. It was the bottom of the ninth inning, one out, man on first and third. We were up by one run—the National Championship hung on this next play. A fly ball, and the game would be tied. Our hometown fans mumbled anxiously, causing the stadium to hum like a beehive. The tension was so thick it was smothering. In the stands, the media people hammered out their news reports awaiting only the title. Would it be **FORTANASCE, MVP MANAGER, DOES IT AGAIN** or **FORTANASCE FAILS ONCE AGAIN**? I delivered my orders. With hands on my hips, I confidently strode back to the dugout to the roar of the crowd. The pitcher, Orel, blazed a fast ball, high and outside, as I had instructed. The runner on first, as I had anticipated, was darting toward second. The catcher fired toward second base as the man on third was signaled to go home.

Orel cut the throw off from the catcher and caught the stunned third-base runner dead in his tracks. Another managerial triumph. The cleanup batter then hammered a drive to the warning track, which was caught easily by our center fielder. The game was over. The stands burst into a chant, "Fortanasce, Fortanasce," as the players carried me in triumph to the center of the field. Suddenly a gruff voice said, "Hey, Coach, wake up. You have two little kids arguing about who gets to play first base." At first startled, I suddenly realized where I was. My visions of notoriety and an adoring public vanished.

Expectations, expectations. Was this why I had said yes to coaching the Angels team?

As a coach or manager, you must sometimes wonder, as we all do, whatever possessed you to accept the great responsibility of guiding and directing a Little League team. Many claim, "I did it only because no one else wanted the position. It was either do it, or the children don't play." Some do it for "my kid"; still others find it a challenge, something they have always wanted to do. For me it was tradition. My dad coached me when I was a child. I just naturally expected to do the same for my children.

No matter how you come about the position—voluntarily, by default, or through guilt—once you are there you have your own expectations. Like mine, these expectations are both conscious and unconscious. My conscious expectation was to coach a championship team. My unconscious expectation involved the fear of failure—**FORTANASCE FAILS AGAIN** in the headlines.

When you are a manager, you have more than just your own expectations to worry about. Every coach must contend with parental and team expectations and feelings of success or failure—and all of these are ultimately directed at you. "My child did not have a good experience because the coach stunk"—I have heard that remark at least a million times. Of course, they were referring to some other coach than me!

Just imagine: you have at least 30 individual parents with conscious and unconscious expectations for their son or daughter—and you. You also have to contend with all the expectations of the opposing manager, coaches, and teams; often, these set up severe conflicts. Put them all together, and you have expectations running rampant even before the season beings! Any veteran manager or coach will tell you that a competitive opposing manager is enough to kindle latent pride and hostilities in even the most gentle and docile coach. If you are already a fierce competitor in life, Little League can bring you to the brink of insanity and make you say and do things you thought only crazy people did. You could easily end up as so many of us have in the past—mature and educated adults in real life, but jumping up and down in a tantrum on the baseball field, with as many as a hundred other parents and 30 children looking on, wondering who is the adult and who is the kid.

## *Bloopers I Have Known*

"What are you afraid of?" huffed Mr. Gardner, a short, beer-bellied, hard-driving coach. Sweat dripped off his red neck in the hot noon sun. With a small bat riveted to his right hand, he threw another ball with his left and chopped down on it fiercely, causing it to bite into the dry clay and shoot toward the second baseman. He bellowed, "Get in front of it. We don't need no chickens on this team."

Pow! A shot to the left fielder, who dove for the ball but missed it. "What do we have there, a bunch of babies, or are we going to be men?"

A short while later, I eavesdropped as the Hawks sat around Mr. Gardner. "Listen up! You look like a bunch of toddling babies out there, like a bunch of sissies. How are you going to win if every time a ball is hit a little too hard you jump out of the way? You've got to learn to take a couple of hard knocks. You've got to be tough to win, or you'll be losers all your life. Now, anybody got anything to say?"

One little hand went up. "Mr. Gardner, Dicky wet his pants again."

Mr. Gardner sneered down at Dicky, a three-foot tot—only two feet sitting. "Why didn't you tell me you had to go to the bathroom?" he demanded.

Dicky whimpered, "You said in the last practice, no one was ever allowed to go to the bathroom again, Mr. Gardner, and if we did, we should do it in our pants." He then cried. His teammates empathized with him; they all stared sadly down at the dirt.

A coach must recognize his children's stage of development and capacities, or he will doom his little bright prospects to failure, just the opposite of his intent. If you met him on the street, you would think Mr. Gardner was a bit rough around the edges, but a well-meaning and very dedicated dad. He simply forgot that these children were not on the gridiron with the Raiders, but on the Little League diamond, being children. His expectations and those of his players were definitely not the same.

## I Cannot Believe I Said That

Nothing saddens me more than hearing a parent or coach openly berate a Little Leaguer at bat. I cringe every time I hear one of the more benevolent coaches bellow out, "This one can't hit it," or "Hit it to second 'cause he can't catch."

Few adults realize how powerful their words truly are. We may think kids never listen, but certain words penetrate and are never forgotten. I learned this too late, in my second year as a T-ball manager.

One of the more talented children, Tammy, seemed depressed whenever I played with her. After the third practice, I put my arm over her shoulder and said, "What's wrong, Tammy?" She ignored me and walked away. Being well-versed in child psychiatry though, I began to expertly probe, hoping I would hit a nerve that would open her up.

"I notice your dad isn't here. Does he play with you?"

"Sure," the girl said solemnly.

Tammy had not played with me last year, but I had notice her talent and made sure to draft her in my second year as coach. This year, I had said to myself, I would have a first-place team! After a number of oblique psychological references, I saw I was not getting anywhere. I decided to try the honest approach.

"What's wrong, Tammy?"

She answered curtly, "You said I stunk last year, and I don't like you, I don't like baseball. My dad makes me play it."

I was shocked. Me? The great therapist had said this kid stunk? I later learned she overheard me telling on of my players to hit the ball to a certain base, because that player could not catch. My Little Leaguer hit it to Tammy—and she remembered that a full year later. Had I unintentionally destroyed the confidence of a talented child? Just imagine what I had done to the confidence of the child I had really directed that comment to! Why, I asked myself, was I so insensitive to these little children, saying things like "He's no batter. Infield move in, he's an easy out." We coaches and parents must learn that our words can burn like a wildfire, or heal like a miracle. They wound the spirit of a child like a bullet, or instill confidence like a magical potion.

I started thinking back, remembering other remarks I had made without thinking. At one pregame pep talk I had said, "Okay, kids, watch their infield—you see their third baseman has no arm."

Mary had yelled, "Yes, he does, Coach, he has two."

Another remark: "The second baseman can't catch."

"Yeah, I know," Carlos agreed. "He goes to school with me, and I already told him that. I will tell him you said so, too, Coach."

I think back on all the games I played with six- to 12-year-olds in the past 14 years. I long ago learned that winning or losing was not important to them as long as after the game I smiled and said, "You guys did a great job," and their parents hugged them and acted proud. I started doing this that second year, and we had a winning season pretty much from then on—despite the fact that I stopped recruiting talented kids and started looking, instead, for interested and loving parents. By the end of the season, no matter how many games we had lost, the children's faces would gleam, and their only sorrow would be that it was over until next spring.

## *Oh, Yes, They Hear Us*

By the way, in case you ever wonder if your children are listening, let me tell you of a conversation I had with a fellow physician, my age, just the other day. We had been talking about children when I gently inquired why he and his wife had never had any. Thinking I would get the usual biological-problem explanation, I was stunned to hear it was due to his parents, who often spoke about him when he was well within earshot. What stood out most in his memory, he said, was his father's comment to several other coaches on the Little League field: "Sometimes I wish I had never had a son when I see how uncoordinated and goofy he looks out there." My friend was 12 at the time. From that moment on, he said, he decided not to have a child, because he did not want it to go through the same humiliation. I could not help but wonder if he was subconsciously afraid of humiliating his own son, or of his father doing it.

Please, parents, remember: children may not seem to be listening, but believe me, they hear every word, positive and negative, that we say about them. Every child wears an invisible sign that says **NOTICE ME, MAKE ME FEEL IMPORTANT.** Every time you look at the number of his or her uniform, see that sign!

## *Where Are They Now?*

Well, Dr. Fortanasce is now a guilt-ridden author who writes parenting books to try to make up for his blunders. He hopes some of the children he has coached over the years have finally forgiven him and that others are not waiting to get even.

# 11

# CHILDREN'S
# EXPECTATIONS

*"Happiness can be measured in smiles."*

—**Momma Fortanasce**

**GREG LOOKED LIKE A MODERN VERSION** of Rodin's "Thinker" as his brow furrowed and his mighty chin rested on his hand. A scholarship to Notre Dame, the 2002 Olympic team, a small jaunt at triple-A baseball, then right to the majors with a minimum of seven digits a season plus a healthy bonus. Ahhhh!

Greg's son snapped him out of his daydream. "Gee, Dad, why can't I get one of those nifty green-and-yellow uniforms the A's have? When can I pick up the bat and hit the ball? Can we get a hamburger and fries after the game?"

Did you ever ask yourself what a child entering Little League for the first time thinks about playing baseball? What are his expectations? Most will answer, "I don't know," unless they have played with neighbors or their brothers or sisters. If you persist, they will say they want to have fun, which is exactly what adults initially say they want for their kids—that is, until they get indoctrinated by veteran parents and coaches to enter the world of competition and think about "winning." Competition means competing against others, trying to be better than your opponent—trying to beat him. Is that what a child really wants to do, compete and beat? Or does he want to play, like he did in preschool, and have fun with other children? Play is the work of children—it is their job, the way the learn social skills.

This is a test. Do not panic. Just pick A or B.

A child of six, seven or eight would rather:

(a) slide in the dirt

(b) button his uniform and keep his hat on straight

(a) hit a ball and run

(b) keep his shirt tucked in his pants

(a) have his parents cheer and smile at him

(b) have his parents tell him to be quiet and listen

If you picked all Bs, you are a typical coach and average Little League parent. If you picked all As, you have a good sense of what children cherish and expect, and what Little League is all about. Surprised this chapter is so short? Children's expectations are short and simple—and make a lot of sense. Some of us should listen to them sometimes and have fun and play. It is obvious, isn't it?

> *"Listen to your children and have fun!"*
>
> From the Gang:
> Tommy Lasorda, Mike Scioscia, Dr. Frank Job, Rob Dedeauax,
> Tom Boyle, Mike Legg, Luke LaPorta, Jim Chavez,
> Tony Monteleone, Micky Haggert,
> Tommy John (Cy Young Winner, NY Yankees),
> Orel Hershiser and Al & Al

# SECTION 3
## CHARACTER

## *Lasorda's Hall of Honor*

**EVERYONE KNOWS** that Tommy Lasorda loves to win. But if I had to win through dishonesty or by cheating I would have quit the game years ago. My World Series rings, my pennant wins would be worthless. Winning is valuable but meaningful when it is earned through hard work. Any Little League coach who teaches this wins, no matter the score, and so do the children. They learn the most valuable lesson: Honesty is the only policy. Integrity is built on honesty. Winning is fleeting but honor endures forever.

You can't legislate honesty, it comes from within. If there is one thing a Little League coach must teach it is to honor honesty. With honesty comes team spirit and loyalty, the building blocks of sportsmanship. To teach honesty you don't need to know much about baseball, nor do you need a college degree. All you need to know is right from wrong and how you like to be treated. The Golden Rule. Maybe this is why many parents, especially moms, make such great coaches.

What gets me upset is seeing Little League games where the coaches put winning ahead of honesty. I have even heard them say, "Good guys finish last," "You gotta get even," "If they cheat, you gotta too." Others laugh ho-ho-ho at honesty. But if you take the HO out of honesty, you're left with

NASTY. You may laugh at this—which is good—I want to see you keep the ho-ho-ho in honesty. It also leads me nicely on to my next point: keeping baseball fun for kids. Little League is about having a good time with friends. It's about working together and learning how to get along. It is about life and life's lessons.

When I was a youngster, there was no Little League, no organized sports and no umpires or coaches, just us kids. We'd walk five miles, uphill all the way, through Norristown, Pennsylvania to get to the ball park. There we'd play a team from a nearby town. You might think that without adult supervision and umpires we must have been a disorganized rabble, with nobody to keep everyone honest, no one to stop fights breaking out. But there were no such problems because we all had honor; we all honored honesty. Cheaters were not tolerated. We all realized that unless we were truthful and stood up for what was right, winning would have no meaning and the game would not be any fun. And after all, that was the reason we were all there: to have fun. That can only come with honesty and equality for all.

Remember this: if you win by cheating, in my mind it is a loss not a win. The great game of baseball will become a mockery. A Little League coach who doesn't make himself an example of honesty and integrity but tells his players that it's OK to bend the rules (a nice way of saying cheating) is doing harm to both the children and the game of baseball. Such a coach is saying, "I am the adult and I say it is more important to win any way you can."

As Mike Scioscia said in the foreword, winning is never final and losing is never fatal. Unfortunately, statistics seem to reign as most important in today's world. If it were up to me, I'd start the Lasorda Hall of Honor, which would hail those who helped their teams excel because of their honesty and their undying efforts to set a great example. Men like Connie Mack, Orel Hershiser and many more.

There is no room for the D words in Little League: deceit, dishonesty and dissension. Little League coaches need to remember that the word coach starts with a C, the same as character, courage and camaraderie that all build community and cohesion. This is the essence of baseball and the Lasorda Hall of Honor.

# 12

## SUCCESS: WHOSE? YOURS OR YOUR CHILD'S?

*"Is success the same thing for a child as it is for an adult?
If it is, then why don't adults like playing in the mud
and children like staying clean?"*

—Micky Haggert
**Angels coach**

**THE FIRST RAYS OF EARLY MORNING SUNSHINE** kissed the empty bleachers surrounding Triumph Park baseball field. I took a deep breath, savoring the clean morning air, and allowed myself a wry smile. This is what life is all about, I thought. Spending a summer morning with my son and my Little League team. Marvin, my assistant coach, shuffled past without a word. He stopped by home plate and stood motionless, his eyes pinned on the distant horizon.

"What's up, Marv?" I asked with a cheerful smile.

"Nothing," he mumbled without looking over. I'd known Marvin for 20 years. He was a senior sales executive for a medical supply company and was normally a bubbly, enthusiastic man, never short of something to say. The uncharacteristic scowl on his face and brooding look on his face told me something was most definitely up.

I patted him on the back and asked again. "Come on, what's wrong?"

He took a deep breath and finally turned to look at me. And then he poured out his story. He had worked for the same company for 15 years and for the past year he had spent every waking hour trying to secure a huge new account. That week the deal had fallen through and in less than five minutes 15 years of dedication and service had been forgotten. Instead of becoming the new VP of Sales, Marvin had been fired. Just when he thought he was on the brink of success and felt secure, the rug was pulled out from underneath him. I felt such empathy but nothing I could say was going to change the look of failure he had on his face.

Marvin's son, David, took up his usual position in center field and the first ball was thrown. Today my Angels were facing the league champions. Marvin watched quietly from the dugout, his mind clearly not on the game. David was in the thick of all the action. He dived to make catches in the field, swung with all his might when he was batting. He dropped a couple of catches and was struck out twice but he was focused, having fun, and he never gave up. He tried his very best and put every ounce of effort and enthusiasm into the game right up until the final out. Despite all his efforts, though, the League Champions proved to be too good for the Angels, and we lost 11-7.

I watched as David ran over to his dad at the end of the game, his shirt soaked in sweat and his face glowing with the satisfaction of having given his all. "Hey, Dad, how d'you like my home run?"

Marvin shrugged. "It was for nothing," he muttered. "You lost." And with that, David's face dropped and he silently trudged after his father to the car.

# Second Place is No Place
## —or—
# Do or Die

There is not a parent I've met who doesn't want the best for his or her child. We all want our children to be successful, but have you ever asked yourself, "What is success for a child and how does it differ from success for an adult?"

If you asked Marvin, he'd tell you what happens when you don't succeed. For him and most adults, success is closing the deal, being the champion, the millionaire, the number one. In other words, success is winning. Success is determined by results alone. Marvin and any Major League baseball player will tell you, second place is no place at all. Sometimes this adult quest for success necessitates the need to be less than honest.

In psychology, we talk of a child's world since a child's world is so different from an adult's world (thank God). In a child's world, life does not depend upon results, unless we, the parents, say it does. In fact, from a neurological standpoint, it is the repetition of continued effort that enhances brain cell maturation and the development of neural connections. Effort and repetition enhance a child's innate abilities, not winning. In fact, it is important for a child to NOT get it right the first time, because repetition is needed for neural maturation. Positive reinforcement can occur whether a child wins or not, because success in a child's world lies in the eyes of the parents and their acceptance. You can reinforce effort or winning, but know that the winning is everything attitude fostered by adults condemns a child to failure, since the statistics of winning point to only one thing: everyone is eventually a loser. In sports you always have a 50-percent chance of losing. Why give your child such bad odds when it is you who determines the odds in the first place?

## *The Door to the Room of Success Swings on the Hinges of Determination*

Success for a child is not measured by the outcome of the game but in the amount of effort he puts in and by determination to pick himself up when he is down and things are going badly. Success for a child is trying, never giving up and enjoying the game. This means every child can be successful, because every child is capable of trying his or her best.

Marvin made two mistakes with David. First, he failed to recognize his son's success in never giving up despite being on the losing team. In fact, David felt satisfied with himself because of the positive comments made by his teammates and the other parents during the game. Everyone except his father applauded his efforts, even when he made mistakes. His father, on the other hand, simply imposed the adult measure of success on his son, that winning is everything. Marvin devalued the one factor that would truly make Danny a success in life: his determination. When a child continues to try, it means he's enjoying himself. This positive feeling makes the child want to repeat the actions that caused it, in this case, trying hard on the Little League field. The positive feelings derived from baseball develop into feelings of self-confidence that are then transferred to other endeavors later in life.

The second mistake Marvin made was to lose sight of the fact that success is not determined solely by his career or his performance in the work place. Success is more about the quality of your closest personal relationships. Success is the smile on your child's face, the warmth in your spouse's embrace when they look at you.

Adult misconceptions of success lead to five myths about winning:

1. Winning is final.
2. Losing is fatal.
3. There is more to be learned by winning than losing.
4. Success is a place, a destination.
5. Success equals happiness.

## Myth 1: Winning is Final

For the Giants' coach, Guy, winning was always final. He was a successful businessman and now he would be nothing but the best Little League coach and lead the championship team. What he forgot was reality. What he forgot was that each time his team played, there was only a 50/50 chance of winning, that the chance of winning was dependent upon the kids, the players in his team, not Guy himself. Guy hadn't asked an essential question: did anyone else care?

The odds of winning are always stacked against him, and even if he does win, then there is next year to deal with. Only one team in any competition can wear the crown in any one year. No team manages to repeat the feat year after year. What pressure, what nonsense it is to believe that winning is final. Yet that is what many coaches and parents think. Worse are the parents who think their child will make it to the Major Leagues. Only about one in

150,000 kids who play Little League will go on to play in Major League Baseball. So no matter how successful a child is in Little League, chances are he will never make it to the big leagues. So winning is never final.

Unfortunately, many parents, in their determination to make their child the best, harm their child's feelings of self-confidence in the process. Sometimes winning can be fatal.

### Myth 2: Losing is Fatal

In the fourth game of the 1998 NBA Finals, the Bulls were one point down with six seconds left on the clock. Michael Jordan drove toward the basket, tripped, and the ball was taken away from him. He lay on the floor dejected and humiliated. He had failed to score and his team had lost the game. But this was nothing new for a player who was named as one of the 10 best athletes of the last century. In fact, Jordan missed the winning shot in the last seconds of the game no fewer than 131 times. Yet he is still arguably the greatest player to have ever played the sport.

Apart from the fact that they were all great hitters, Babe Ruth, Mark McGwire and Mickey Mantle have one thing in common. They all had the highest percentage of strikeouts, especially with the bases loaded. What they and Michael Jordan realized was that without trying there would never be any reward, and that losing is always a possibility when you try. They also proved that losing—if you've given your best—is never fatal.

For children, losing isn't fatal unless someone convinces them otherwise. Unlike many adults, children are resilient to defeat. Adults will stew over mistakes and mishaps for days or weeks after a game. Children's attention, however, is always focused on the "here and now" which gives them the ability to keep trying without becoming discouraged—unless an adult convinces them to do otherwise.

Losing determination and effort, however, can be fatal.

> *Instill the desire to be determined in your child rather than the desire to win and your child will be successful no matter what the final score.*
>
> **—Rod Dedeaux**
> **Baseball Coach of the Century, USC**

### Myth 3: You Learn More from Winning Than Losing

Coach Vic was in charge of a very talented bunch of players, the Rangers, but he always demanded perfection from his young Little Leaguers. Even after a victory, he was critical and unappreciative of his players' effort.

Brett's team, the Jaguars, on the other hand, were less talented and lost their first five games of the season. Brett, though, always recognized the effort his players had put in, regardless of the final score. The players appreciated and respected Brent, and he was able to use their losses as teaching tools so that they would always go into the following week's game with great excitement, determined to play better and show Brett that they wouldn't be making the same mistakes again. Their losses were never fatal but rather lessons to be learned. When the Jaguars and the Rangers met, Vic's team ran out 7-4 winners, but the smiles on the faces of the Jaguars showed which team had enjoyed themselves and at the same time learned an important life lesson: you can still learn from defeat. It's trying one's best and being appreciated for that effort, not being the best, that makes one a winner in life. Determination stems from positive reinforcement of effort. Parents and coaches should never forget that.

Brett's team was less talented but they did go on to eventually win the league. Vic's Rangers fell quickly from first place to mid-table. The following year, the true measure of success became clear. Brett's players all returned for another season, Vic's players turned to other sports or dropped out all together.

Since everyone will eventually lose, the most that can be learned from that experience is that it's "OK to lose, just don't lose the lesson."

### Myth 4: Success is a Destination

The idea that success is a destination, a place you end up is reinforced by popular media images. Lose 20 pounds and your destination will be a beach and a bikini and the chance to walk off into the sunset with your perfect mate. Success is the Mercedes in the driveway, the expensive watch on your wrist, the place you end up.

In reality, success is a process, part of a long journey. Success on the journey known as Little League is when your child learns a life lesson as he plays, picking up the qualities such as honor, responsibility and compassion.

After Larry had finished pitching the final inning of a game, I saw his father walk up to him and proudly ruffle his hair. During the inning Larry had thrown a pitch that conceded three runs and knocked our team out of the playoffs. "I'm proud of you, Larry," his dad said. "Because you kept pitching your best to finish the inning, even though you knew you weren't going to win." His dad was right. Larry had determinedly stuck to his task even though he had no chance of winning, and in that process had proved himself a winner.

## Myth 5: Success Means Happiness

Julie was a confident child, captain of her Little League team as well as the League's best player. At the end of the season, she was voted MVP of our team, but she showed little enthusiasm when she collected the award. She looked sullen and bored, a complete contrast to her father who beamed from ear to ear. We all knew why. Julie wanted to sing in a rock band, but her father refused to let her waste her time on a pursuit he regarded as shallow and a waste of time when she was obviously such a natural ball player.

For Julie, all her success was meaningless, devoid of any happiness because her passion lay somewhere else. Her dad was an overachiever parent, who thought he knew what was best for his daughter. Remember, success is getting what you want, but happiness is liking what you get.

### FROM MANAGER MIKE SCIOSCIA'S DUGOUT

*Remember: It is better to have tried and lost, than not tried and succeeded. We can never be certain that things will always go right, but we can be certain that things will eventually go wrong. Adults and children have little trouble dealing with success, but it is how they deal with losing, with disappointment that makes the difference in their lives. We cannot protect children from the world, we can only prepare them for it. Remember, winning doesn't breed success, it's effort, determination and discipline that breed success.*

*Parents must understand:*

1.  *Adversity is the mother of invention: it provides coaches and parents an opportunity to teach children how to deal with disappointment.*
2.  *Winning does not build ultimate success.*
3.  *Effort, diligence, discipline, and determination (i.e., character) build success.*

*If parents and coaches recognize only the score, then all children will at some point be losers. But if we recognize effort that leads to character development, then all children, regardless of talent, can be winners.*

> **"Remember: success is building character and will end in a happy child."**
>
> —**Tommy Lasorda**

## *Where Are They Now?*

There was a reason Marvin's son David never gave up. He had the example set by his father. Marvin soon got a new job at a computer company and quickly rose to the position of Vice President. David is currently in graduate school; computers are his game as well.

# 13

# CHARACTER VS. TALENT: SOLID VS. SLICK

*"You gotta have character to recognize it."*

—Tony Monteleone, DA Little League

*"I've known a lot of characters but only a few good men."*

—Jim Chavez, DA Washington Little League

**WHAT IS CHARACTER?** I asked 200 coaches this question and less than ten percent could provide a clear answer even though the majority said they thought they could recognize someone who had it. Many of them gave me a definition of talent rather than character. Of course, if we don't know how to play a game, we can never teach it; the same is true with character development. If we don't have a clear concept of what character is, we can't do a good job of instilling it into our kids.

One of the major problems in Little League and, indeed, all youth sports, is the confusion many coaches and parents have distinguishing talent from character. Talented kids are showered with adulation and special privileges, while less talented kids who demonstrate good character aren't shown any appreciation. In fact, it often seems that parents and coaches who DO recognize character are somehow out of sync with the modern winning-is-everything attitude. Take a look at the trouble that many of our sporting heroes get themselves into, the ones whose names fill newspaper columns for all their off-the-field problems. In most cases, there is no doubting their talent, but their exploits serve to highlight the difference between talent and character or conscience.

# *Talent Without Character*

Pat was simply our best player. He looked it and he played like it. With him, our team couldn't lose; without him, that's all we could do. When I first saw Pat play, with all his skill and self-confidence, I have to admit I was envious. I wished my son had the same talent, the same self-assurance. Pat had such speed, such agility in the field, such power in his hitting. His father was a lucky man, I thought. His son had a real future in baseball.

It was another of those pivotal games in my first season as manager of the Angels, and I needed Pat to be at his best. He arrived at the field a little late and his teammates greeted him like the prodigal son. They knew as well as I did that we had no chance of beating the Orioles without him. As always, Pat was a little aloof and warmed up on his own, sprinting, practicing his swing, etc. His teammates just looked on in awe. Then the game got underway. Pat went up to bat with his usual confidence but the Orioles' pitcher fired the ball past him. Then again and again. Pat struck out.

Each time Pat went up to bat, the Orioles pitcher comfortably struck him out. He tried crowding the plate, tried intimidating the pitcher, but was reprimanded by the ump. Pat turned around and taunted the pitcher with language that turned the air blue. I will always remember the rage that seemed to envelope him. He clenched his fists red with fury, spitting out obscenities. But nothing did him any good. Despite all his skill, all his power, he couldn't get the better of the Orioles' pitcher. Even cheating got him nowhere.

At the end of the game, Pat hadn't scored. In fact he hadn't even come close to hitting the ball. He stormed off the field and never returned to play for us again, despite our persistent attempts to coax him back. This young boy whom I so admired, who I wished my son could play like, turned out to be a talented but self-centered child used to always getting his own way. Vince Lombardi once said, "When the going gets tough, the tough [those with character] get going." Instead of being a boy with the "right stuff" to succeed, Pat turned out to be an endorsement of the motto, "When the going gets tough, quit."

He lacked something, even though that something was definitely not talent.

So what is character and how does it differ from talent?

My dad, who was also my Little League coach as a kid, summed up the difference between talent and character best. "Remember," he told me, "talent will get you to first base, but it is character that will bring you home."

## *Worshipping Talent Instead of Character*

Suzie walked out to bat like Britney Spears walking out on stage at the Hollywood Bowl. I watched in astonishment as the parents in the bleachers stood up and cheered like fans worshipping their idol. Suzie's mother was incredibly aloof and refused to even acknowledge other parents whom she deemed below her social standing. An icy chill always seemed to descend on me when she was near. "Hello, Doctor, how are you?" she'd say and then completely ignore my assistant coach standing next to me. Suzie was just the same. The team seemed to take on another dimension when she arrived. There may not officially be any royalty in this country, but there was no doubt that Suzie's talent had earned her the status as crown royal, even at just nine years of age. She could be late, slack off in practice and even treat her less talented teammates with disdain and everyone ignored it. There was one set of rules for her and another for the rest of team; a situation not unlike many major league teams, where star players are afforded royalty status despite being only too human.

> *"The adulation that parents and coaches shower on young athletes with talent while continually excusing their bad traits is a major problem in sports. In the long run this attitude does damage to both the player and the sport."*
>
> —Tommy John, Yankee great

John Nabor was a five-time Olympic swimming gold medallist who was disqualified from the Olympic trials for failing to touch the side with his hand during a turn. Because of his status in the sport, he could undoubtedly have had the call overruled and been reinstated onto the Olympic team. However, he insisted on doing what was right even though it cost him the chance to defend his Olympic title. He wasn't sure, but believed the judge may have been correct in her call. "If the rules are broken for the best," he said. "What does that teach the rest?"

Adulation and positive regard must be given in the same proportion to those who demonstrate character rather than just those who have talent. Little League players who have talent but no character must be taken to task as the umpire did with Pat. Players need to learn that it is not enough just to be talented, it's not enough just to hit home runs, and it's not enough just to throw strikes or be fast around the bases. A child needs to learn so much more.

# *True Character*

Character is not just about doing what you have to do; it's about doing much more. Character is about doing what is honest, what is fair, what is kind. But since so many coaches are unable to define character, we have a problem. A teacher who doesn't know his subject is a danger to his pupils. Parents or coaches trying to teach character when they can't clearly define it is like a swim coach trying to teach algebra. The children won't learn much, and the little they do learn won't be of much value.

True character is what shows up when we are tested, when we are at the point that might cost us dearly. Character embraces the qualities of trustworthiness, respect, responsibility, fairness, conscience and courage.

# *"Character Needs Courage"*

—**My cousin Gina**

Character and conscience are important, but without the courage to stand up for these virtues, the character-less and conscience-less people will always prevail.

I once watched a Little League game from the bleachers with three of the players' mothers: Missy, Cindy and Gina. One of the team's coaches kept having some of his players swap shirts so his best hitter, Simon, could move up the rotation and get more at-bats. When one of the fathers pointed out to him that this was cheating, he launched into a vicious tirade at him. Missy turned to me and said, "The coach completely demeaned that man. That's disrespectful and sets a terrible example to the kids." In so doing, Missy recognized some of the central virtues of character: caring, respect and being a role model.

Cindy, Shawn's mom, said, "This is so wrong. The coach is cheating by swapping shirts." Cindy demonstrated conscience, an intrinsic recognition of the difference between right and wrong. Although Cindy and Missy recognized the wrong in the coach's actions, how he had trampled upon every pillar of character, neither possessed the courage to air their views to him.

Gina, however, possessed plenty of courage and marched over to the coach, planted herself in front of him and forcefully told him that what he was doing was wrong. She even explained to him why his actions were so deplorable. Unfortunately, her words had little effect because there were too many gutless wonders like myself who lacked the courage to speak out. You can have character, you can have conscience, but without courage to demand that the principles of character and conscience be upheld, the win-at-all-costs attitude will prevail and the only losers will be the kids.

Of course, it's easy to talk about showing courage and taking a stand, but what is the best way for a parent to address these concerns without being confrontational? Al and Al advise the following:

1. Know your Little League coach. If the coach is defensive or inaccessible, then speak to his senior about your concerns.

2. If your coach is accessible, tell him directly and ask him to get feedback from other parents who have the same concerns.

3. Remember that timing is very important. A telephone call or a practice is often the least emotional and stressful time to confront your coach rather than in the heat of a game.

---

### FROM THE DESK OF DR. VINCE

*In a survey, 200 parents were asked what they most wanted their children to learn from sports. Character was near the bottom of the priorities. Another poll asked parents what single quality they most wanted for their child's future spouse: intelligence, wealth, good looks, creativity or good character. The overwhelming majority chose good character. In the battle of Character vs. Talent, Character emerges the victor.*

---

## *Where Are They Now?*

Pat, I still don't know. Have you seen him? Maybe he's become one of the "Ice Men." See Chapter 31, "The Ice Men."

Gina is now a lawyer. She defends those who can't defend themselves. She is courage.

# 14

# CHARACTER: THE WHAT

*"It is character that makes the world go round."*

## Mike Scioscia's Four Bases of Character

Why all the concern about character?

When you are in trouble or whenever you relate with other people, it's your character that makes you or breaks you. Character is what people see; it is how people judge you. It is you.

Character is also like a baseball diamond with four bases that you need to make the game. If one is missing you can't make the game of baseball work. If there is no first base there is nowhere to start. If home is missing you'll never score. So too, if any of the four bases of character are absent, something essential is missing. The same analogy can be made with a car. You'd never want your child to drive in a car with a wheel missing or a wheel that's unreliable. When they needed it most, they'd be in danger.

The four bases of character are:

First—Honesty

Second—Responsibility

Third—Respect

Home—Courage

Honesty gets it all started. Responsibility takes you to second. Respect gets you ready for home, and that is Courage. When you have courage, the ability to stand up for what is right, you are home and ready for Barry Bonds with the bases loaded.

I tell Little League parents you either have character or you don't. You aren't partly a character, or maybe you are, if you get my meaning. A man with character is a man with character.

> *"We must be what we want our children to become."*
>
> —Tommy Lasorda

Frances, an eight-year-old girl with a blond ponytail approached me after one practice with an earnest look on her face. "Coach, you're a doctor. What is that?"

I smiled and told her, "It's a person who cares for others."

Her little face frowned again. "Cares for what?"

"Illness," I said. "Disease. Like strokes or head injuries."

Like most kids at that age, she had all the questions. "And what is disease?" she asked. Soon, I realized that you cannot really explain what medicine is without first explaining about the disease it cures. So, too, it follows with character. It is hard to understand clearly what character is until you see what happens without it.

### First Base—Honesty

> *"God help me to be honest and law abiding, even when no one is looking."*
>
> —Uncle Mike

I watched Mr. Cox explain the finer points of the game to the freckle-faced Kevin. "Look, you got to learn about life, kid. Good guys come in last. Life is tough and you gotta be smart," he said. "Try this trick. Make believe you're throwing the ball back to the pitcher but hold on to it. The runner is tricked into thinking you threw it, so he'll lead off and you can tag him out!"

Seven-year-old Kevin furrowed his brows and in a gentle voice asked, "Isn't that cheating?" Mr. Cox winked. "It's not cheating as long as the ump isn't looking."

Later that afternoon Kevin's mother caught him taking a candy bar from a concession stand. Furious, she asked him what possessed him to steal. He replied innocently, "The ump wasn't looking." His mother obviously had no idea what he was talking about but, in the ultimate irony, when Mr. Cox found out, he benched Kevin from half the next game as punishment. Kevin couldn't understand why. No one saw him do it. The pain on his face denoted a mixture of confusion and a loss of respect for adults. Quite simply, he had been punished for following what he had been taught—to be dishonest, that honesty depended upon being caught rather than from doing what is right all the time.

In the last few years "character education" has become fashionable. After my first book, *Life Lessons From Little League* was published, I have had the pleasure of spending a great deal of time teaching children. I lecture about the challenges children face and encourage them to develop strong values by providing examples of daily behavior that are a reflection of good character. During these lecture appearances, in community after community, I have been left with one conclusion: the most important lesson of all is the role parents play as the primary teachers of our children. The first question I ask is: "Where do your values come from?" I then recount the story of Kevin and Mr. Cox.

Kevin could be respectful, responsible and courageous, but if he is not honest no one will ever trust him: not his wife or his fellow workers, and he will have no deep friendships. Honesty is the best policy and the most important of the four bases of character.

## *An Excuse Is As Good As Its Truth*

I overheard Fred, the manager of the Hawks, say after their 12 to 1 loss to the Giants, "Look guys, it wasn't our fault. The way the umps called those close calls, I think the Giants paid them off. I'm gonna have the League president check their pitcher's birth certificate. No way is he eight years old!" The Little League Hawks who, ten minutes prior, had smiles on their faces, feeling they had lost fair and square, were now outraged. "Yeah, Coach, we were cheated and shouldn't have lost the game!" shouted Jimmy.

During the week, while consulting with a colleague, Dr. Withers, he said to me, "Did you hear about the Hawks? They were cheated by the Giants. They paid off the Ump."

## *The Devil Made Me Do It*

Often I am convinced that the single biggest barrier to effective character education is the difficulty parents have in accepting total responsibility for how their children turn out. I know lots of parents who point to the fact that they raised two children in the same household, and they turned out to be very different people. Children are not a blank slate to be written upon as a parent chooses, or an empty container that parents can fill with their own wisdom and knowledge. Child rearing is a complicated strategy. What I do witness is that our complex society suffers from victimization, self-created and perpetuated as an excuse for misdirected imagination. It's an unhealthy tendency that many of us have, whereby we see ourselves as mere victims of forces larger than us, like the media, the government, society as a whole. Somehow we use this as an excuse to get us off the emotional hook.

I stress to youngsters time and time again that the most important sign of personal maturity is the willingness to accept total responsibility of your own life, your future success or failure, and your impact on others. Arthur Miller, in his play *All My Sons*, illustrates how a father can lose his children's respect by not accepting social responsibility for his actions. When Joe Keller speaks to his son, defending his position as a factory owner he says, "Son, I'm no worse than anyone else." His son replies, "I know Dad, but somehow I thought you were better."

## Second Base—Responsibility

> *Responsibility: "Don't look around. Baby, it's you."*
>
> —Tommy Lasorda

Responsibility has two meanings. First it means dependability, the ability to follow through with your obligations. Second it means accountability for one's conduct.

Mike Scioscia often sees players he wants. He evaluates whether they have demonstrated responsibility. He's looking for them to always strive for a win, to give every game their all and to accept defeat as graciously as victory. He wants to see each player taking responsibility for his part in the team. They don't set poor examples by blaming defeat on the umps or bad coaching or other players. One must remember that if parents blame defeat on unfair umpiring or a coach, they are teaching the children to do the same and someday blame them for their shortcomings.

A person with character needs to learn to accept responsibility for his or her mistakes because it is only when taking responsibility for one's shortcomings that one can learn from it and understand what that you must do in order to avoid making the same mistake again. Remember the old adage that "It is OK to lose as long as you don't lose the lesson."

Players with responsibility are consistent and have endurance. Often that is the difference between success and failure. Many believe the difference between success and failure is a large gap, but any coach will tell you it is often just a thin line. Ralph Waldo Emerson said, "The heights of great men are dependent upon not never failing but on rising up every time they fail."

The challenge of self-examination extends to parenting as much as any other facet of our lives. When parents blame peers or ineffective preaching from clergy, or the power of the media, or the influence of rock stars for the behavior of their children, they are ignoring the most potent reality. Parents are a child's primary teachers. What they say, do and the example they set sticks for life.

Regardless of our age, and even long after our parents are gone, most of us still search for ways to receive their approval for who we are and how we act. It is this power of approval that every parent holds that needs to be safeguarded. As stated by the late writer, James Baldwin, "Children have never been good at listening to their elders, but they have never failed to imitate them." It is in the imitation of our parents that the most effective character education takes place.

> *"Children hear what we say but do as we do."*
>
> —Mike Legg

As a parent, everything you do teaches by example. How you talk to your spouse or partner; how you treat strangers on the street, what you say about your neighbors when they aren't in the room; how you speak about employees or co-workers; how you talk about other drivers while on the road; whether you show up at piano recitals or to your children's Little League games, everything teaches your children how they should behave in similar circumstances. Every single minute that your children are around you, they are learning from you. If it's a babysitter or the Little League coach your children are with, it's the babysitter or Little League coach who they're learning from. That's why I always stress that parents should get to know their coaches and coaches should understand their responsibilities to the kids.

The parents' job is to recognize and accept the responsibility for being the number-one moral role model for their children, and to act accordingly. Whatever you say or do, your actions are constantly demonstrating to your children your values, goals and family values, whether you want them to or not. The willingness to accept full responsibility for the moral education of your children is crucial, and it is so important that parents not merely react to a child's behavior, but also take the time to explain to them why they should act in a certain way.

*Third Base—Respect*

> *"You don't have to like it, but you do have to respect it."*
>
> —Tommy Lasorda

Respect includes courtesy and tolerance. A player, parent or coach should not argue with umpires but respect and accept their decisions. Parents can help teach respect by demonstrating it themselves by not arguing or abusing coaches, officials or other parents. Instead, they should encourage politeness and gratitude. A respectful person cares and has consideration, and it is through respect that team spirit and loyalty remain firm.

There are three habits that one can adopt for teaching children respect:

1. Make sure that they always say thank you.
2. Encourage them to ask if someone needs help.
3. Get them in the habit of asking permission. "May I have . . .?"

> *"The only job you start at the top is digging a hole."*
>
> —Tommy Lasorda

Randy was always the first boy at pitching practice or when snacks were given out. However, he was nowhere to be seen when it came to putting away the equipment. Randy rarely rooted for others and made fun of those who were smaller and less coordinated than him. He did, however, show respect when it was the means to an end. For instance, he showed respect to an ump or a coach when it would benefit him. His parents, too, often pushed and manipulated to get any advantage they could for their son. The behavior of Randy's parents created the opposite of mutual respect. It created anger and distrust and finally disloyalty.

> *"Those who row the boat don't have time to rock it."*
>
> —Tom Boyle, former Western Little League Director

*Home–Courage*

> *"The only thing necessary for evil to try triumph is for all good men to do nothing."*
>
> —Edmund Burke

Courage is standing up for one's values when everyone else is afraid to. It is the ability to do whatever has to be done despite the consequences.

Mr. Cox had his favorite players, including his son. As soon as practice began he would take his five favorites and put them in the infield and spend all his time with them. The others he relegated to the outfield and gave them little eye contact and even less time. Since he had won three straight championships in four seasons, no one stood up to him. That is until Gayle went up to him and said what had been on the minds of the parents whose children were being treated unfairly. She demanded that all the children be given equal time in practice; the same number of swings when at bat, for example. This was no easy feat for Gayle, who stood 5'2" and weighed not much more than a bag full of groceries. She showed great courage in standing up to a man who not only towered over her but was capable of belittling anyone and taking his revenge out on her son.

> *"Remember: courage is risk taking."*
>
> —Mike Scioscia

> *"Get up to bat and never be afraid to strike out."*
>
> —Babe Ruth

You give honesty, respect and responsibility. If you can't stand up for those values, the baseball diamond is going to collapse. Believe me, your children see you saying nothing and it tells them that what is going on is OK. More, it tells them that fighting for justice is just not that important. Courage is when the tough get going; it's when you find out if you have character or not.

### FROM MANAGER MIKE SCIOSCIA'S DUGOUT

*The greatest compliment anyone can give you is to say what a thoughtful, respectful and responsible child you have. It's a reflection on you, so be proud. Parents and coaches, you are the example to your children. Be all that you can and so will your children. Remember:*

1. *The soul of character is honesty and from it grows trustworthiness.*
2. *The heart of character is taking responsibility; from it grows diligence and discipline.*
3. *The body of character is respect and faithfulness and from it grows loyalty.*
4. *The mind of character is courage; from it grows the strength of our nation.*

# *The Field That Feels*

I can see who has character.
They walk with certitude, their steps do not wander.
They speak with open hearts that leave no wonder.
Like the three musketeers, one for all and all for one.
Make no mistake, even in defeat they have won.

# 15

## CHARACTER: THE WHY

*"It is the spirit that transcends the rules and gives meaning to honesty. There is no victory without honor."*

**IT WAS A BIG DAY.** My son Vinny's Padres team faced the first-place Marlins. The Marlins had beaten every team they'd faced because of their explosive speed around the diamond and led the league in stolen bases. The Padres had size, discipline but little speed and a knowledgeable coach in Angry Alan, so today would be a real challenge. The regional commissioner would also be in the bleachers to see this game. He had already reprimanded Alan for encouraging overaggressive pitching and would be watching Alan closely this morning. I myself was softening on Mr. Angry. He was devoted to the game of baseball, even if he did care too much about winning. But that I'm sure came from his background in the Marines. "A loss is not a win no matter how you cut it," he'd say.

Once again, I had confused the start times and arrived early at the field. This time I was greeted by the bizarre sight of a lone figure hovering at one end of the field. When I walked closer, I realized it was Alan and he was watering down the clay in the infield and was covering the clay around home plate with fresh dry dirt. How wonderful, I thought, Alan had his faults, but he was certainly dedicated. "Hi Alan," I called out. "Getting the field ready for the big game?"

Alan spun around in surprise. "Oh, hello, Dr. Vince," he said, then hurried over to turn off the water. I watched him walk off guiltily, like I'd somehow caught him with his hand in the cookie jar.

Twenty minutes later, the bleachers were filled with spectators, all buzzing with expectation. The umpire started the game and the Marlins' lead-off batter went up to the plate. He cracked the first pitch deep into right field and took off for first base. However, rather than speeding across the clay, he slipped and skidded and finally sank into the wet clay. The sure-footed Padres' first baseman retrieved the ball and stepped on first base before the hitter. One out.

I looked over at Alan. There was a self-congratulatory snicker on his face. Then my veil of naivete lifted and I finally realized what Alan had been up to. By drenching the field he had reduced the powder keg Marlins to wet squibs, slipping, sliding and sinking in their short cleats. Meanwhile, Alan had insisted all his players wear long cleats that day.

I walked over to him and asked him directly if he had deliberately cheated by watering down the field to counter their speed around the bases. "I broke no rules," he retorted with a smirk. "If I did, show me where."

The Padres went on to win the game 7-5 and Alan made no secret of his tactics. Richie, father of one of the Padres, thought it a "stroke of genius" and called it "gamesmanship" as no rule was broken. Technically, he may be right, but then there are rules and there is the spirit of those rules, or why the rules were made.

There are two kinds of rules: the ground rules and the rules of fair play.

Ground rules are just that, rules to give consistency to the game. For example, every field is marked out in the same way: three bases and home plate, an infield and an outfield, etc. The rules of fair play, however, are there to protect players and to ensure equality. Rules on throwing a bat or wearing a helmet, for instance, are there to protect children. Guidelines for playing children of similar age and talent levels assure the games will be competitive and give every team a chance to do its best.

Unfortunately, rules and regulations can't cover every eventuality. The rest is up to the players, coaches and officials to observe the rules of fair play, to behave with a sense of right and wrong or "conscience." To hose down a field to give your team an undue advantage is clearly wrong, rule or no rule.

It's common sense. The best way to judge what's right or wrong is to ask yourself if you'd think it fair if it was done to your team. If you think yes, then it's probably fair. If no, then chances are it's wrong. If you say, well I should have thought of it first, then my reply to you would be, "You need help."

I've seen coaches teach kids to bend the rules when the umpire isn't looking. They call it bright baseball. Football coaches have their defensive backs wear gloves the same color as their opponents' shirts so the referees can't see them holding on. Basketball coaches teach their players to hit the shooter's elbow with their elbow, again so the referee can't see the foul. Soccer coaches teach their kids to foul when the ref's attention is elsewhere. What they are teaching is beyond bad. You can't tell a child that it's wrong to steal, then flaunt the rewards in front of him, or tell a child that stealing or cheating is OK, just as long as you're not caught. It infects a child's conscience and character. Remember if you cut corners, your children will learn to do likewise.

# *The Bright Side: Coach Terry*

Once a year the Little League manager who best symbolizes the spirit of the game receives a trophy. Patty, a dedicated league president thought up the idea. I remember the year Terry, the Athletics' manager, won the prize.

The Athletics had two runners on base. Ping! The batter hit a ground ball between the first and second baseman. The umpire, behind home plate, watched as the right fielder timidly placed his glove on the fresh, dewy grass and let the ball run into it. He then quickly picked up the ball and threw a strike to the astonished first baseman—just a second too late. "Safe!" the ump yelled.

With the umpire's attention on the first base side, Daniel—being inventive, as children often are—tried a sneak play. Running from second, he decided the best way to make home plate was a straight line from short stop to home. As the umpire turned he saw Daniel in the baseline passing the dugout with his teammates cheering him on toward home. The second ump, behind second base, also missed Daniel's clever base running.

Daniel touched home plate before Kiel, our big first baseman, could throw the ball home, but Ronnie, our third baseman started jumping up and down. "Hey mister, he missed the bag! Hey, he missed the bag!"

Terry was coaching third base and had seen what had happened. All the youngsters had seen it, as well as the parents on both sides. Our guardian angels had seen it, and I'm sure God had made a note of it too. It had been obvious. It was also obvious though, that Joe and his team needed this run. The game was in the last inning and would decide who would win the second-half championship. If Daniel was called out, the Athletics would have two outs and would still need two runs.

I looked at Terry. She stared intently at Ronnie, who now had tears in his eyes. Terry's eyes went blank and she turned away. The ump did not know quite what to do when our shortstop, Stefan, chimed in, "He cheated! He cheated!"

Terry called Daniel to come over. She placed her hand on his shoulder right in front of the dugout where his teammates were sitting. "Did you touch third base, son?"

"No," he said meekly.

"Well, you'd best tell the umpires that, because they didn't see it."

Daniel went up to the home plate umpire who towered over him like Goliath over David. In a soft, innocent voice he said, "I didn't go to third base, sir. I just ran home. I'm sorry."

The umpire patted him on the back. "Honesty is what baseball is all about. You're a real sportsman, Daniel."

The ump called me and Terry over and said, "Look, I have to call them like I see them. I didn't see him run out of the baseline or miss the bag. I must call him safe." He then announced this to all the players. Terry, however, insisted that the play be called the way it really occurred, for the benefit of the children.

As you can imagine, in addition to all the contented chatter from the parents on both sides, the Little Leaguers learned quite a lesson that day. They saw an adult stand up for the truth, even when it might cost her the game and the championship. My respect for Terry rose considerably. I don't know if I would have had the same courage to do what was right, rather than hide behind the rules of the game. With one move, Terry taught her players that honesty was more important than winning.

I have played against at least 100 coaches in the past 12 years but it is funny—only Terry, and a couple of bad eggs, stick out in my mind. I recommended Terry for the Little League Manager of the Year award that season. Everybody else who played against her did, too. Terry exemplified what we wanted our children to learn: honesty and integrity. Too bad what happened that day occurs so infrequently.

## *Rules Are Meaningless Without Truth*

I do not think incidents like the one with Terry are so rare because most people are dishonest but rather because many parents do not have an overall sense of morality, that compulsion to do the right thing even when the rules say it is okay to be wrong. I don't think these parents realize what they're teaching their children either.

One father, for example, referring to what Terry did, said, "Well, it is not what is right or wrong, but what the rules say."

Another agreed. "You are out only when the ump catches you. If you fool him, well that is smart baseball."

After the game, though, Terry had said, "If I don't set an example for my young team, and insist on telling the truth and being honest, then I have taught them nothing. After all, later on in life, who will ask them if they stole a base or shagged a fly ball or fooled an ump? Everyone, however, can tell an honest person from a cheater."

Terry is right. It does not take long, for example, to assess someone's integrity in tennis, golf, or cards. Children do not learn integrity from lectures, they learn it by watching the most important adults in their lives—their parents. The fellow who constantly misses line calls in tennis is teaching his child to do the same; the accountant who never misses a number when he is adding up a bill but cannot seem to add up a score above par for any hole on the golf course, is instructing his child to play "smart"—not fair. You know your assessment of these people—do they really fool anyone? Do we really think we are fooling our children? Sometimes saying nothing is worse than telling an outright lie.

> *"Conscience and character come from within,*
> *not from without."*
>
> —Rod Dedeaux
> Baseball Coach of the Century, USC

True gamesmanship is training harder, learning discipline, developing the courage to never give up, and improving baseball skills. Watering down a baseball field when the faster players are wearing short cleats to cause them to lose their footing in the wet clay and then letting your players think that this is OK, does double damage to kids. Other parents or coaches who witness such acts need to have the courage to stand up and stop it.

## Sports Build Character

Many people believe that sports build character. They do not. Sports provide us with the opportunities and the challenges to build character. It is up to coaches and parents to use those opportunities and challenges to build good character. Alan had done the opposite and shown how to bend the rules for personal gain. The excuses for such behavior are always the same: well, "everybody does it," "it's smart play," "it's gamesmanship," "it's ingenuity." The best excuse of all is "if I don't do it, my team doesn't stand a chance!" Kids should learn it now, because later in life it'll be too late. All these excuses refer to cheating, to dishonesty. In children's sport, as in any sport, there is no victory without honor. Kids will never feel that they've won if they had to bend or break the rules. If coaches resort to cheating or breaking the spirit of the rules, the children will always be left with the knowledge at the back of their minds that the other team may well have beaten them.

# The Ends Justify the Means

As we walked back to the car after the game, I asked my son Vinny if he realized that Alan had cheated by watering down the field. "Yeah, Dad," he said. "I know it wasn't fair, but we did win."

My son had learned that "the end justifies the means." There is no wonder why children think little of cheating on exams. Fifty-five percent say they do so regularly and 22 percent say they steal from stores without remorse. Where did they learn such things? From any coach who thinks it's OK to bend or break the rules, for a start. From any parent who keeps quiet when it happens. By saying nothing, we say so much.

## FROM LASORDA'S DUGOUT

*1. Bending the rules is bad.*
*2. Breaking the rules is worse.*
*3. Bending/breaking the rules, and then justifying it, is criminal.*

*Remember, winning by cheating is never OK because there can be no victory with dishonor.*

# Where Are They Now?

I was surprised to run into Coach Terry one evening after I had been inducted into the Little League Hall of Excellence at Dodger Stadium. I had been invited to join Peter O'Malley, then the owner of the LA Dodgers, to watch the game in his private suite. Terry was there as well. I asked her, "Do you know Peter O'Malley?"

"Yes," she replied. "He's my brother."

No one in our league ever knew it. She wanted no special treatment. She gave, however, special character to us all. It was then that I realized why the O'Malleys are considered the royalty of Major League baseball.

# 16

# CHARACTER: THE HOW

**PARENTS AND COACHES CAN BUILD CHARACTER** in a child by instilling conscience. It takes the right words and a unified message from adults, be they parents, coaches or umpires. Unfortunately, it is mainly moms who read books like *Life Lessons From Little League: Revisited*, rarely the coaches teaching Little League or by umpires who are enforcing its rules. So now is the time for Little League moms to insist that all the umpires and coaches read this book (or at least this chapter)!

## *Sportsmanship: The Golden Rule*

As parents, we need to help our children understand sportsmanship. Sportsmanship is doing what is fair, what is right, what is one's duty. Following the rules often makes us fall short of sportsmanship and our obligation to the truth. You can't use the rules to get around what is fair.

We as managers and coaches must recognize that Little League rules are guidelines first, to ensure fairness and safety, and then they establish the rules of the game, such as three strikes and you are out. If the managers and coaches mutually agree that a play was miscalled, I believe the umpire should be allowed to reverse his call based on the integrity of these adults and the need to demonstrate real sportsmanship on the baseball diamond to young, impressionable minds. That would reinforce the concept of honesty being the best policy. These children are not professional ballplayers and Little League is not about winning baseball games. Little League is about fun and growth and learning life's important lessons. To teach sportsmanship, one of life's most crucial lessons, we the coaches, managers and parents must all agree to emphasize its cardinal rule: how you play the game is more important than anything else—even the game itself.

# *The Sinking Eagles*

It was my tenth game of the season as coach of the Eagles. Despite my good intentions and emphasis on fun and character development over winning, my team had lost every game and my pride was hurting. I've said over and over that if you have courage and build character, you will win. Well, clearly many of the parents didn't agree with my assessment that, even though they were losing every game, their children were still winners because they were building character. I really needed a win but still wanted to adhere to the principal that right must overcome might, with "might" referring to the other coaches who would do anything to ensure victory. They stocked their teams with only the most talented players, taught questionable ethics and let everyone know who had just won and who were the losers. Even the Little League Bulletin used headlines like "Eagles Sink instead of Soar!" The reports never mentioned the fact that I played kids no one else would give a chance to or reprimanded any of them who cheated or deliberately endangered an opposing player. How could I teach these children right from wrong when there was so much pressure to just win?

Frannie shook me from my daydream. "Coach," she whined. "Bobby keeps hitting me with the ball when I turn around. How do I tell him that it's wrong?"

I knew exactly what I wanted to tell her to do: punch him on the nose. That'll teach him a valuable life lesson. Instead I simply said, "Tell him to stop."

"I did," she replied. "And I even told him I'd give him half my candy bar if he'd stop." That's great, I thought, reward him for doing the wrong thing. Soon Bobby would be running a protection racket, demanding rewards for not bullying.

"Tell him it's against the rules of this team," I told her finally. Frannie walked away and I watched from a distance as she spoke to Bobby. He nodded but when Frannie turned away, he bounced the ball off the back of her head again. So much for my bright idea.

# *How Do You Teach Right From Wrong?*

"You're out!" bellowed the umpire. Tears welled up in Paul's eyes. "Never throw the bat again," the umpire continued. Paul stared at his feet. Then the Hawks coach chimed in with, "He should be thrown out of the game, too." Paul, an Angels' power hitter for T-ball, had the dangerous habit of letting the bat fly at the end of his swing.

Two innings later Paul was up to bat again. And again he let go of the bat, and without any explanation, the ump threw him out of the game. Oh, terrific, I thought. One of my best hitters was out for the rest of the game. As Paul trudged off the field, I thought of Frannie and her question to me before the game. How should I tell Paul what he had done was wrong? How should the umpire have told him?

1. Because if he doesn't obey the rules, he'll be punished.
2. Because if he does obey the rules, he'll be rewarded.
   Well, neither had worked for Frannie with Bobby.
3. Because it is against the rules and the rules say it is wrong.
   I thought every kid would have to carry a rule book with them and have a rule for every conceivable eventuality.
4. Because your teammates won't like you for making the sides uneven and losing the game.
   I thought all these reasons sounded like it's wrong only based on whether it gets you in trouble or not. Maybe that's why so many coaches break or bend the rules because they only act from these first four methods of explaining right from wrong.

The fifth, and best, reason:

5. Paul should not throw his bat because it could hurt someone and he wouldn't like someone to do it to him and hurt him in the process. The rules are there to protect everyone. You don't cheat, because you don't like to be cheated.

As Paul approached the dugout I knelt down to his eye level and lifted his chin. "Paul, there are rules in the game," I said. "One is to hit the ball off the tee. The other is to run to first base after the ball is hit. And the last is to never throw the bat. If you throw it, you will be called out. If you don't throw the bat, you can run around all the bags, get a home run and everyone will be happy. The reason we have this rule is so that no one gets hurt. You wouldn't want a bat thrown at you, would you?"

"No," he responded softly. He walked away with a contented look having learned a lesson about sportsmanship, one of the most valuable lessons of all. Treat others as you would like them to treat you.

One of the most compelling ways to nurture a child's moral development is by giving him or her the reasons for the rules and the consequences of not following the rules. As a sport, baseball can assist a child to make the crucial mental and emotional connection between their own behavior and its impact on others. As a parent, one can teach his child that what he says and does is an important matter. The only way this can be done is through having a child make the connection in his own mind about actions bearing consequences. One of the greatest challenges of parenting is to live your life in such a way that your children emulate your behavior and make you proud of the outcome. Your tone of voice, your sensitivity to the child's dilemma also enhances his emotional intelligence. Help him accept his behavior and recognize the need to be aware of others' safety and feelings.

At the end of the game, Paul walked over to the ump and apologized for throwing his bat. The ump knelt down next to him just as I had done and told him how proud he was of Paul's courage to come over and apologize.

Paul demonstrated character by accepting responsibility for his actions. He demonstrated conscience by realizing that he was wrong to place another in danger. He learned the most valuable lesson. He learned the difference between right and wrong. He learned the Golden Rule: don't do something to someone else if you wouldn't like it done to you. The same follows with cheating or stealing candy bars.

If a child is constantly reminded why something is wrong, he'll soon develop an innate knowledge of right from wrong and will always do what is right, what is fair.

# *Example*

Character is taught by example. As adults there is a danger in allowing basic instincts to win, to be the best, to come out on top and overshadow our good character traits. As parents and coaches we must always recognize where we are and remember our responsibility to help instill character, respect and courage in our children. We have to be examples of good behavior.

It is this behavior that is our legacy, our only legacy to our children.

The money and material things that we can leave our children are meaningless when compared to leaving them a legacy of character. That is, to be honorable, courageous and to stand up for what is right, no matter what it costs. If we are dishonest, our children will be dishonest. They will learn to cut classes, to steal and take advantage of others at every opportunity.

The wonder of children is their natural honesty, their naivete and their instincts to have fun and see the world as a safe haven. One person can make the difference and that one person can be you.

### FROM ROD DEDEAUX
#### NCAA BASEBALL COACH OF THE CENTURY WITH
#### 10 NATIONAL CHAMPIONSHIPS

*Little League keeps parents off the street and in the baseball park with their children. It's the best way I know to build family and community spirit. The adage "the family that plays together, stays together" is what we need more of in the 21st Century. It's highly unlikely that a major league team will need your child, but every child needs her mother and father. Little League gives parents that opportunity. Don't miss that opportunity because it only comes along once in a lifetime.*

*It's rare that a child will make it to the Major Leagues but if he makes it to the Major Leagues in your heart, you've done a job well worth doing, and he will become a young person with character.*

### FROM MANAGER MIKE SCIOSCIA'S DUGOUT

*A coach who has character himself is not enough. He needs to learn how to impart the principles of character in his players. My hints for teaching character are as follows:*

*First, be an example. Character is taught by example, not words. So be responsible, be on time, be respectful to the umps and the players, parents and coaches of both teams.*

*Second, remember every problem or conflict on the Little League field is an opportunity to teach and demonstrate character. If you see one team or one child breaking the rules, that is an opportunity to tell them how to do it the right way. In fact, one of the best opportunities for teaching character is when you have made a mistake yourself and then admit that you were wrong. Children can be self-critical, so accept their mistakes and help change them.*

*Always admit when you are wrong. Let a child see that there is nothing wrong with admitting faults; that we all have them, we are all human. A survey of college students found that what they respected most about their parents was their ability to admit that they were wrong. It helps increase trust and makes you, the parent, approachable. It's hard for anybody to relate to someone who's perfect. Be perfectly imperfect.*

*Finally, reward your child for her effort when she demonstrates good character. This means being grateful and never giving up.*

---

**FROM THE DESK OF DR. VINCE**

*Conscience is knowing what is right and wrong.*

*Character is following that conscience.*

*Moral development is how one builds a conscience.*

*Having a conscience means understanding right from wrong. The concepts of right and wrong come from universal principles. It applies to all races and cultures, to the intelligent, the talented, and the handicapped alike. Some of its accepted, universal principles are you do not steal, you do not hurt others, you do not kill. These are held true by all reasonable people. From these concepts of right and wrong come duties to protect those principles. Remember, children learn right from wrong, they do not inherit this knowledge, as they do not inherit character.*

---

## *Where Are They Now?*

Paul is a plumber, an honest one. He told me once he wanted to be a doctor, but it just didn't pay as well.

# SECTION 4
## HARMONY

*"Spend less time concerned with who is right
and more time deciding what is right."*

—Jim Chavez
**DA Washington Little League**

**SOME THINGS IN LIFE** are simply not taught in grammar school, high school and college. They must be learned through life experience. Little League, too, has ingredients that cannot be found in books (even this one), nor in the usual baseball camp. Focus, consistency and harmony must be learned on the diamond with the bleachers full, the sun blazing, and the parents, coaches and young players interacting.

# 17

# FOCUS:
# MOST JUST DON'T SEE IT

## *Keeping the Attention of the Playstation Generation*

**MAJOR LEAGUERS ALWAYS TALK ABOUT FOCUS**—focusing their eye on the ball, focusing their attention on the play, focusing their energy. With proper focus, the pros claim, one can anticipate every potential eventuality, make the correct choice without hesitation, and predict and outsmart one's opponents. Orel Hershiser, Tommy John, Micky Mantle, Willie Mays, and Hank Aaron all focused and made things happen. The great managers, such as Tommy Lasorda, Joe Torre, and Casey Stengel seem to be born with focus.

In Little League T-ball, farm, minors, and even majors, focus primarily comes down to paying attention. If a first-time coach does not know the average attention span of a six- to twelve-year-old child—or if he expects to have a field of Babe Ruths, Ty Cobbs, Mike Piazzas, Tom Seavers, and Jim Palmers—he is in for unexpected hair loss (from pulling it out in frustration), headaches (from slamming the palm of his hand into his forehead in disbelief), and upset stomachs (from jumping up and down in mini-tantrums). I am sure you have seen this coach before. He is the rookie—and Little League goes through many rookie coaches. Fifty percent of all coaches do not return the following year, a statistic rarely quoted in the league. The ones who do return either have given in to the guilt piled on by their league presidents and vice presidents or have learned the trick of keeping their sanity:  keep the team alert and focused.

Sixth inning of the crucial game. The score was…well, being the kind of manager who was more concerned with my ball players, I did not care about the score, but if the Hawks managed to make four more runs, my hopes for a first-place team would fade into the horizon.

José was up for the Hawks. The ball, sitting innocently on the tee, was just two feet from him. He swung and missed five times in a row. The only safe place for the ball was on the tee!  My pitcher, Alan, raised his hand as soon as he saw I wasn't looking and yelled, "Coach, I have to go to the bathroom."  Just at that moment, José swung for the sixth time and, wonder of wonders, hit the ball to second base. An easy grounder—if Brent had not been lying down with his head nicely propped up by his glove, that is. The ball rolled to the outfield. I screamed, "Danny, get in front of it!"  Danny, however, had nodded off. My shout jolted him momentarily to reality, but he had no idea where the ball was.

"Did it pass me?  Is it in front of me?  Where am I?"

Suddenly, Danny saw the ball lying next to him. He picked it up and tossed it to left field, where Amy was watching dandelions grow. At the last moment, she raised her hand and caught the ball on the fly. She held up the shiny white sphere for all of us to admire, and proudly yelled, "He's out. I caught the ball on a fly."

In the meantime, Mr. Sane Coach was having a mini-tantrum. I was jumping up and down screaming, "Throw the ball, throw the ball, throw the ball home!"  José was skipping around second and going toward third. By now, all the players had gotten the message and were on alert. Amy, however, was not aware that the ball had been thrown, rather than hit, to her, and would not give it up. José crossed the plate to the howling of the opposing crowd. I had bruises on both thighs from hitting myself, a sore throat from screaming, and had made an utter fool of myself in front of all the parents to boot.

To save face, if not your sanity, the next time you find yourself in a similar situation, you might take note of some facts I have acquired since then.

First, the average attention span of a six-year-old in the outfield is four to six minutes. A seven-year-old with one year of experience can last five to seven minutes, and an eight-year-old with two years' experience might make it ten to 15 minutes. A nine-year-old with experience is good for ten to 15 minutes, while a child ten or older should be able to stay focused for 15 to 20 minutes. Take off one minute in each category for players with no experience. In T-ball, take off another minute for each inning played.

What all this means is that a child of six can be expected to pay attention for no more than two to three minutes in the third inning of a T-ball game. In other words, if your T-ball team is all first-year rookies, they will be "gone" by the time they reach their positions in the outfield and turn to face home plate. In fact, I once had a player go all the way to the snack bar 300 yards away before he realized he was supposed to stop in the center field! You, as the coach, must do something to refocus them—that is, if you haven't already nodded off yourself.

Coaching T-ball is not an easy job, nor is it one for someone who is not ready to use his lungs for something other than breathing.

## *Cheer Them On*

You could have fried an egg on home plate as the sun blazed down on Pasadena Little League Field at Hamilton Park. The ballplayers looked like they would gladly run in if anyone suggested it was nap time. They would probably have even run to the dugout to do homework, just to get out of the sun. It was top of the third inning. The first batter up for the Giants hadn't yet gotten to the batter's box, but Chris, on third base, had already squatted down like an Indian ready to pass around the peace pipe. Not ten seconds later, all the outfielders joined him. I bellowed, "Who are we?"

Several feeble, squeaky voices said, "Da Angels."

I hollered again, "Who are we?"

Now added to the voices of the several were the distant calls of the outfielders. "The Angels."

I shouted one more time, "Who?"

With moderate gusto, they whooped, "The Angels!"

"Are we ready?"

At that, the team was awake. In unison, they yelled, "Ready!"

"Ready positions," I called with authority. They jumped to their "gorilla" position, arms hanging from their shoulders to the ground and swaying gently back and forth. My team was focused…for a while.

The outfielders were all first-year rookies, so they were good for four to six minutes, less one minute for each inning and two minutes for severe environmental (heat) factors. That made five minutes off their optimum six-minute attention span, which meant they needed to be refocused every few minutes. In a situation like this, I could only hope they would continue to face homeplate—some do not. The best way I found to combat the doldrums and keep their attention was the series of cheers—"Who are we? Are we ready? Do we ever give up?"—that I used throughout my 12-year career as a coach and manager. They were so effective that by my second year, other coaches began using them and making up more of their own.

Do not worry about your team getting tired of doing the same few cheers over and over. Young children love monotony; they can hear the same story endlessly ("Dad, tell me again about the Three Little Pigs"). Remember, repetition makes memory. In Little League, above all, it focuses attention, which is what prevents some child from being hit by a ball because he or she got distracted, and it even gives the players an opportunity to make a catch.

## Just When I Had Their Attention

It was the fifth and probably final inning. I stood at the entrance to the dugout, a baseball in one hand and a bat in the other. We had played a long but fruitful game and were down by only two runs. The real problem, however, was that my Little Leaguers were fading quickly, like a red chameleon on a green leaf. I had to refocus them. I called them to gather round, but my series of "Who are we?" cheers had little effect. Looking at their tired faces, I tried my next trick: "Who would you rather be—the ball or the bat?" I stretched both out to them. Several yelled, "The bat!"

"Yes," I said with enthusiasm, "because the bat always clobbers the ball!" They liked this, as usual. I gently sent the ball flying off the bat. "Who has the bat now?" I queried mischievously.

"We do," several answered.

"Who?"

"We do!" they all chimed.

"Who has the ..."

Before I could finish, Sean yelled, "Look, there's a frog!" All heads turned away from me suddenly, but no one moved until the magical word was spoken: "It's a bullfrog!"

With that, I found myself like a mime, frozen with arms outstretched and vivid with expression—standing alone. All my Little Leaguers abandoned ship to chase the bullfrog. Did I feel bad, ignored, in doubt about my sense of leadership or ability to instill enthusiasm and focus my team? You bet I did. I had lost their attention—but I did not lose the lesson. Next time, I'll use going to the zoo as a motivator!

## *Cheer the Parents*

Cheering works just as well with parents as with children, and is a nice way to break up your own feelings of monotony. As I would notice the dads and moms drifting off into mundane and boring conversations, or getting the too-many-hot-dogs-before-the-game nods, I would yell, "Do your children ever give up?"

"No!" they would holler in return.

Then: "Who are we?"

"Padre Parents!"

"Who?"

"Padre Parents!"

"Louder!"

"Padre Parents!"

I would most often lead the parents in cheers when our team was down or having a hard time focusing despite their cheers. Somehow, when the dads and moms cheered, it inspired the boys and girls on the field. Everyone gets inspired when they hear their family root for them. I have heard profession-al players say, "This one is for you, Mom," or an announcer remark, "Orel's parents are in the park today." Somehow, having your folks in the stands lends an air of mystique—everyone knows that a professional ballplayer will be so much "more" for that particular game because his mom and dad are in the stands. I do not know if a study has ever been done to see if parents' pres-ence makes a difference in professional baseball, but my statistics definitely prove they count in Little League. Give me a stand full of parents, and I will give you a field full of contented, focused Little Leaguers. Get the picture?

# 18

# CONSISTENCY: SECRET FOR PARENTAL SUCCESS

*"Strength and confidence don't come from physical and mental capacity but rather from consistent parenting."*

**CONSISTENCY,** in the American and National Leagues, means reliability. A "golden glover" will rarely make an error; a .300 hitter with a .450 slugging percentage can be counted on to bring home the runners who are in scoring position, no matter what. In professional baseball, consistency refers to a person who, when the pressure is on, always rises to the occasion. Practice is probably one of the main ingredients for developing that consistency, but I will bet there is an additional element, one that instills the self-discipline to practice: consistent, supportive parents. Self-discipline in children does not come automatically or overnight, but is bred by their parents. In Little League, then, consistency really refers to reliable parents.

Several interesting studies have shown that children grow up feeling more secure when they have consistent parents. Consistent does not necessarily mean strict discipline; it means that regardless of whether the parents are strict, somewhat liberal, or in between, they are consistently that way. (The extremes of neglect and smothering were, of course, found to be harmful.)

Parents who respond to problems and situations in a like manner all the time make their child feel secure. The child does not need to agree with them; he only has to know he can count on their sensible response. Another major factor in a child's sense of security, the study noted, is having both parents respond in a similar manner and agree on what is significant or important. Continual conflicts between parents cause confusion and are often a sign of a shaky marriage, something children can sense, even when the yelling, finger wagging, and arguments occur in supposed secrecy. Children get frightened by their parents' conflicts, and some find ways to use it to their advantage. Either way, they learn some disturbing lessons from our inconsistent ways.

# The Old Divide and Conquer

As I stood in front of the stands, chubby-cheeked Mario went up to his mom. "Mommy, can I have some money for a hot dog and nacho chips 'n cheese?"

"No, Mario," she answered seriously, "I have a nice, nutritious lunch ready for you at home for after the game. Remember our talk about good food and losing weight?"

Mario's cherub face frowned and his head drooped. "Aw, but Mom!"

About 15 minutes later, after the game, I stood in line at the snack bar— ready to order carrot sticks and yogurt, of course, to go along with my hot dog. In front of me I heard a familiar voice. "Gee, thanks, Dad."

"Two hot dogs with nacho chips and extra cheese and a Coke, please," Mario said. His dad bent over to talk into Mario's ear.

"Now, don't tell Mom."

"Don't worry, Dad, your secret's mine."

I wondered if Mario's dad did this often. Maybe that was why Mario always found a way out of running the bags, was always the last one on the field, and generally did the least he could to get by—and he was only eight.

# *Open Warfare*

When George managed, he was obviously the boss, the one wearing the pants, the one calling the shots—that is, until Cheryl, his wife, would arrive in the stands. A big man at 250 pounds, George seemed to grow a deeper red as each of his orders to his ballplayers was second-guessed by his wife. Their son, Jeff, would sag lower and lower as the game progressed, obviously embarrassed.

Whenever Cheryl contradicted George, he would tell her to shut up and go to x%$#! She would respond with similar expletives—yes, right there in the middle of the ball field. The first time I heard them, I almost expected to see Roseanne sprouting from some portable television. Some of George and Cheryl's exchanges were quite inventive and funny. If you listened long enough, though, you realized they meant what they were saying to each other. Many of the parents, including me, felt very uneasy as their interchanges grew progressively nastier. Jeff would simply try to disappear. Then it happened.

It was a Sunday afternoon. George's team, the Twins, had just lost their third close game in a row, this time on a squeeze play he had called but which had backfired. As the Twins shuffled to the dugout for the final "2-4-6-8" cheer, Cheryl yelled out, "Well, you blew another game, you idiot! I hope you're..."

Before she could finish, George spun around and roared, "That's it! I'm quitting! I'm quitting Little League, and I'm quitting this marriage!" Well, those were not his words exactly...but the sentiment, sans expletives, is the same. What happened to Jeff? I do not know. He never showed up again on any Little League team I know of—he probably spent the rest of his childhood trying to fade into the woodwork, just as he had spent his Little League career trying to fade into the outfield.

# Inconsistency, Indecision

Chad stood on second base. As the ball was hit, he took five or six quick steps toward third, then froze. The third-base coach yelled, "Run, run!" You could see the indecision on Chad's face as he bit his lower lip and anxiously looked around. The shortstop came running up with the ball in his hand. As he reached out to make the tag, Chad began to run, but it was too late. Chad started to cry and stomp his feet in frustration. He tore his hat from his head and walked toward the dugout, his chin down near his belly.

This behavior was not unusual for Chad. Anyone who knew his parents knew why he was this way. If I asked them to be at a specific practice, they would hem and haw, finally saying yes, and then not show up—or, even stranger, they would say they could not make it, and then come. They often dropped Chad off late; sometimes he did not get to practice at all. Frequently he did not have his equipment and had to borrow other children's. His parents were rarely at the games; if someone did show up, it was always one or the other, never both. On more than one occasion, either his mom or dad would arrive before the game ended and pull him out to go home; they would flatly state he had been playing long enough. I never knew what to expect from them—and neither did Chad.

Children who are brought up without consistency, like Mario, Jeff, and Chad, become confused, chronically anxious, and frustrated. They never know when the other shoe will fall. They take on their parents' uncertainty and turn timid. Their reaction to their environment becomes inconsistent and a source of frustration. They develop into what all parents hope their children will not be: a child who is insecure, indecisive, and frightened. When they are under pressure, they do not have the inner security needed to see them through the rough spots in life.

What can help children like this? What do they lack? Harmony. Harmony comes when a child's environment is healthy, safe, consistent, and predictable; when he can count on and trust the behavior of parents, teachers, and coaches; when his parents support each other. Harmony is the element that will allow your child's natural abilities and talents to flourish.

### FROM THE DESK OF DR. VINCE

*If you think you and your spouse have this problem, it is urgent you rectify it. Lack of harmony is the main reason for anxiety in children.*

*Try to sit down with your spouse and discuss how you can act more consistently. Remember: you can only change your own behavior.*

*If this fails and your child is anxious, doing poorly in school and you openly argue frequently, then consider counseling. Do this before it is too late. Fifty percent of marriages end in divorce; it can be prevented.*

### FROM JO LASORDA'S KITCHEN

*As Tommy Lasorda's wife of 47 years, I know a lot about harmony. Harmony is like a good Italian sauce. It takes attention, a touch of parental discipline and a lotta love. Remember, you get the best out of others when you give the best of yourself.*

# *Where Are They Now?*

Chad, the indecisive boy with the inconsistent parents, went to live with his grandparents when his folks got divorced. I am told he is doing well.

# 19

# PREPARATION:
# IT'S PRICELESS

## PREPARE YOURSELF
## FOR THE GAME

*"I've noticed the better prepared I am, the luckier I get."*

—Tommy Lasorda

**COACHES CAN VIRTUALLY RECITE** the rules and regulations noted in the *Official Little League Guide*. They usually advise parents to read it to learn about playing Little League baseball. If you were to plod your way through it, you would know a lot about a little, and a very little about the nitty-gritty of what you need to know. What you would find is this:

1. Shoes with metal spikes or cleats are not permitted.
2. All Little League bats must be official Little League size: not more than 33 inches in length, not more than two and a half inches in diameter, not less than 1 $1/_6$ inches in diameter at their smallest part.
3. Home base shall be marked by a five-sided slab of whitened rubber. It shall be a 12-inch square with two corners filled in so that one edge is 17 inches long, two are eight and a half inches long, and two are 12 inches.
4. Sleeve lengths may vary for individual players, but the sleeves for each individual shall be the same length . . . huh?
5. Any part of an undershirt exposed to view shall be . . .

Isn't this trivial? Well, yes—and no. No, because children must learn that discipline and rules help everyone have an equal opportunity. Yes, because in the development of a child do you really think it matters how he or she is dressed, or what his or her sleeve length is?

This chapter is really about the nitty-gritty of preparation—not the rehearsed, Hollywood version, and not how you imagine Little League will be. I am talking about the down-and-dirty truth of where the game begins.

## *The Great Equipment Scavenger Hunt*

Preparation for the preparation begins at home. Is it important? Why, yes—possibly even more so than the game. Your preparation, Mom and Dad, will actually set the tone for the game. It is all your choice and under your control—sort of. I offer the following story in an attempt to save you from having a similar unforgettable experience. If you have never had a child in Little League, you may find it somewhat farfetched—but if you do have Little League kids, I am sure you will find yourself with sweaty palms and a parched mouth as I take you down Memory Lane.

My son had a weekday game and I had just rushed home from work to get him there on time. Although my body was in the front hall my mind was still in the office. "Vinny, are you ready? It's time to get to the baseball field. Remember, I told everyone to be there 20 minutes before the game starts. Make sure you tighten your belt buckle. I'll meet you in the car."

"Okay, Dad, I'll be ready in a minute."

I patiently beeped the horn once and my Little Leaguer skipped gleefully out of the house with his tanned-leather fielder's mitt tucked under his arm. He jumped in the car, his face beaming. "Let's go, dad."

I looked him over. "There's something missing, Vinny. Your hat—where's your hat?"

Absently, he said, "My hat. Oh, my hat."

"Yes, your baseball cap."

"Huh? I don't know. I had it before."

In a fatherly way I reminded him that he cannot play without his baseball cap. "Run in and get it."

Faster than lightning Vinny raced through the front door of the house, which he had left open. I glanced at my watch. I could still be on time if he hurried and the lights were with me. Two minutes ground by. My work anxieties dissipated as I drummed my fingers, waiting. I beeped the horn twice—one a chirp, the second an unconscious warning blast. My grip on the wheel tightened as my back muscles followed suit.

Ah, here he came, and with his cap. As he skipped past the open door, I noticed for the first time his sneakers. "All Little Leaguers must have rubber cleats or they won't be allowed to play" rumbled from deep within my cranium.

"Vinny, where are your cleats?" I said as mildly as I could, although it came out rather strained, the "eats" of "cleats" ending in a grunt.

My son looked down at his feet. "Gee, I don't know."

Brow furrowing, nostrils flaring, I now gave the issue of my loins the unequivocal message that he had done something terribly wrong. "Where did you leave them? They must be in your closet! Get them now!"

Off he trotted again, albeit at a somewhat disheartened pace.

The back of my neck was by this point as hard as a brick. My hands were gripped to the steering wheel. My neighbor glanced over from the easy chair on his porch. He saw a grown man sitting in a parked car, looking as if he was doing 236 mph in the Indy 500. I glanced at my watch once again. Even if I caught all the lights, took the shortcut behind the strip mall, and drove 236 mph, I would still be late! My neighbor fell off his chair as I gave the horn three sharp blasts. No, no, no, I told myself, almost in the same rhythm, I will not lose control.

Vinny had gotten the signal. He once again ran past the open door and into the car, once cleat tucked under each arm. I realized it would be much easier to get out and close the door myself rather than remind him. Back in the car in five seconds flat, my pulse now 140 (not necessarily from the sprint to the door), I zipped out of the driveway and pulled into the street. My son looked up timidly, no doubt reading my facial expressions like a Gameboy screen. It was time to be quiet and meek, or else.

I heard a thump but there was no time to stop—probably just the neighbor's cat. . . . A car, coming in the right direction at the wrong time, just missed us. I took it in stride, since my pulse was already maxed out. This was a matter of life or death! If I was even two minutes too late, the consequences could be disastrous! All the lectures I had given the other parents, all the reminders about being on time—what would they think of me now, late, late, late, when they had busted their you-know-whats to get there at the appointed time? I just had to be on time!

As I sped towards the field, I told Vinny to put his cleats on.

"Dad, I can't get the knot out," he whined.

Oh, no! Not The Knot! How do they do it? No wonder he would just slip his shoes off and leave them. Too bad they could not just be slipped back on. Houdini himself could never have unraveled the knots Little Leaguers get in their shoelaces.

Out of the corner of my eye I saw a street person stare as I sped down the road, steering with one hand and fighting the knot with my teeth. Have you ever tasted clay? Even the street person was gagging!

Yes! The field. We had arrived. I spit out the shoe, abruptly slowing down so I could pull into the parking lot gently. Vinny raced across the field to greet his friends while I said hi to another parent in my most hypocritically casual voice. She cheerfully greeted me with, "What a beautiful day for a ball game."

Just as the past ten minutes of anxiety seemed to be ebbing away, Vinny came racing back across the field to stop in front of me, his face a mixture of fear and excitement. Before he got up the courage to say anything, though, my mind's eye did a fast reverse. I recalled him jumping into the vehicle with his two cleats, one tucked under each arm. I also remembered him carrying his nice, shiny brown-leather glove back into the house as he went to get his hat. Did he ever bring it back out? My mind flipped through the scenes in rapid succession, over and over. Yes, my worst fear had been realized. No, the rage that had me in its gnarling grip was not totally irrational. No, I definitely needed to resist the impulse to shake my wife's kid until the stuffing came out of him.

I looked at Vinny. He looked at me. He knew what I was thinking—he could feel it. Like a five-year-old, I could not hold it in—I had to say it. "Where is your glove?"

The obvious! Yes—I asked the obvious. What's more, I knew the answer. He knew the answer. Every mom and dad in the country knew the answer, but I had to blurt that out, too. "You left it at home, didn't you? Didn't you! Didn't you!"

Of course he did. Why do we have such unwarranted, out-of-control responses to such obvious and incidental mistakes? Well, okay—maybe you would not have that kind of response. Maybe I am the only father who ever wanted to strangle his child the 16th time in one season we went through this scavenger hunt. Maybe I was the only "jerk" parent to ever participate in Little League.

But I doubt it.

# *They are the Children, We are the Adults, They are the Children . . .*

A young child has a short attention span. He lives in the now, the present. Past and future are adult concepts. Children do not begin to participate in activities on a regular basis without your reminders until they are about nine or ten. Even then, of course, they do not necessarily recall what they are supposed to do, nor will they necessarily do it, should they happen to remember. Baseball is a wonderful opportunity for you to teach your child good habits. On the ball field, the coach will hit ball after ball, encouraging your youngster with the same monotonous instructions every time: Keep your glove down. Get in front of the ball. Cover the ball with your hand. Take your time throwing. We parents need to use the same techniques, the same monotonous encouragement at home to reinforce the pre- and postgame instructions: Get your hat. Find your cleats. Get your glove. Put everything in the bag. Put the bag in the car.

Yes, I am a respected medical professional—but I am also a jerk. Not until halfway through my second season did I realize the problem was not my son, but me. Children are normally disorganized. We must help them learn organization—but that did not finally dawn on me until my third year of coaching.

# Schedules and Stuff

The two most common questions asked by parents at home concerning Little League are, "Where is the schedule?" and "Where is your equipment?" Here are some hints for things that I had to learn the hard way:

First, make two or three copies of the baseball schedule and put them in obvious places, such as on the kitchen door, the refrigerator door or on the calendar, placed at your child's eye level. If it is on the refrigerator door, it will get seen an average of 18 times a day. If you are a mom, double that number. (By the way, sticky refrigerator doors are not an uncommon cause of shoulder and neck pain in women).

Displaying the schedule constantly reminds your child of the next game and keeps you from having to call the coach or team mother to find out where and when you are supposed to show up. Remember though, most children do not know how to read a calendar. You must teach them to cross off each day so they can tell when the big game is coming.

The best way to prevent the weekly Great Equipment Scavenger Hunt is to buy a baseball bag. All sports stores have them. They are long and thin with a special zipper compartment for the bat and enough room for all the equipment. Alternately, you can use an old school bag or Dad's old army duffel.

When do you place everything in the bag? As soon as the game is over and you reach your car. Get everything from your child before he goes running off to get a snack, knock his friends' hats off or chase the other players around the field. This is normal behavior for Little Leaguers. They have just sat quietly in one place, the cage, for an hour and 45 minutes without bashing one another over the head inadvertently with a bat, making mud pies near the water fountain or rolling in the dirt. Once the game is over, they need the release of going a little wild. Their memory, though, seems to get released with their energy.

"Where is your cap?"

"Uh, I dunno."

"Where is your glove?"

"Over there, somewhere?"

"What happened to your shoes?"

"Uh. . .uh . . . uh . . ."

"Where is your head?"

We cannot expect our children to act like adults—especially since the cries of "Where are my keys?" and "Has anybody seen my appointment book?" often compete for the same airspace as "Which one is your hat?" The time to start the right habits—your habits, Mom and Dad—is as soon as the game is over. Grab your child's glove. If he is under eight, grab his hat as well, but let him carry his bag to the car.

Step two comes at the car. Off go his cleats, which you clean on the pavement by hitting them against the ground and yes, untying the knots in the laces. Place all the items in the bag. Put the shoes in a plastic garbage bag if you do not want them to mess up the rest of the equipment. Next, neatly fold up his hat, then store the glove. If he has a ball and bat, make sure they get in the bag too. Once home, make sure his belt is placed in the bag along with a clean set of socks. Now he is ready for the next pregame check.

Go through all the equipment in the bag again the day before his next game. Why? Because he will have taken the glove and hat out during the week to play. In time, you can remind him to check his own equipment. If you see him do it by age nine, you can bask in the glow of having a precocious child.

Little League is great when you are prepared, Mom and Dad—and when you realize you are not alone.

## One Last Hint

Many children, caught up in the frivolous fray of postgame euphoria, inadvertently wander off and get lost. Do not expect them to remember their own telephone number. Write it on their shoes, glove and hat. By the way, hats are often misplaced and unintentionally taken, especially early in the season, when they are all clean and look the same. Later on, you will be able to recognize your child's belongings by the mustard, catsup and other indelible stains they manage to acquire during the season. Nevertheless, do not leave responsibility for your child's possessions up to your child, unless you have a saintly amount of patience and an infinite limit on your Visa card.

# 20

# OVERCOMING "NATURAL" INSTINCTS

*"Children may be children, but parents should be more."*

**I HAD JUST SAT DOWN AND TURNED ON THE TV.** With my remote control, I swiftly raced through the channels until I hit a ball game. As the pitcher threw the ball, the batter dove out of the way to avoid being hit. In a flash, the batter raced to the mound with flailing fists. Before he could do any damage, though, he was tackled by the third baseman. Both dugouts emptied. Soon, I could not distinguish one team from the other; the players seemed to meld into a chaotic mass that ebbed and flowed with grunts, groans, and a mixture of unintelligible words. The broadcaster excitedly recounted each blow. Was this baseball? Where did all those guys go, who used to stand with their hats over their hears as "The Star-Spangled Banner" was belted out by the soprano?

Harmony is the opposite of such chaos; it is order, teamwork in an atmosphere of mutual respect. Some team sports, like football, maintain a delicate balance between harmony and chaos. One moment everything is symmetrical and orderly; the next moment, the field is filled with mayhem and twisted bodies. Baseball, of course, is (supposedly) more civilized. At times, though, something takes over that destroys the order and camaraderie.

Did you ever wonder which comes more naturally to human nature, harmony or chaos?

History demonstrates that survival of the fittest, and the establishment of boundaries and pecking orders, is "natural." Children, especially, quickly determine who is the toughest in the class, who is the prettiest, who is the best, who is the fastest. Unfortunately, the other side of the coin is fixing who is the ugliest, the slowest, and the worst. Children effortlessly decide who is "in" and who is "out"; who is rad or cool, and who is a nerd. We, as adults, know this is immature, and it makes us angry. We shake our heads over how children can be so cruel to one another. Yet, when you think about our own "grown-up" behavior, is it all that different?

Take a look at this exchange:

"Hi, my name is Leon. Nice to meet you, Kevin." Leon and Kevin shake hands. In ancient years, handshaking was a way of making sure your adversary did not have a weapon. Now, it is a ritual of manliness; Leon shakes Kevin's hand firmly and decisively. "Which child is yours, Kevin?"

Kevin points to his son, who towers over all the other children.

"He's a big boy," Leon says in a surprised voice.

"Yeah, he gets it from his mother's side. Her brothers are all six-five or more. Which one is yours?"

"Jeremy, over there, is my son."

Kevin's son towers over Leon's boy by a head. Leon now feels a little intimidated, especially after noticing that Kevin's son is as talented as he is big. After a little while, he asks Kevin, "Do you live nearby?"

"Yes, over there near Poor Pines Road."

"Oh, on Poor Pines Road? I live up the hill in Big Bucks Manor. What do you do for a living, Kevin?"

"I'm a carpenter."

Kevin recognizes the game, so does not bother to ask Leon what he does. Still feeling somewhat inferior, though, or maybe just irritated because he let himself feel that way at first, Leon tells him just the same.

"I work for the Sue Them All firm as a lawyer. That's spelled a-t-t-o-r-n-e-y."

This conversation, of course, is a complete fabrication. I'm sure none of us have ever met anyone so crude, because as adults we are above these kinds of childish status games, are we not? Our sophistication and hard-won wisdom have taught us to abandon such puerile comments as "I am the toughest," "I am the best," or "I am the prettiest." All we care about is who has the biggest house, the best car, the best job, and the most money.

Interestingly, the first question most adults want to ask of an individual whom they do not know is not their name, but what they do, what their job is. In other words, what is their status? Asking about someone's occupation is the adult way of finding out who is the toughest, who is the best.

Yes, most of us really are still children. We are simply more adept at disguising our basic competitive traits, which if left unbridled, can become destructive and chaotic. Fortunately, we developed other attributes as we grew to adulthood that counteract our fundamental chaotic tendencies. We have acquired compassion, generosity, and empathy, the hallmarks of civilized society. These are the qualities we hope to instill in our children, the virtues all parents wish for their children. They make us feel sorry for those who are less fortunate, ill, in danger, or in need of help. They are not easy to impart, though—especially in Little League, where, some would have you believe, the entire purpose of the game is to beat your opponent.

How can we, as parents and coaches, teach our children harmony and provide for them the kind of safe, trusting environment that will start them out on the road toward being good, moral and wholesome people? First, we must teach it to ourselves and then each other.

Some men are little because they are afraid no one can accept them if they really knew them. Other men are not afraid to admit they are not the best and can be themselves and be consistent. These are the big men.

Be a man, be genuine and people will like you, and your children will see you as someone they admire.

# 21

# TEACHING CHILDREN HARMONY: HOW TO GET ALONG

*"Little League is a song,*
*The bat leads the beat,*
*The ball carries the tune,*
*The cheers are the choir."*

CHILDREN FLOURISH WHEN THEY FEEL SAFE. They look to us for safety, security, and protection—at times, even from one another. After all, Little Leaguers can get hurt in plenty of ways other than by being hit by a ball or called out on a strike. Words and actions can leave invisible scars that create defenses within and shape negative reactions for life. These kinds of words and actions happen when a Little League coach does not make harmony—teamwork, order, safety, mutual respect—the most important part of the game.

## *Children Will Be Children*

Everett could only be described as awkward, thin, and lanky. It seemed, at times, that his left foot loved to step on his right. His brown locks were always in disarray, and his nose, like Jimmy Durante's, seemed to eclipse his tiny mouth and soft brown eyes. He was gentle and shy—just the kind of child to make everyone else feel he was different.

Don was a talented Little Leaguer, but as young as he was, he could be as demeaning and cruel as any adult. He was the kid we all feared in our own childhoods—the proverbial bully, the one who got his self-worth from pushing others around. The object of his contempt today was, as usual, Everett.

The Yankees coach hit the ball to Everett. It went into his glove, up his arm, into his chin, and landed on the ground in front of him. A demeaning giggle came from Don. "You stink, Everett. You really stink."

"Good thing it didn't hit you in the nose," chimed in Ky, "or it might have got stuck up there." That brought titters from everyone.

"Hey, anteater-nose, you don't need no bat, just swing your nose. You're bound to get a hit." This brought a greater roar.

Children learn destructive behavior so quickly. All they need is an instigator. When the team came off the field, the onslaught continued. Don took Everett's hat, bent it, put it on his nose, and walked around the dugout bumping into everyone, mimicking Everett's awkward walk. Some of the other children mocked Everett, who could only frown and try his best to hold in his tears.

"Hey, Don, give Everett his nose back—I mean his hat," said the coach as he smiled and chuckled. "And stop picking on him," he added halfheartedly. As soon as he turned around, though, one of the other children grabbed Everett's hat again and started swatting him with it.

Soon, the mischievous bunch turned their attention to picking on "Chubs," as they had nicknamed Bobby. Don took Everett's hat and bumped into Richie, who threw out his belly to mimic "Chubs." The other children laughed at the two boys.

Bobby began to cry, which was, of course, the signal for all the little men to chime in with a chorus of "Cry, baby, cry. Stick your finger in your eye. Tell your mother it wasn't I. Cry, baby, cry." More than simply the words, it was the children's whining, demeaning tone that hurt Bobby and deprived him of any respect for himself. Yes, Bobby was learning peer pressure. His mom and dad had never done this to him. They loved and respected him. Now his friends were telling him he was not acceptable because he was fat. To a child, being "not acceptable" is the same thing as being bad or rejected. Seven years after this incident—and many more like it, unfortunately—Bobby told me, "I cannot trust people anymore. They will hurt me."

Did he remember where he learned this? Oh, yes. Not surprisingly, Bobby does not like team sports today. Bobby and Everett blame the other players for what happened to them. When Everett's parents complained to the coach, he pulled out the old, worn, "Well, children will be children!" There was nothing, he claimed, he could—or should—have done to stop them. "You can't control them. Kids have to fend for themselves. That is how they learn to grow up."

Separation anxiety, the fear of being left alone, is a child's first and greatest dread. Children feel safe when an adult is around. They bloom with firm, loving control. When left alone—physically or emotionally—they, like adults, compete to stay in the "in" crowd, even if they do not like the people in it, just so they will not be by themselves. Remember, though, to be in the "in" crowd, someone must be in the "out" crowd. After all, how would you know who is "in" if you did not know who is "out"?

A coach does not—and should not—have to tolerate the kind of behavior that made Bobby's and Everett's Little League careers so miserable. Children do not have to be permitted to "do what comes naturally," to be cruel. They can be stopped, and guided to a safer, more harmonic road—but only if someone is there to teach a higher level of civilization than dog eat dog. Never accept the unacceptable.

## *Coaches and Parents in Harmony*

Have you ever wondered where bullies—the children who throw their weight around, the ones whose tone can hurt much more than a fist—come from? Some parents like to think they learn these behaviors on their own, or from their friends, but they do not. They learn them at home. It never ceases to amaze me how much children mimic their parents in all ways, including the expletives and four-letter words they heard Dad and Mom use—not base, ball, and bats, but the F word and the S word. These are damaging, not harmonious words. They hurt the people they are used against—and they hurt the people who have gotten into the habit of using them.

"Damn it, Mark. You can't hit a barn with a bat!"

Mark missed the ball sitting on the tee, but his was not his coach or his dad talking; it was Mark himself. He was seven years old. His hat was crooked sideways. He stood just a little taller than a tee. He stopped trying to hit the ball, and started kicking the tee as he yelled, "Shit, shit!"

I remembered hearing Mark's dad make the exact same remark just two days earlier: "Damn, you can't hit a barn with a bat." Obviously Mark had added the other expletive on his own—but, of course, he must have learned that at school!

As coach, you can and must set the stage for the parents. Just because they have jobs and have produced children does not necessarily mean they ever grew up. Listen to them and the other coaches at your next Little League game. If you close your eyes, it will be hard to distinguish the children from the adults by their conversation. You can—and must—establish what words and behavior you will and will not tolerate from your team's parents. Make your point at the first meeting, then make it again just before the first game, and then again at every game after that, if necessary.

### AL AND AL'S COACHES CORNER

*At your first parent-coach meeting, you the coach must in no uncertain terms stress that the words and behavior adults use at Little League games are extremely important and powerful tools—tools the children will copy. What is said and how the children are treated by the team parents will influence not only how those children treat their friends, but also how they will treat Mom and Dad later in life, when the roles of who is supporting whom become reversed. All parents must:*

*Never laugh at or criticize a child for something they, as adults, might consider an error.*

*Never curse or criticize a child in front of the child's friends. Talk to him after the game, or talk to the coach. Exceptions, of course, included correcting a child who was doing something dangerous, such as swinging a bat.*

*Never openly criticize the umpire, another coach, or someone else's child.*

When a coach or manager establishes these criteria, he creates a harmonious atmosphere that fosters teamwork and mutual respect. In such an environment, children also learn respect for authority—and remember, umpires are the authority in Little League. Demeaning them ("Hey, ump, what are you, blind?") gives a strong message to little people. Open criticism of coaches and other players in front of the children is also ill-advised and often potentially destructive. A one-on-one confrontation, or a discussion with the league president or vice president, is the best way to air any complaints about a coach's, manager's, or umpire's wrong or inappropriate conduct. If you do talk to the umpire or coach, always do it in private. (The one time any parent must stand up publicly to a coach or manger, however, is when that person is being destructive to a child. Making sure the children feel protected comes before everything else.)  If you wonder if you are making the correct decision, ask the other parents if their perception of the situation is the same. Then act.

Children also need to see that you, the parent or the coach, respect authority. They learn how to deal with life's inevitable conflicts from watching you. You can teach them to treat their adversaries with honesty and respect, or with derision and destructiveness. Don't forget, though, that if you choose the latter, you will be teaching your child rudeness and unruliness, and will eventually bear the fruits of those teachings yourself, when your children reach their teenage years. You will have taught them how to deal with you!

## *Someone Is In Control*

Miguel giggled and yelled, "You stink!" as Lewis missed the ball on the tee for the third time in the practice. Giggling and making fun of someone else is infectious to T-ballers; several of the other children began to laugh, too.

Suddenly, the coach bellowed, "Who said, 'You stink'? Speak up! you think laughing at someone is funny? Well, I think it is not very nice. I never want to hear or see anything like this again! Miguel, tell Lewis you are sorry, immediately."

Miguel looked up defiantly and said, "No."

The coach marched right over to Miguel and sat him on the bench. He then turned to the rest of the players and told them that anyone who laughed at another teammate for missing a ball, or any other reason, would be off the team.

The little boys had never seen their coach like this. He was always smiling; he always spoke in an enthusiastic tone. Were they afraid? No. There was no fear on their faces. Quite the contrary—they looked calm. Someone was in control—someone who would prevent them from getting hurt, who would allow only praise and good comments from and for one another, and who would protect them from being laughed at by the others. Children flourish when they feel safe. They look to us parents and coaches for this protection, this peace. They expect it—and they deserve it.

Remember Don, Everett, and Bobby? They were Yankees. The Yankees team had a problem. Many of the parents noted signs of anxiety—squirming and discomfort—in their children as the players approached the field. Several Yankees could never seem to find their equipment; others developed muscle and tummy aches before every game. Although they never voiced the truth, they were afraid of the bullies, like Don, who made their Little League experiences painful, like Everett's was. Their fear was well founded, as no one was in control of their team.

The Yankees coach did not realize that his hands-off attitude and lax behavior was allowing the children on his team—his charges—to be hurt. Their pain was not from physical injuries that would leave visible scars, but from invisible wounds to their confidence and feelings of security. He was not teaching trust, order, and mutual respect; he was not providing them with an atmosphere of harmony—his greatest of all responsibilities. All was chaos on his team, and in chaos, children do not flourish—they cower.

## *Harmony Can Work*

The positive, safe, and mutually respectful environment I call harmony builds a nurturing atmosphere that allows good feelings and positive self-regard to grow. These ingredients of self-confidence and discipline help children do their best. A harmonious atmosphere also teaches children morality of the highest type: respect for others and consideration of their feelings and needs. When children learn to treat others as they would like to be treated, they carry the concept of unconditional positive regard with them wherever they go. One of my daughter's teachers once told me this story:

> *I've never seen anything like it. The boys were rough-housing and picking on one another, when Kaycee put her hands on her hips and yelled in an authoritative voice, "Stop it, this is not very nice. No one is to hit or pick on anyone here!"*
>
> *All the seven-year-old boys stopped and sat down as Kaycee sternly looked them in the eyes. She went on, "Be nice, or you're off the team." I did not know what team she was talking about, but whatever one it was, the boys sure didn't want to be kicked off!*

Yes, sometimes children do listen; sometimes they learn, sometimes they copy your behavior. What you teach them through your actions and your words is important. Words—the right words, the positive words—can build an environment of hope and safety, respect and regard.

Can you hear the harmony?

## *Where Are They Now?*

Everett, lanky, long-nosed and awkward, won a college scholarship for math where his skills are appreciated. He remembers being made fun of and it still hurts him, but he says, "I'm over it." Some scars do not show on the outside; we can only guess how much they ache on the inside as time goes on. Some people, like Everett, are empowered by these hurts to succeed despite all the odds. As coaches, we have an obligation to make Little League a harmonious place in which to grow.

Kaycee, the "be nice or you're off my team" girl, suffered from encephalitis. She was paralyzed for one week on her right side and unable to talk. Subsequently, she also suffered from epilepsy. Several years later, at age 14, she was awarded the Grand National Karate Championship for Red Dragon Karate, then repeated the feat the following year. She was the first girl to ever be Grand Champion and the first person—male or female—to ever win it twice. Currently, she is in college. She is the epitome of "where there is a will, there is a way."

---

# 22

# CHEERING: IS IT JUST NOISE?

## THE SONG OF SUCCESS

*"There are those who make things happen;
others who watch what's happening;
and others who wonder what happened."*

—Tommy Lasorda

**MR. CARTER YAWNED** and Mrs. O'Brien nodded off. Mr. Sackheim stretched out to catch some rays and Mr. Torez tapped his watch and held it to his ear to check that it was still working. The bleachers were full but the energy was on empty. If a pin had dropped, it would have echoed between the parents sitting like bowling pins on the benches. Their bodies were present, but their minds were absent.

Have you ever been to a Little League game where the strawberries growing in right field made more noise than the parents cheering for their children? Where the arguments of the managers and umpires were the only enduring memory of the game? Just what does parental cheering and participation in Little League mean, and does it really matter to the outcome of the game, or more importantly, to the ultimate development of your child?

Baseball is unique in that it has no cheerleaders. Go to a basketball game and you will find a pep squad arousing the fans at crucial moments to urge their teams on to triumph. Of course, no sport uses cheerleaders for generating crowd participation more than the behemoth sport of football: "Hold that line! Hold that line! Defense! Defense! Go Team!" Pom-poms twirling, the head cheerleader leaps ten feet in the air, coming down in a perfect landing with arms outstretched to the thunderous ovation of thousands of fans.

Ask Jimmy the Greek—or any casino or bookmaker—if home advantage is a prominent factor, and he will tell you the odds are always with the hometown prizefighter, player or team. Check your own newspaper today for the home-versus-away statistics in any sport, and you will find a definite difference, be the game baseball, football, basketball, soccer or hockey. Generally, the scores favor the home team by about 70 percent. In college basketball, for example, many teams go undefeated at home year after year. Is this due to the ball or the basket or because the length of the court or the angle of the lighting is different? Definitely not. Is it the exuberant cheering and applause of the home crowd, the yelling and screaming of thousands of home fans? Unquestionably, yes!

What does cheering do? Medically speaking, excitement and encouragement heighten the release of adrenaline, which is stored in little bubble-like vesicles. When released into the brain and bloodstream, adrenaline increases alertness, muscle tone, readiness, pupillary size, breathing capacity and cardiac output. All of these physical reactions are needed for the human body to react optimally to the environment. In other words, when excitement and encouragement release adrenaline and other hormones into our systems, we get stimulated to a state of peak psychological and physiological readiness, prepared for any eventuality. In simpler terms, you can tell if children are at their best by the skip to their step, the gleam in their eye and the sunshine in their smile. To doctors, that skip is the adrenaline in their arteries going to their muscles, and that gleam is the epinephrine in their wide eyes, and that smile is the limbic emotional brain saying this is fun. *Cutting edge, momentum, intensity, focus* and *concentration* are not just words; they are physical body reactions.

Since we know these physiological characteristics of readiness, why are too many Little League games so slow and lackluster that the only response they engender at times is a good yawn? Well, when was the last time you saw a cheerleader at a Little League game? Why has baseball, especially Little League, not fostered a cheering squad like other sports? Well, I'm told that the reason is that baseball started as a kids' game before it was picked up by adults. Whoever was available played, so there was no room for cheerleaders. But, again, isn't that true for basketball and football as well?

## *Back to the Eagles*

Top of the first inning. The Eagles' parents were huddled together in the stands, full of anticipation, their eyes riveted on their own youngsters. Vinny was up first for the Eagles. He smacked a dribbler to third base. The ball was caught, but overthrown. The Eagles' parents cheered. Next, Philip hit a long ball to the outfield. The parents were on their feet waving, clapping, hooting with joy. The face of each Eagles parent beamed with pride. The little ballplayers with bright yellow Eagles hats stood proud, their chests trying to protrude out of their oversized uniforms. If you asked them who they were, they would have screamed in unison, "Eagles!" As each peewee player crossed the plate, he was met with enthusiasm of all the team moms and dads. The children skipped around the bases; they all had a zing to their swing. The adrenaline was flowing, the epinephrine coursing through every muscle.

An hour and a half later, bottom of the sixth. The Eagles were now on the field, the score 21 to 19 in their favor. The Lions, though, had already scored five runs this inning, with two men on base and three batters to go. The Lions' parents were in a frenzy. Sparks of their enthusiasm were igniting their little batters. Gary, the next Hawk to bat, strode up to the box with determination and pounded the plate with his bat. Adrenaline coursed through his arteries, fed by the Lions' parents and coaches chanting praise and encouragement: "Hit the big one! Clean the bases!"

In the stands, on the opposite side, a gray cloud hung over the bleachers. The faces of the once-proud Eagles' parents had turned sour. They sat cowering, as if sleet and rain were pelting down on their heads, as if they had just heard Lou Gehrig tell them he was leaving baseball. The Eagles themselves were slump-shouldered and droopy-armed as if drenched, already accepting defeat. Their gloves looked more like anchors than instruments for catching a speeding ball. The spigots of their adrenaline had been turned off, both in the stands and on the field; their tanks were on "empty."

Tommy peered out from under his cap at his mother and father sitting there glumly, wringing their hands. Some moms and dads were slowly shaking their heads no. Tommy's heart pushed a big tear up to his eye. I guess I am bad, he thought, a real loser. Look how sad I'm making Mom.

Neither he nor the team parents were conscious of it, but those adults were conveying a definite message to Tommy and all his teammates. The juice, the momentum was gone—the smell of defeat saturated the air. Had the parents' behavior affected the children, or the children's playing affected the parents?

# *Three Cheers for Cheering*

Labeling these parents as "losers" is an easy out. Sure, what these children needed was obvious, at least in hindsight, but how many times have you cheered your team on when it was losing? Logically—which is how adults think—one would not cheer if the Dodgers or the Yankees or the home team were getting trounced and had lost its juice. Logically, then, one also would not cheer—meaning, be happy—when one's own kids were getting beaten. The problem is that children do not understand logic the way we grown-ups do. Losing is just not as important to them as it is to us. They are more interested in the fun of playing the game and having something to be happy about. When we tell them differently by our disapproving mood, who really loses—our kids or us? Who has their priorities right, who is being logical? We know that cheering and encouragement turn up adrenaline, which gives the children spirit and focus to do their best. Logically, then, when we do not cheer, we are the ones being illogical.

Cheering is not simply a way of rejoicing when the team is doing well; it is a way of showing acceptance and love and giving children a vote of confidence—especially when things are not going as hoped.

> *"Children need praise the most when they appear to deserve it the least."*
> —**Tommy Lasorda**

A child's self-concept (what he thinks of himself) depends on the reflection his mom, dad, and other significant adults such as coaches and managers, give him. This is why some children are so confident with themselves despite their shortcomings, while others are so discouraged about their abilities, despite all their gifts. Cheering when the child or team is doing well is also definitely important, of course, as it encourages repetition of the behavior and enhances self-confidence. Cheering when your team is down is even more important, because it specifically augments the physiological response that increases physical prowess, to make your child the best he can be. In other words, cheering is the home advantage.

> *"Cheering is winning. It is the rally monkey."*
>
> —Mike Scioscia

After my second year as manager, I could plainly see that children with positive, participating parents had winning teams. Pick the right parents and you had a team that loved to play, a team in which, at the end of the season, everyone was looking forward to getting back in the game the next year. To me, a winning team consisted of parents who would bring love, affection and a touch of tenderness to their kids. The children were secure and cooperative with their friends. Nothing was boring to them. They seemed to have it all because their parents were always at their sides to guide and mold them into beautiful, harmonious sculptures with genuine grins and hearts full of contentment.

These children did not cringe with grief because they missed a grounder or overthrew first base. They knew that if they made the effort they would always be rewarded. Their parents' cheers were not rewards for the runs scored or the plays made; they were hymns of support, trumpets of solidarity behind their children. The glee that emanated from these kids as the Little League season rolled on was the music that made me come back to coach year after year.

**FROM THE DESK OF DR. VINCE**

*Cheering has certain senses:*

1. *The visual: a smile, a look that says, "Hey, you're my child and I'm proud!"*
2. *A sound: one that resonates warmth, encouragement and has a beat full of heart and excitement.*
3. *A voice: words that are positive.*

*As noted in previous chapters, a child has two memories or two brains. One is the limbic system, the feeling brain that immediately reads mom and dad's real message. It is an automatic reaction that they learn starting from one year of age. Cheering and chanting is so enthralling because it is the heartbeat of emotional intelligence. It enables a child to rekindle a pleasurable primal feeling that is positive at a time when his cortex, or thinking brain, is depressed due to circumstances that surround losing.*

# *The Field That Feels*

I can see the sparkle in each child's eyes, a reflection of the energy their moms and dads make, like the light of a full moon dancing on a shimmering lake.

I can hear the heartbeat of each child quicken with the chants of "2-4-6-8, who do we appreciate!"

I can feel the little feet patter.

That makes the game really matter.

# SECTION 5

## THE GOOD, THE BAD AND THE UGLY

### *Introduction*
by Dr. Frank Job
(Orthopedic surgeon for the LA Dodgers and
Originator of the Tommy John shoulder surgery)

THERE ARE PARENTS who have their eyes on fame instead of their children. I operate on too many 16-year-old shoulders with the Tommy John procedure I pioneered 30 years ago. Then it was only the Major Leaguers who needed it. Parents have forgotten it's real children, not their own dreams they are dealing with. Children depend on their parents to protect them. As Dr. Fortanasce has said, a parent or coach who doesn't protect his children might be considered the UGLY.

There are also parents who seem to forget their children need their encouragement and attention. They need to be made to feel important. The parents who aren't present at every game are the BAD.

Finally, I say there are those parents who just have fun with their children and are a positive influence on their development. These are the GOOD.

## 23

---

# DEVELOPMENT: PHYSICAL, MENTAL, SOCIAL

## IQ AND NATURAL TALENT ARE OVERRATED

**DO YOU EVER . . .**

. . .feel your heart drop down into your gut as you see how clumsy your child is compared with some of the other children?

. . . feel like a failure because your child sits on the bench half the game?

. . . wonder if your child will be a failure forever if he plays right field, ending up a janitor with the pitcher as his boss?

. . . wonder if girls should be on the same ball field with boys?

. . . feel like pulling your hair out in aggravation when trying to teach your child to play?

Well, so did I.

## *My Child Can't Catch*

If necessity is the mother of invention, anxiety and competitiveness are the necessities behind this chapter—the anxiety I felt when I compared my child with other children; the competitiveness I saw generated by some of the win-at-all-costs coaches and managers of Little League. Why would a person like myself, with 21 diplomas on his office wall, be anxious and competitive in Little League of all places? Well, let me tell you of my first year.

I had volunteered to coach the Angels. I remember sitting in the dugout, gazing out to the ball field. My third baseman, Stefan, had his eyes riveted to the Yankees batter, who hit a slicing line drive down the third base line. Stefan dove and speared the ball with his glove. Off balance, he slung a side-arm toss to Wayne, the first baseman, then quickly spanked off the clay from his trousers. Wayne, meanwhile, noting that the runner on second was on his way to third, fired the ball back again to Stefan, who adroitly applied the tag. A double play. Not bad for two seven-year-olds.

The Angels parents were in awe, as was I; Stefan and Wayne had stifled their opponents again. They were the "iron curtain," as some of the other teams had named them by mid-season. Bob, Vinny and Mike, three Angels parents, sat silently along with me in the dugout. We all smiled in fascination. We all then looked at our own little Angels, and our smiles evaporated into frowns of concern and fear. Staring up and to the left (a sign of contemplative thinking) I wondered, is my child normal? Is he developmentally delayed? Is he brain damaged?

As I sat wondering, I remembered my dad throwing me a ball at least 90 miles an hour when I was six years old. I could catch it without any difficulty; I could hit the cover off it. I stared up to the right (a sign of imaginative thinking). Ah, well, the older we get, the better we were. With age comes wisdom—or is that amnesia?

The clank of the ball off the tee shook me from my reverie. Todd, Mike's son, got in front of the ball. He bobbled it in and out of his glove, then picked it up and tossed it over the first baseman's head, just 20 feet away. Mike softly groaned.

Heather of the Yanks, hit a soft pop fly just beyond midfield, out of reach of the Angels' shortstop. Vinny's son, Philip, was playing left field. He staggered and stumbled and lunged for the ball, which had now stopped in front of him. As he reached to grab it, Stefan swept it up and flung a perfect toss to Todd on second base. Unfortunately, Todd bobbled it again; by the time he had a handle on it, the base runner was standing on second with her arms folded smugly. Vinny and Mike groaned in unison and their heads sagged down to their shoulders. I am sure they were feeling the same anxiety I was:

how come my child's not like Stefan and Wayne? There must be something wrong with him, something terribly wrong!

## *What Can They Really Do?*

Comparing your child's achievements to those of another—whether it is SAT scores, IQ scores, or skills on the baseball field—can cause distress for parents. However, unlike baseball, school tests enable a parent to justify the results, even outright lie about them when a child does badly. The tests are flawed, they're meaningless, my child was sick that day, etc, etc. On the baseball field, the parents have no such excuses to hide behind. It is obvious to everyone watching which children are talented and/or skillful and which are not. I should point out that there is a difference between talent and skill, just as there is a difference between IQ and achievement tests. Talent and IQ are inherited abilities. Skill and achievement test scores demonstrate learning. Some children with average IQs have high achievement scores, which means you and your child's school are doing a good job. Neurological research shows that children who use their brains also increase their brain connections and thus increase inherent abilities such as IQ and athletic abilities.

## *To the Birds*

"Pay attention!" Tommy's mom screamed at him from the bleachers as the ball bounced past him in the outfield. Tommy, like many eight-year-olds, was more interested in the pigeons that flocked over the outfield than in the ball. He loved watching the birds flap their wings and take off en masse as he ran close to them. While Tommy's mind was on the pigeons, the Hawks scored yet another run. His mother glared at him, then bellowed more abuse. "Why don't you wake up, Andrew? Come on, you're letting us all down!"

A week earlier I had been to Tommy's birthday party with my son. His parents had a trophy cabinet full of awards that highlighted their own athletic accomplishments, and I decided that Tommy must have "good athletic genes" and would turn out to be an accomplished sportsman. But, by the end of that game, it became obvious his mother didn't share my view. Tommy stood close to her, but she, unconsciously I'm sure, ignored him and walked off to the parking lot. Her behavior looked even worse in contrast to the other parents who eagerly chatted with and congratulated their children. I heard Tommy apologize to his mother as he reached the car and then promise to "clean my room." His mother continued to ignore him, however. He dropped his head and stared at the ground, then tried to grasp her hand. His body language spoke very clearly. "My mom thinks I'm no good."

I'm sure his mother was not consciously aware of the message she was sending to her son by her tone of voice and body language, but it was clear to Tommy. She had confused his inattention with disobedience or inability, rather than recognizing it as a natural effect of his immature development. Even if Tommy was naturally talented, he had many other attributes that she could recognize, appreciate and love. Many successful doctors I have known spent their childhood playing on the bench and many dropped out of athletic activities because of a lack of talent.

Remember Frankie and his dream?

## *How Parents React*

Many parents show their disappointment with their child in several unconscious ways.

- Their tone of voice and body language are cold and stern.
- They accentuate the negative. "You aren't trying. You're not paying attention."
- They avoid being closely associated with their child, thus provoking the child into attention-seeking behavior.
- They refuse to accept their child for whom he or she is. "You've let me down. You're embarrassing me."

Children pick up on the body language and disapproving statements and translate them into "Mommy and Daddy don't find me valuable." It is natural to act disappointed, but parents don't have to act in a rejecting way.

As a parent, when your child is not living up to your expectations, you may be tempted to look for a quick fix, one that may well make the problem even worse. The quick fix is often to tell your child everything he did wrong, followed by how great you did everything at his age and then by a command such as, "I'll get you lessons" or "I better give you extra chores until you learn to catch a ground ball." This attitude suggests your child has failed, as has your relationship with him or her.

Parents often reprimand their children solely because they think people will think less of them if they do not. This is a face-saving technique that only saves a parent's face at the expense of the child.

# *How Children Interpret Those Reactions*

Tommy knew exactly what his mother was saying. A child learns to respond to a parent's slightest change of voice tone or body language. Between the ages five and 12, children believe they are responsible for everything, and because they see what we say, parents are unable to hide behind words. From age five to nine, children interpret a parent's reactions personally. They feel responsible for their parents' change of mood.

Tommy interpreted his mom's frown and translated it into: "She doesn't love me. She's ashamed of me. I am responsible for my mom's unhappiness."

The reaction of a child on the field as he sees his parents' unhappy expressions in the bleachers varies from "Mom's crying; Mom's mad," to "Dad doesn't like me; Dad is upset about what I've done."

Tommy regressed to baby talk and childhood games to try to reconnect with his mother. This only increased her anxiety and her admonishments to "Grow up, Andrew. Act your age."

Alice, a ten-year-old, utilized delaying tactics to avoid experiencing her parents' disapproval. Whenever it was time to play baseball, she complained of physical ailments or pretended she couldn't find her equipment. Delaying tactics are used when the child is saying, "Mom, Dad, I don't want to disappoint you anymore. I want to avoid situations in which I do."

For children, negative attention is better than none at all. A 12-year-old, Jessie, used bad behavior as his way of saying, "You're right, I'm no good," or

"If you think I'm bad now, I'll show you what bad is all about." This attitude becomes prevalent during the teenage years. It is both a way of reacting and retaliating against disapproving parents.

All these behaviors, of course, confirm the parents' initial perceptions and result in further rejection techniques such as referring to the child as "My husband's son." One successful businessman friend of mine even said he once overheard his dad saying: "I don't know how he is so clumsy. Sometimes I wonder if he is really my kid." This friend had no interest in sports but, as he has told me, he now makes more money in one year than his dad did in his whole life. But all these years later, he's clearly still angry and hurt about his dad's comments.

---

### FROM THE DESK OF DR. VINCE
#### WHY ARE SOME CHILDREN BETTER THAN OTHERS?

*From my coaching experience there are six clear factors that separate average baseball players from outstanding players. These are:*

1. *Living in a neighborhood with other children who also play baseball.*
2. *Having older siblings who play baseball.*
3. *Having a mother or father who spends a considerable amount of time teaching them baseball.*
4. *Having had a positive experience with any previous coach.*
5. *Natural talent.*
6. *Maturation.*

*The first four have to do with learning the skills of baseball and can increase the child's inherent abilities. The fifth and sixth points deal with inherited potential.*

*Some children physically mature faster than others; some are born with better eye-hand coordination. I differentiate between these two (maturation and natural coordination), because as a child matures, becoming physically larger and stronger, his abilities appear to improve. Other children will catch up to him later, when their own bone and muscle development occurs.*

*Dr. Ysuiri, a physician who examined Little League World Series players, said he could predict the winners in 90 percent of cases just by examining them for physical maturity.*

# The Difference Between Maturity and Maturation

Maturity is the process of physical maturing of a child's body. It is often gene related. For example, children of Latin origin often reach full body maturity (muscle and bone growth) by 16 years of age. Teutonic, English, Swedish, and German children, however, usually don't reach this maturation until 18 to 21 years of age. Those who mature earlier are stronger and quicker from 10 to 16 years of age and can expect to appear as better players. Those who mature later soon catch up. I remember so well as a high school freshman being the only one at 5'10" to touch the rim. One of my friends, Tommy Breen, at 5'6" could barely touch my outstretched hand over my head. By senior year, Breen towered over me and over the basketball rim.

# Child Development

Children's development is best understood when we see it in a practical sense; a helpless infant develops into a mobile toddler, then into an inquisitive dependent child, and finally to an independent, skillful adolescent. In medical terms, development can be defined as a systematic intra-individual change that is age related. In other words, with each progressive year, a child develops mental, physical, psychological, and moral capabilities that he did not have a year before. These capabilities are called developmental milestones.

*At each developmental milestone a child tends to assume that everyone thinks in the same way that he or she does.*

When a two-year-old grabs ice cream with his hands, his five-year-old sibling yells with confidence, "No, that is wrong." The seven-year-old certainly can't understand why his teenage brother wants to hold hands with a girl. The 12-year-old looks at the seven-year-old and can't understand why he can't pay attention to the soccer coach and maintain his position on the field. A mother can't understand why her 15-year-old daughter can't keep her room clean. A father can't understand why his 12-year-old son cannot remember to take out the garbage. All children cannot understand why Mom and Dad are so grouchy when they get home from a full day at work. A grandfather can't understand why his son doesn't spend more time with his family, and his son secretly wishes his father had.

The greatest problem for many parents to face is the fact that their child isn't a miniature adult or a "Mini-Me".

Development is dependent upon the brain, hearing, visual and sensory perceptual development of a child. If the child cannot hear, it is hard for him to follow instructions. If he cannot see well, it is hard for him to follow the flight of a baseball. If his gyroscopes or coordination centers are out of line, he cannot tell that he is falling down or needs to make adjustments to catch himself before he hits the ground. Likewise, if his brain isn't fully developed, it will be difficult for him to learn or remember.

### FROM THE DESK OF COACH VINCE

*Q: Coach, is it safe for a child of six or seven who has never played baseball before to catch a fly ball at 45 to 60 feet?*

*A: No. About 60 percent of girls and 45 percent of boys would be hit by the ball. Many will instinctively get out of the way to avoid being hit. Never use a regular baseball with newcomers to Little League; use a tennis ball instead. A child injured at the beginning of the season may not learn to catch at all, due to fear of the ball. In fact, one of the major fears of farm-team players is being hit by a pitched ball.*

*Q: Why did 15 percent more girls get hit?*

A: As any parent who has had both a boy and a girl can tell you, girls pay attention better at this age and tend to be more obedient. If you tell them to catch a ball, they will stand there and try to catch it.

Q: Coach, how well can children of this age hit, catch ground balls and throw?

A. Good question. Six- and seven-year-olds batting off a tee have a 50-50 chance of hitting the ball beyond the 18-foot perimeter used for "fair" in T-ball and a 20-percent chance of hitting a fly out of the infield, with little statistical difference between boys and girls. Ground balls will be caught about 40 percent of the time, dropped 40 percent of the time and missed completely about 20 percent of the time. Catching grounders is safe for all children; catching the heavier T-ball is easier than catching a tennis ball, as it gives a truer bounce that can be anticipated and also sticks in the glove better. Boys of six and seven can throw a distance of 45 feet with ease 60 percent of the time, with 40 percent accuracy. Girls can throw a distance of 45 feet with ease 30 percent of the time with 60 percent accuracy. Basically, boys throw farther, but girls are more accurate.

After one year of experience, 80 to 90 percent of children can catch a fly ball at 45 feet. However, only 50 percent of fly balls are caught at 60 feet, while 80 percent of grounders are caught consistently.

After two years' experience, close to 100 percent of the players will likely be able to catch fly balls at 45 feet, 80 to 90 percent will catch them at 60 feet, and all of them should be able to catch ground balls correctly.

# *Where Are They Now?*

Stefan, part of the "iron curtain" infield, was the MVP in baseball, soccer and whatever else he touched. When he got to college, he found himself faced with a negative coach who could not accept himself and projected all of his problems onto the ballplayers. Stefan had character besides talent, though, so he transferred schools and moved on. He recognized that his self-worth did not depend on a coach's or anyone else's evaluation of him. He was made of the right stuff.

# 24

# EMOTIONAL POTENTIAL

*"I am certain genius is one percent inspiration and
99 percent perspiration."*

—Thomas Edison

## Sometimes The "Have Nots" Have It:
## The Factor That Makes A Difference

**"DAD, ARE WE GOING TO WIN AGAIN TODAY?"** asked little Vinny as
his brown eyes met mine.

"Winning isn't important," I replied. "It's how you play the game that
counts." Not that I was counting or anything, but we were 3-0 for the season and about to play the only other undefeated team, the Hawks. I had
never met the other coach but had heard that he was "really good with kids."
The previous year I had been chosen as Manager of the Year and prided
myself with that honor. Though I hate to admit it, 4-0 sounded much better
than 3-1, especially to us doctors where 4.0 and A+ mean everything. Of
course, I didn't let little Vinny or anyone else know that!

In my usual self-confident way, I absentmindedly wrung my hands, anxiously waiting to see the Hawks practice. I wanted to assess their potential,
see if they had a chance to beat us—not of course that that was important to
me. Then I noticed their coach. Gee, did he look familiar. His eyes met mine
at that moment and he yelled over, "Vinny?" No one calls me Vinny anymore, I thought, I'm Vince. I still couldn't place him. Then he trotted toward

me and awkwardly tripped over the pitcher's mound. In a flash of temporal lobe activity, I matched the clumsiness to the face. Josh, the misfit from my old grammar school, St. Bonface. It couldn't be! I watched him trip again. Yup, it was Josh all right. I sighed with relief. As a kid, he struggled to get out of the dugout, let alone beat someone on the field.

## Four and O—Here We Go

Josh was one of those kids who could never do anything right. Even when he was made to stand in the corner (a regular occurrence) with the proverbial "Dunce" hat on, he'd struggle to keep it on his head. He was awkward, clumsy and certainly no academic heavyweight. The closest he ever came to scoring 100 was on his IQ test. Subsequently, our teachers never held much in the way of expectation for Josh, but just hoped he wouldn't end up in jail.

Despite all his shortcomings, though, I had always liked Josh. Once as I sat alone in the schoolyard, upset that my dog had just been hit by a car, it was Josh who ventured over to console me. "What's wrong, Vinny?" he quietly asked. When I told him, he patted me on the back and said, "Hey, I'll share my dog with you."

Yeah, Josh was a nice kid. But like him or not, today he was going to be 3-1 while I would go on to a perfect 4.0!

## A Natural Knack

*"You learn the full value of a man by how he treats someone who can do nothing for him."*

**—Luke LaPorta**

I watched Josh move methodically among his Little Leaguers, encouraging and instructing them with a relaxed, jovial air. He was good with the kids, but it was clear to me that my team was more talented. The final score was 15 to 4, no contest. Yup, Josh was now 4-0 and Vince was standing in the corner with the funny hat. I watched as the parents and their children approached him after the game. It was astounding to me to see so many people regarding him with such respect and healthy familiarity. Then came the real cruncher. A gleaming limousine pulled up and a man in a chauffeur's uniform walked over to Josh and said, "Mr. Smith, your car is ready, sir. May I carry the bags for you?" It turned out that "Jailman Josh" was in fact the president/CEO of a large toy company.

How did the Dunce turn into the Duke? He was at the lower end of his class academically, and in terms of physical prowess, a close second to the Hunchback of Notre Dame. I remember an old saying at college: What do you call the class nerd 10 years from now? Boss. Today, however, that old adage had been proved wrong. Josh as a lad had little intellectual and even less athletic ability. So what happened? Did he inherit the toy company? Nope. Was there something that no one saw, a type of intelligence not measured by the standardized IQ, SAT, GRE and the three R's and not measured by batting average, home runs and All Star team selection? Is there a secret something that is an essential ingredient to success and happiness as Josh was showing? Is there something we should be teaching our children and learning ourselves, something that is not taught in the classroom or on the baseball diamond or in the batting cage? The answer is YES, YES, YES, and that something is called "emotional intelligence."

## *The Secret Something*

We've always known about emotional intelligence. Some people call it "common sense" and certain children and adults just seem to have it in abundance. Recent advances in brain science clearly show that IQ and aptitude achievement tests can be changed significantly if a child is properly taught. The same is true for athletics. Studies have shown that not only does practice and training increase a child's knowledge of the sport but they also cause changes in the brain neurons that enhance actual ability and potential. Neuroscience shows that we are not stuck with what we're born with, but we can make improvements. People born in the middle ages believed that you were born to the class of kings and princes or slaves and serfs, and would remain there throughout life. This concept was obviously untrue, as we in a democratic society are now aware. Similarly, it is equally false to believe the adage "once a klutz, always a klutz."

What is this emotional intelligence, how important is it, and how do we help our children acquire it? First, how important is it? Well, the story of Josh tells you what effect it can have. Recent studies have conclusively shown that IQ has little to do with whether a child will ultimately be successful, either professionally or emotionally. A study of 80 valedictorians, those with the highest grades in their graduating classes, showed that 10 to 20 years later, they did no better than the average or below average students in their classes. Another study showed that only 2.5 percent of people who graduated in the top 10 percent of their class went on to become millionaires. This figure is three times lower than was expected. But why?

Orel Hershiser and I figured out that natural talent is only one ingredient to success in baseball. Statistically, only one person in 144,000 who plays baseball as a child will make it to the Major Leagues. Hershiser was not even the first-string pitcher at college. Hershiser felt that it was his ability to learn and know who to learn from that made him a success. In addition, his ability to get along and mediate with teammates contributed to his longevity as a baseball player. Teams needed him for his leadership skills and as an example to younger players. This ability to empathize, nurture and manage relationships is one part of emotional intelligence that Orel Hershiser has in abundance. This emotional intelligence is inborn, not taught. Emotional intelligence I feel is the most important factor of success, if success is defined as happiness with oneself and with one's relationships with others, and being in control of one's destiny. In other words, being the manager, the owner, the proverbial "leader."

Emotional intelligence has two parts: common sense about oneself and common sense about other people. Josh, for example, realized that he had a real talent for getting along with others, and he didn't kid himself that he was something he wasn't. His parents didn't kid themselves either, but accepted him for who he was. I was once told by a father with a child much like Josh,

"I realized that I could not change the color of my son's eyes, but I could change the sparkle in them."

Josh and his parents had a solid level of self-knowledge. In baseball terms, they played within themselves. They didn't try to make Josh a rocket scientist when he would have crash landed, and didn't try to make him a major league star when he would have been a major league flop.

Josh had a natural gift, that if measured in IQ terms would run somewhere in the 160s. He was sensitive to others' feelings, took time to think of others and tried to help them instead of only thinking of himself. By eagerly running over to me at the Little League game that day, by offering me his dog years ago, he demonstrated something even more than just common sense. He had compassion and empathy, the things that make a real friend. People like this are those whom you always enjoy being around. They make you feel good about yourself, about life. They bring confidence just by their presence.

How does one measure emotional intelligence? Well, a survey of children in a school playground was conducted recently. In separate interviews, each child was asked where everyone was standing and playing that afternoon and who was best friends with whom. Those who were considered to have low emotional intelligence didn't know where others were standing in the playground and were poor in pairing best friends. Those who were considered to have high emotional intelligence often knew where every child was standing in the playground and were especially adept at pairing best friends. These children were aware of others and their feelings. These abilities, however, had no correlation with their IQ levels.

How do you recognize your own emotional intelligence and· develop it within your children?

Recent advances in genome research (the study of human genes) have revealed that the expression of a gene tract depends on both nature and nurture. A simple example of this is the increase of average height. In the 18th and 19th centuries, the average height of a male was 5'1". Now it is 5'9". The average lifespan was 40 years and is now 76. The genes are the same (nature), but environment (nurture) has changed to make the difference. You can make the difference in your child's emotional IQ if you nurture it.

## FROM THE DESK OF DR. GAYLE FORTANASCE

*Emotional intelligence is an inborn quality of awareness of one's own feelings as well as the feelings of others and the ability to draw upon this to guide one's behavior.*

*Emotional intelligence is not the same as character. Character is a set of values or virtues, a learned behavior one obtains through example and reinforcement.*

*Emotional intelligence has two central factors:*

*The Me-factor—the ability to immediately assess one's own feelings accurately and use these feelings to affect your life in a positive way.*

*The People-factor—the ability to accurately gauge other people's feelings to guide one's own behavior, also known as "empathy."*

*People with strong People-factors often become successful salespeople, politicians, teachers, doctors, and religious leaders—the Orel Hershisers, the Tommy LaSordas, the Tommy Johns—leaders in their own field.*

*People with a high emotional intelligence become:*

*1. The real leaders, captains of the team because they unite their teammates.*
*2. Helpers, the nurturers of relationships.*
*3. Peace makers, the settlers of conflict.*
*4. Therapists, the analysts of social situations.*

*When we talk of intelligence quotient or IQ, we should really change it to PQ, or Potential Quotient. IQ is just one part of a child's natural inborn abilities. For me, there are seven parts to a child's real potential for success:*
*1. Mathematics, logic PQ (formerly part of IQ, Intelligence Quotient).*
*2. Verbal PQ, the second part of IQ.*
*3. Spatial relations PQ, artistic ability.*

4. *Kinesthetic PQ, athletic ability.*
5. *Musical PQ.*
6. *Intrapersonal (Me-factor) PQ.*
7. *Interpersonal (People-factor) PQ.*

*Children with good emotional intelligence:*
- *Know their emotions and are self-aware.*
- *Can manage these emotions. (This can often be taught and/or greatly influenced by parents and coaches).*
- *Are capable of nurturing themselves and others. The optimist.*
- *Have empathy, the ability to know how another person feels and share it.*
- *Know how to handle relationships.*

*If you want to know who has emotional potential remember:*
1. *These are the people, when asked who are friends with whom, can provide an accurate answer.*
2. *When asked how they feel, they can accurately identify their emotions—happy, sad, angry—and the reasons for them.*
3. *When asked to help, they often beat you to the question, offering before you've had to ask.*
4. *When you don't feel like asking a question, they're there asking you how you feel.*
5. *As children, they are usually not the most popular or the star, but are the ones who care and are there.*

*Yes, emotional intelligence, like the intelligence quotient or IQ, is inborn. However, it can be greatly enhanced by the parent, either positively or negatively. If you are now feeling overwhelmed, don't be. It is simple to do a good job. It just requires time, effort and reading the rest of this book.*

# *The Field That Feels*

That's the child listening to a friend.
Never gives up, there to the end.
There for all, through thick 'n' thin,
When others walk out, this child walks in.
Caring and kind, this child doesn't bend.
Some call him sportsman, I call him friend.

## 25

---

# AFFLUENZA:
# YOUR WORST NIGHTMARE,
# IT'S CONTAGIOUS

*"When the going gets easy, watch out!*
*You may be going downhill."*

—Tommy Lasorda

**I FIRST HEARD OF AFFLUENZA** when I bumped into one of my old colleagues, Dr. Habib. He told me of a strange infection he was seeing in a lot of young children. I asked what the physical symptoms were—fever, cough, rash?

"No. No, physical symptoms," he said. "Just attitudinal symptoms."

"Attitudinal symptoms?" I echoed. "You mean the ones you only get in high mountain ranges?"

It wasn't until I started coaching Little League that I finally learned what the disease of affluenza was really all about.

## *"The Finster"*

"Give me it, it's mine!" screamed Finster as he snatched Mikey's new glove. Strange, I thought. Finster had a new glove himself. In fact, Finster had a new glove, a new bike, a new bat and it seemed like a new designer T-shirt at every practice.

I remember our first practice when I told everyone to line up and started hitting balls to them one at a time. After two rounds, Finster got out of line and walked to the bench and sat down. I went over and saw the sad look on his face and his arms crossed over his stomach. "Got a stomachache, Finster?" I asked.

His response still echoes in my head to this day. "I'm bored. Take me to Burger King!" Those weren't exactly the words he used, but the attitude of "You owe me, entertain me, give me what I want right now" was spot on.

I learned that Finster didn't catch this attitude of entitlement but inherited it from his parents. I know you're probably thinking, "Oh, some rich, snobby, better-than-you types!" But you'd be wrong. Affluenza has no socioeconomic, gender or race bias. It's found all across America, and teachers will tell you it's a major factor for school failure and future disillusionment in life.

Finster's parents in fact were hard working, down-to-earth people who earned every penny they had. When I asked them about Finster's fine array of new T-shirts, they told me, "We want our son to have all the things we didn't have as children. We work hard so he can have the best." Finster, I thought, was everything his parents were not.

What they really owed their child was their work ethic, making him learn that things have to be worked for, have to be earned. The secret to a child's success and happiness begins at home and is continued on the Little League field. Al and Al, the Official Coaches of Little League, recommend the following:

1. Give each child a job to do, such as preparing the field and equipment, putting things away, keeping the dugout clean, picking up the bats and gloves, etc.

2. Insist on politeness. Encourage kids to say thank you.

3. Insist on kids showing gratitude, thanking coaches for their hard work, etc.

4. Give them the pill that kills affluenza. Show them they are NEEDED. Every time you make a child do something for himself, he learns that he is needed and capable.

You may believe that it's easier to do it yourself rather than get your child to pick up after himself at the Little League field or help you at home. Yes, it probably is easier for you, but it's not the best thing for your child. It does take work, persistence and even fortitude to get your children into good habits. Habits like earning things, and being helpful.

## FROM LASORDA'S DUGOUT

*Gifts are given, character is earned.*

*Teach your children to get up to where you are by themselves. Don't carry them. All you owe your children is your presence and your example. That example must be one of honor, diligence, responsibility and respect, with a touch of gratitude to God and country. It sounds old fashioned and maybe it should, because the people who built America did it by earning everything; nothing was given to them.*

*When your kid says things like, "Well, Johnny's dad gave him a new bike. Annie's mom lets her drink all the soda she wants," be firm and fair and say, "Yes, but in this family we do it differently. We love you and the greatest gift we can give you is to teach you this life lesson: You can accomplish anything by earning it yourself; you can accomplish nothing if it's just given to you."*

*When everything is just given to kids, they learn that they don't have to work for anything, that the world owes them. This is how affluenza begins. That is how moms and dads infect their children, by just giving them everything they want.*

*To me, it is a worse disease than many physical ailments. A child can be blind in one eye or in a wheelchair like President Roosevelt but still accomplish great things and be a productive, inspirational figure. But one infected with affluenza, however talented and intelligent, will accomplish far less because they are handicapped by thinking that the world owes them a living.*

*There is not a ball player I know (and I've known many of the best) who has made it to the majors without humility, the knowledge that it takes hard work and diligence. It takes character to make it to the majors. After all, isn't every endeavor in life like striving for the majors, be it Little League, high school, college, your first job, your family? How you act in any one of these environments is how you act in all of them. Let it always be with honor, respect, responsibility, and courage to do the right things.*

*Remember, Mom and Dad, be the person you want your child to become. If you worked hard to get where you are, then realize the greatest gift you can give your child is the example of your hard work. The easiest way to know you're doing the right thing is to think of the last time that you gave your child something. Was he appreciative? Did he earn it, or did he just take it like you owed it to him and then ask for more?*

*It's not Johnny or Annie's affluenza nor their parents'. It's only you who can make your children selfish, greedy and lazy. And it's only you who can teach them that everything in life has to be earned. It's not what you give your children, but what you teach them to do for themselves that counts.*

# 26

# THE CELL PHONE INVADERS

## *The Team Ringer That's Truly A Loser*

IT'S THE FINAL INNING of a tied game, two outs, bases loaded. Spectators are on the edge of their seats. The batter swallows nervously. The whole game is hanging in the balance. The pitcher takes a deep breath, prepares to fire in his final curve ball and . . . a shrill, persistent ring shatters the atmosphere, breaking everyone's concentration.

We all remember the story of the body snatchers. Now, since the explosion of wireless phones in the 1990s, we are in the era of the "cell phone invaders." Even those parents who do care enough to come to the field can now be found talking on their cellular and digital phones rather than watching the game.

How are coaches and umpires supposed to deal with this? There was a time when we could throw someone out of a game, be it a player, coach or unruly fan. But what do we do about throwing out these cell phones that are more invasive and troublesome than they are helpful to players on the field? They are not part of baseball or part of socialization. They are merely a distraction.

Stevie had finally persuaded his father to come and watch him play baseball. When he stepped up to bat, he took a deep breath, summed up all his strength and cracked a home run over left field. It was the first home run of his life and his dad was there to see it. Stevie looked up jubilantly to see his father's reaction. His father, though, was in the middle of a heated cell phone call, one finger in his ear, his head turned away from the game. He had missed Stevie's moment of glory. Stevie's expression sank from jubilation at his great play to total disappointment as he realized his father had missed it.

### FROM THE DESK OF DR. VINCE

*The function of cell phones must be kept in perspective. Using one on the road can kill you. Using one at the Little League field can kill the atmosphere and the fun of the game.*

*Unless there is a good reason, they should be left in the car. A good reason is an emergency or something serious.*

*They are there for our convenience, not the other way around.*

*If you must carry it with you, put it on vibrate. Nothing breaks up the atmosphere of a game quicker than a cacophony of ringing cell phones.*

*Coaches should insist that parents not use their phones during games. They aren't allowed to use them in a movie theater so they shouldn't be allowed to use them at a Little League game.*

**FROM THE DESK OF DR. GAYLE FORTANASCE**

*Studies have shown that a continually ringing phone increases the anxiety of both parents and children. This in turn reduces a child's adrenaline levels and therefore adversely affects preparedness and performance.*

# 27

# VIOLENCE: HOW TO STOP IT

*"Fighting fire with fire only leaves ashes."*

**—My Dad**

**I SLAMMED ON THE BRAKES,** pounded the steering wheel and screamed at the top of my lungs, "How the *%#@ did you get a license!!!!" A stream of expletives flowed from my mouth and I pounded the steering wheel again, wishing I could do the same to the driver in the SUV that had just cut me off. There's nothing like Los Angeles traffic to get the pulse racing. I took a deep breath and let my road rage dissipate. It's ridiculous, of course, for a normally rational person to become so angry at a stranger's bad driving, but it's perhaps even more ridiculous to see this same rage erupt on the Little League field. If you've ever played or been involved in Little League, or any other youth sports, you've almost certainly seen it or fallen victim to it yourself. I call it "Little League Lunacy."

It's amazing how a carefree children's pastime like Little League can bring out the worst in normally calm people. Moms and dads, grandmas and grandpas, even experienced coaches can be transformed from polite, rational human beings into seething homicidal maniacs.

# *Just Another Game*

Brad, a contractor by day, coach of the Indians in the evening, had his mind elsewhere as he drove to the Little League Field for the game against the Angels. He was still fuming about the last client he'd seen, who'd refused to pay his invoice. The client told Bill that he charged more than a doctor but had "half the brains of a gorilla."

At about the same time, Debbie, coach of the Angels, was also battling Los Angeles traffic, her thoughts firmly with her chauvinistic boss who had just threatened to fire her again. Whenever a deal fell through, Debbie always seemed to bear the brunt of his temper.

The game itself was as hot as the evening, and Debbie and Brad's moods did nothing to cool it down. Then it happened. A match was dropped into the kindling. Debbie heard, or at least thought she heard Brad threaten one of her players, specifically her daughter. She yelled at the ump about it, calling Brad a "dim-witted monkey." Barely had the words left her mouth, when Brad's face turned a deep shade of crimson and he raced over to the Angels' dugout. Debbie reached for her pepper spray. The result was irrational and devastating to the small children watching. The ump watched with his mouth hanging open, stunned into silence, as Debbie blasted Brad with the pepper spray.

Thankfully, events this violent are not frequent, but even just once a season is too often. There are plenty of lesser conflicts, though, that seem to erupt every game and inflict terrible damage to the Little League experience. Brad and Debbie were not normally aggressive, hostile people, but under a certain set of circumstances they were still consumed by Little League Lunacy.

## *Three Steps to Biological Explosion*

Just as with the detonation of a bomb, there are some defined steps before detonation of a coach or parent. Emotions provoke overreaction, whether it's in a Little League lunatic like Brad or Debbie or in a road rager like me.

• The stressful day (who doesn't have one?) increases one's adrenaline and therefore aggressiveness. Stress also decreases serotonin, a neurotransmitter that governs social control of the neocortex, or thinking brain.

• Fatigue or hunger (games are often played before dinner) activates the hypothalamus (central part of the brain next to the rage area) for "fight or flight." This is why it's never a good idea to step into the cage when the lion is hungry—or to drive in front of me before I've had dinner.

• For the involuntary part of the brain in charge of rage to take over, one often needs to depersonalize the perceived foe through name calling (like dim-witted monkey). This allows a loss of social respect and frontal lobe control of our brain.

• Perceived injustice or threat is the final straw that ignites the explosion of the limbic unconscious brain, causing a complete loss of neocortex control and an outbreak of violence.

# Debbie and Brad Revisited

Primordial protection was the major factor affecting Debbie. With Brad, it was pride. Both had experienced a stressful day and both were hungry, which increased their adrenaline by the time they reached the field. Debbie's primordial protective instinct for her daughter caused her to react appropriately by addressing the ump. But then she took an extra unnecessary step that was borne of her instinct to protect her child. She depersonalized Brad by demeaning him and calling him a "dim-witted monkey." Brad's pride and prowess were offended. This was a weak spot for Brad, because he never did well in school. He perceived an injustice because someone belittled him in front of others. He lost his cool (neo-cortical control), and his animal instincts (limbic brain) propelled him across the field. His threat was curbed by pepper spray, a totally appropriate reaction if it occurred in a subway or alley at night, but totally inappropriate on a Little League field in the presence of eight-year-old children.

For most of the children, it was the first time they'd seen violent conflict between their teachers. The most damaging aspect of the incident was the bad and very sad example it set for the children.

## AL AND AL'S COACHES CORNER

### Prevention always beats cure
*How can parents and coaches deal with this? It starts with:*

1.  *Set up a friendly environment. Give opposing sides a chance to meet. Parents from each side should mix, shake hands with each other. Meeting, speaking and mingling with the other side prevents depersonalization and reduces the possibility of perceiving them as a threat.*
2.  *Before assuming an injustice, ask the referee for clarification. Debbie thought she heard Brad call her daughter a "pushy bitch." The ump heard him say "push up, people."*

3.    *Know your warning signs. Have something to eat before the game. If your hands are clenched or your teeth gritted, it's a sure sign you're in the "pre-detonation" phase. Walk away from the field, take a deep breath and count to ten.*

4.    *Remember: never confront someone after the game (when most fights begin) if you or they are "hot" after a perceived injustice. Talk to the ump, call them on the phone later if you have to, or talk to the region commissioner. Better still, just let it go.*

5.    *Always remember that it's a game, and remind everyone else that they are there to have fun with their children and to be an example of honesty and goodwill to the children.*

6.    *As a fail safe, have a mantra, "The family that plays together, stays together."*

## *Courage vs. Confrontation*

I know I've already told you that you must have courage to stand up against the intolerable, but at the same time, you must recognize the difference between courage and confrontation. Courage also requires tact. In other words, you need to know the appropriate time and place to speak out. If you approach a problem from an incendiary or offensive position, you'll provoke a confrontation, and confrontation is like fighting fire with fire; it only leads to ashes.

## FROM THE DESK OF DR. VINCE

*There are some key points to remember.*
*The four basic factors that can bring out the worst in adult behavior are:*
- *Primordial protection. Parents are biologically protective of their children. This is especially strong in women.*
- *Perceived injustice.*
- *Pride and prowess. Especially strong in men.*
- *Biological reaction (neocortal limbic violence system or "fight-or-flight" reaction).*

*Additive emotions provoke overreaction:*
- *Stressful day—increase in adrenaline and aggressiveness, decrease in serotonin due to stress provokes loss of social control.*
- *Fatigue, hunger activates the hypothalamus rage area for "fight or flight."*
- *Depersonalization (name calling, etc.) allows loss of social respect.*
- *Perceived threat provokes limbic explosion causing complete loss of neocortex control and outbreak of violence.*

## AL AND AL'S COACHES CORNER

*Head off the threat of violence by:*
*Shaking hands with the other parents. Meeting, speaking and mingling with the other side means neither they nor you will be depersonalized and perceived as a threat.*

*Before assuming an injustice, ask the ump for clarification.*
*Know your warning signs. Take a breath, count to ten and walk away.*
*Never confront someone after the game if you or they are "hot" after a perceived injustice. Talk to the ump, the coach or the region commissioner.*

*Always remember that it's a game and remind everyone else why they are there: to have fun and make it a safe haven for our children. Life will give them a lot of ups and downs. This is one down that can be avoided on a Little League field.*

# SECTION 6
## THE COACH

By Al and Al
(Al Herback and Al Price, Official Little League Coaches)

**THERE IS NO GREATER OPPORTUNITY** that life can give you than to be a coach. It is by being a coach that you get taught the consequences of life's lessons and have the opportunity to help others learn from those lessons and from your own experiences. You have heard of the power of one. Well that one can be you, the coach.

As a coach you can make a difference, sometimes a critical difference in a child's life. Remember, C-O-A-C-H stands for:

C—Caring for children, community and character

O—Objectively building a child's confidence

A—Attitude that's always positive

C—Courage to do what is right and honest

H—Humor, making Little League fun.

Little League baseball is a great game, a great opportunity to make a difference.

# 28

# CHOOSING A COACH

*"He who has no fire cannot warm others."*

—Al Milham
Former DA Little League District 18

MARY TURNED AS THE DOOR OPENED, and her husband, Reginald, meandered in without looking up or greeting her. "What's wrong, honey?"

"You know that car I've been looking into?"

"Which one, Reginald? Our bedroom is covered with flyers from the hundred or so dealerships you have visited in the last two months. Our dresser is overflowing with every automotive magazine published in the past two years!"

"Well, I had decided to buy the Lanca 2AQXRM-7 Turbo, so when I saw one in the parking lot this evening at the Pavilion, I waited until the owner came out. When I asked him how he liked it, he said it was the best-looking car he had ever owned—it was just too bad it spent more time in the dealer's garage than in his! Mary, I am so tired of looking for a car. The harder I look, the more confused I get."

"Well, think about something else," Mary advised. "Little Reggie made a Little League team. You have to drop him off at the field tomorrow. His coach's name is Trisant, of the Dodgers."

"What'd you say?" Reginald responded absently. "Mr. Tyrant from the Dodge dealer? I don't remember looking at any Dodges, though I hear Chrysler cars are really good this year."

Somewhat exasperated, Mary said, "No, Mr. Trisant of the Dodgers."

"Listen, Mary, Dodge doesn't make a Triumph, that's an English car." Reginald saw his wife grind her teeth together and realized he had better stop. He had really misheard her at first, but the second remark was supposed to be a joke—one Mary obviously did not appreciate. Changing to a serious tone, he said, "I'll drop Little Reggie off at the field, and maybe while I'm waiting, I will visit the Dodge dealer—it couldn't hurt."

Reginald drove Little Reggie to the field the following morning and spotted someone wearing the Dodgers team hat. As he got closer, he noted a slightly built middle-aged man, whom he figured must be the coach. "Hi, my name's Reginald Fender. Are you Mr. Tyrant?"

"Trisant," said the coach. "Is this your kid?" He turned to Little Reggie. "Run out to the field so I can hit some balls to you."

Little Reggie, all seven years of him, skipped out to the field.

Reginald turned to Mr. Trisant. "You'll keep him entertained for an hour or so?"

"Yeah."

"Well, I'll be back then."

As Little Reggie reached the field and turned he saw his dad walking toward the parking lot. The gleam in his eyes dimmed, the smile on his face drooped. He had imagined all night that he and his dad would be together. He so wanted his dad to be with him. "He didn't even say good-bye." Little Reggie sighed. "I guess I'm really not so important to him. What did I do to disappoint him?"

Most parents give little more time to inspecting their coach than Reginald did—they spend more time choosing tomatoes at the market. Like Reginald, many think Little League and its coaches are nothing more than babysitters. The coach you walk way from and leave your child with, though, may have a tremendous influence on your child's future, not to mention his or her like—or dislike—of sports. Remember your child's sign: **NOTICE ME. TELL ME I'M IMPORTANT.**

# *It Only Takes One "Rotten Apple" Coach*

Shea was assigned to my team in my fourth year of T-ball. I did not know him prior to that first day, but I can still see him in my mind's eye, dragging his little body out onto the ball field—he was the image of a prisoner of war. I could have sworn he had a ball and chain on both legs as he shuffled out at a snail's pace to shortstop. Shea's dad, I saw, had creases of concern over his face. I yelled encouragingly to the infield, "Are we ready?"

All but Shea yelled, "Yes!"

As I hit a ball to Shea, he bent over quiet adroitly, scooped it up, and threw a strike to the first baseman. Wow! "Great catch, great throw," I yelled. Shea's head lifted a little, and I thought I saw a flash of a smile.

When our practice came to an end, I went over to Shea's dad. "Your son is quite talented. How come he looked like he was going to the dentist when you brought him out?"

"She had a terrible experience with baseball his first year," his dad said. "I literally had to carry him to this first practice. He didn't want to play at all; I practically had to force him."

It seemed that at the previous year's first practice, Shea's coach had made an example out of him in front of the other children for talking out of turn. The coach ordered Shea to do ten push-ups. When the boy just stood there, the coach yelled at him until he cried. The coach though Shea was being disrespectful, but Shea did not know what a push-up was. His first-year coach had no idea that a six-year-old could not possibly do ten push-ups, even if he did know what they were.

Remember, a coach is often a coach simply because he was the only one who accepted the position. Many coaches, in other words, get the job by default. Coaches and managers do not have to pass an interview—they only have to say yes to the league vice presidents and presidents, who are frantically trying to coax someone into the position for the following year.

Parental and coaching expectations can differ greatly, and, as we know, the coach is not the only one who may have distorted objectives and expectations. The least a mom and dad can do is call ahead to assess the attitude of their child's potential role models. In the same vein, the coach must be ready to confront the parents' expectations if they are potentially unhealthy for any of the children.

Though you might not realize it, your being there has a special significance to a child between the ages of five and 13. Children's dreams are mainly focused on their mom and dad's love, approval, and time spent playing with them. If you are not there, your approval and love are not apparent to them. Children must see and feel your presence, not imagine or "accept" it on your word. If you doubt your importance, just look into the eyes of your child. If you do not see any love, look into a mirror at your own eyes—they will show you what your children are seeing.

## *Time for New Mandates*

How can Little League help assure that parents make adequate coach choices? First, by requiring a pre-team meeting. Second, by letting parents know the essential questions to ask. Third, by requiring first-time coaches and managers to undergo specific training to learn:

1. Basic norms of child psychology and motor development at the different ages of Little Leaguers. A child hit in the face with a baseball thrown by a teenage coach, for example, will most likely be discouraged from trying again.

2. Basic training in pitching, catching, and hitting.

3. The ingredients and importance of sportsmanship. This is what will make them excel, with or without athletic talent, and (hopefully) make our country a better place to live!

Remember, approximately 40 percent to 50 percent of all six-year-old children cannot catch a ball thrown to them on a fly. Up to 50 percent of them who had never played baseball before, in face, would be in dire danger of getting hit by it. A coach who does not realize this can traumatize those kids in the very first practice, making the rest of the season an uphill battle.

Having well-informed coaches is important. Having coaches with appropriate priorities is essential. Organized Little League must place this as its top priority.

## *Where Are They Now?*

Reggie, whose dad thought that checking out the local Dodge dealer was more important than watching his son practice, graduated from high school with high honors. His mother was as proud as a peacock. His dad, Reginald, could not attend his son's graduation as he had an important meeting. Reggie hugged and publicly thanked his mom for all she had done for him and for helping him to be all that he could be. He never mentioned his father who, I am told, is still looking for the car of his dreams. Some day he may wake up and realize he is alone. But I bet he will never know why.

# 29

# THE MOTHER OF
# ALL MEETINGS:
# YOU GOTTA READ THIS

*"You never get a second chance to make a first impression."*

—Al and Al

THE SUN WAS STARTING TO SET behind the San Gabriel Mountains, filling the sky with the dreamy hue of dusk. My first Little League parents meeting was due to start and I was still a 15-minute drive away. If only I had an identical twin brother, I thought for the nine millionth time, I could see all my patients, stop by the hospital, return all the phone messages I'd missed and not feel guilty about taking on this extra responsibility as well.

I drove as if I was rushing to a cardiac arrest code. I was certain that all the parents would be at my house by now, waiting. What type of manager would they think I was? What kind of example would I set? I decided I had better drop the part in my speech about punctuality, or they might all die laughing. Racing through a stop sign—or rather, making a courtesy slow down—I jotted down some quick notes. First I would do a common sense discussion on the developmental characteristics of Little Leaguers, followed by some neurophysiology and the neuropsychological gestalt of parent-and-child interaction, then finish up with some psychodrama and play therapy. Nah, that would never work. Even medical students fell asleep when I tried that.

7:39 p.m. I had made the 15-minute drive from the hospital to my house in nine minutes. As I opened the door, I switched my distraught facial expression to one that read, "Hiya, folks, I'm your kids' Little League manager." Instead of being greeted by a crowd of enthusiastic parents, though, I found only a handful of adults milling around the room while their little tots ran through the halls. We adults all sat down and had some stilted, quiet conversation, as if we were at a wake. Thirty minutes later, half the parents were still not present, so I got on the telephone. Those not there, however, had excuses: it was poker night or a "bad time." Some honestly said, "You mean we have to go to the meeting to have our kids play in Little League?" It suddenly dawned on me: hey, these parents think this is a baby-sitting service! And here I had risked getting three driving violations to be here—not to mention my life and those of my patients. As I continued phoning the missing parents, I looked down at the stack of notes shoved into my breast pocket—return calls I had yet to make to my patients. By 8:30 I decided to start the meeting, even though a third of the parents had still not shown up.

That first year I began with the topics I thought were supposed to be important—you know: shoes and pants, gum chewing, rubber cleats, the time and date of the opening ceremonies. Of course, by my second year, I realized how naïve I had been. I had forgotten to spell out things like, "Make sure your child's shoes are tied," and "Make sure he or she has gone to the bathroom before practice," and, most importantly, "Make sure you come back to pick up your child." Though these things may seem obvious, I discovered during my first several years as manager that even the obvious needed to be spelled out, because the parents (myself included) were often not much more than grown-up kids. As the season passed, I found this meeting could be both a memorable and enlightening experience—enlightening because most parents entering Little League have little insight into the tremendous potential impact it can have on both their children and their family's interactions. (I've seen families grow and get divorced, right on the Little League diamond). Little League is often the families' first real experience of father-and-son or daughter-and-father bonding. Of 50 parents that I questioned, 45 mentioned their first meeting as being both the most memorable and influential on their outlook on Little League.

# Empty Chairs Have No Eyes

I realized after my first year that no matter how awe-inspiring the first meeting was, unless those chairs were filled with parents—and grandparents, uncles, aunts, guardians or whomever else—it would have no impact. By my second year, I learned some sure-fire tactics for getting families there.

### Lay It All Down on Paper

Before the first meeting, I'd send out a short letter outlining my philosophy, objectives, coaching methods and what I as the coach expected from the parents, as well as, of course, a note on schedule and equipment. I later found out that only a handful of parents had actually read the letter. The rest just noted the date and place of the meeting and filed it in the nearest trash can. My subsequent letters were learning experiences.

The second year, I wrote IT IS MANDATORY FOR ALL PARENTS TO READ THIS LETTER in bold letters at the top of the page. In year three, I learned a fresh lesson, and wrote the message on the outside of the envelope, MANDATORY READING, PLEASE OPEN! It seems many parents had to be encouraged to open the envelope let alone read the contents. I was no different in my first season as a parent in Little League. I never read anything I was given. I was too busy and after all, how much could there be to know about a kid's sport?

## AL AND AL'S COACHES CORNER
## THE LETTER

*As well as noting the date and location of the first meeting, details about equipment and a schedule of games and practices, we recommend coaches include the following in their introductory letter:*

*Dear Parents,*

*Welcome to Little League, one of the first steps in your child's development.*

*My objectives as your child's coach are to build the 3 C's:*
*Character. To demonstrate, through my example, the meaning of honesty, responsibility, loyalty and discipline.*
*Conscience. To help build your child's sense of right and wrong.*
*Courage. To stand up for their conscience, to stand up for what is right. To take responsibility when something goes wrong and to never be afraid to say, "I made a mistake."*

*To do this, I need each parent to:*
1. *Be* present *as much as possible. It is the greatest gift you can give your child.*
2. Understand *your child is not an adult physically or mentally and grows bit by bit.*
3. *Have a* positive attitude. *Praise your child's efforts, not the results. Have five positive for every one negative comment.*
4. *Be* consistent. *Let your words and actions send the same message throughout the season.*
5. Accept *your child for the gifts given him or her. Don't make your child responsible for your happiness. Don't worry if your child is not a great ball player, only if he or she is a happy, contented ball player.*

*Remember, on my team winning is not the priority, building the 3 C's— Character, Conscience and Courage—is. Building ability is secondary to building an honest, responsible and contented child.*

*I can't do this without your help.*
*Signed:*

*Your Coach*

*P.S. Don't be afraid to remind me what I said in this letter at any point during the coming season!*

# *The Meeting*

I once had a professor who said on the first day of class, "For centuries teachers have asked, 'How can I gain the attention of my students?' Jokes will keep some of you awake, informative lectures will keep some of you interested and debates will keep some of you involved. However," he paused to put his hand in his briefcase and pull out some papers, "an exam will keep you all awake, interested and involved!" And so it did!

I decided to try it myself: "I want to welcome those of you who are in Little League for the first time to the beginning of a wonderful journey. As with any trip you undertake, though, you must be prepared. Is there air in the tires? Is there gas in the tank? Do you have proper clothing and enough food? Well, I have a test for you parents who are either new to the game or to my team, to see if you (not your children) are prepared to embark on this journey through Little League."

At that moment, I could usually tell the type of parents I was dealing with. Some would laugh, thinking I was joking; others would begin to chew their nails. Still others would sink down into their chairs with their hands already up, looking for the bathroom.

To the surprise of those still smiling, I would smile back and say, "The first question is: What do you expect your Little Leaguer to learn from baseball?"

As I looked around, the parents' eyes would gaze off in every direction—as long as it was not mine. I always started with the one whose hand was up first, or if no one volunteered, with the one trying hardest not be called upon—that way I could put him or her out of their misery the soonest.

"Mr. Dogood, what do you think?"

After a couple of indecisive gulps, he would say, "To learn to win despite the odds." He would follow this announcement with furtive glances, looking for approval from one of the other parents. I then went around the room in an orderly fashion. The first answer was usually followed by variations on the same theme: to learn to be the best by winning, to learn to compete and win. With each collaborating answer, the parents' focus became more certain and their answers more emphatic. By the time we had gone around the room, they were smugly nodding in unison, "Yes, to win!"

Seventy-four percent of the parents I polled at first meetings answered the same. "So, in other words," I'd say, "you expect your child and his or her team to beat another child, to beat another team?" Instantly, the facial expressions would turn to frowns and the confident postures would begin to dissolve.

"Question two," I would go on without waiting for comments. "What do you think your children expect from baseball?" This was invariably followed by a curtain of silence. Kids are right—parents do not understand them. Nobody could come up with this answer. You would have thought I had just demanded a detailed account of Einstein's Theory of Relativity.

I asked these questions at this first meeting to lay the foundation for the parents' concepts of Little League—since the children would be playing not only with me, but often would continue on in baseball. Why a test? In the academic field, professors know a person's memory for an item is only 33 percent one month after a test if he answered correctly, but it is 73 percent if he answered incorrectly and was then corrected. We do learn better from our mistakes.

Taking a break from the quiz, I would then ask if anyone had questions of their own. I would quickly deal with giving out the times, dates and length of practices so the parents knew when to drop off and pick up their children. I then asked my next quiz question.

"What should you expect from me?" These answers were usually right on the money: "I expect you to set a good example to my child." "I expect you to teach him the basics of baseball."

"I expect you to give him encouragement and be supportive." Some even said they expected me to love their child as they did. To be reliable, to help the child win was often the last request.

Finally, I would ask those parents who had been involved in Little League before what they first asked their children after a game, if they had not been able to attend. The all-time most common answer was, "Did you win today?" The second most frequent question was, "How did you do?"

Starting from this first meeting, I wanted my team parents to re-focus away from "I want my child to learn to win," or the pursuit of perfection to the pursuit of contentment and confidence; from "I want my child to be the best player on the best team"—the pursuit of talent—to "I want my child to be a good sportsman"—the pursuit of character. In other words, at the end of the game, I wanted them ask their children, "Did you have fun?" or "What did you learn today?"

Our interaction in Little League allows us to see the realities of life: we cannot change the children life gives us but we can change our expectations of them and accept and love them for the unique individuals they are. Not every child can be the best player but every child can have a positive experience.

# 30

# STUCK WITH A COACH: WHAT TO DO

*"Never tolerate the intolerable."*

— Al and Al

**THE ATHLETICS WERE HAVING A WILD TIME.** Billy had just filled Wesley's hat with water and dumped it on his head, drawing laughs of derision and taunting from his teammates. Wesley did not seem to enjoy being the brunt of this prank. He slowly wandered off, the tears welling up in his eyes, hidden by the downpour of water still dripping off his brown locks.

Mrs. Haynes viewed the mayhem from afar, unaware of her son's dilemma. She glanced impatiently at her watch. The coach wanted everyone there 20 minutes before game time, but it was now five minutes before the official start and he had not yet arrived.

Mrs. Haynes finally caught a glimpse of Mr. Cox, the coach, lumbering toward the field. He toted a large, bulky, green-gray tattered canvas bag that hung over his shoulder and made him look like Santa Claus with a baseball cap. Huh, more like the Grinch Who Stole Christmas, she thought.

As he approached the chaos on the field, he barked, "Why aren't you guys warming up?"

Jimmy let go of Shannon's hair, and she dropped his hat. Mark swallowed the water he was just going to squirt all over Wesley. All the grinning faces quickly turned to stone.

He's late for the tenth time this season, Mrs. Haynes said to herself, and he's yelling at the kids? Why, he is not only totally unreliable, he takes out his own mistakes on the children. They were just acting the way kids do when unsupervised.

Mrs. Haynes weighed the idea of saying something nasty to the coach but decided against it. Wesley, her son, was quiet and not overly coordinated, but very loving and obedient. He had been practicing hard with his dad all week for the chance to play second base. The coach had been promising him for the past ten games that he would get to play second "sometime," but the season was ending, and so far, Wesley had still not gotten his chance.

As Mr. Cox scribbled down the lineup, Mrs. Haynes timidly approached him in the dugout. "Mr. Cox," she pleaded, "Wesley has been practicing very hard all week so he could play second base. Do you think you could put him in for maybe an inning? I don't want to jeopardize your winning, but it would mean. . . . "

Mr. Cox cut her off without looking up. "Look, your son can't chew gum and walk at the same time without tripping or falling. I'll put him where I want him!"

Mrs. Haynes was crushed and outraged. What an insensitive oaf, she thought. He does not care about me, much less my child—and here I have entrusted my only son to this man. If only Wesley's dad were here!

Before she could regain her composure, Mr. Cox turned to bark at the kids again. "All of you get over here and listen up. Remember last game?" All the little stone faces nodded. Actually, though, most of them did not remember it. Children are blessed with the present. Their recall for the past can be easily erased, unless something very traumatic happens, or we adults hammer their mistakes into their memories. Grown-ups are often stifled by the past and blinded to the present because of our anticipation of the future. We mistakenly expect that children think as we do. Wrong! Experience is in the eye of the beholder—especially for the young. An unforgivable error in the professional leagues is a good try and a positive effort in Little League. Remember five-error Tony?

As the children looked blankly at Mr. Cox, Mark smiled a little. "What are you smiling about?" the coach demanded. "You see what that dog did over there on the ground?"

Mark looked at the small brown heap, and his smile quickly dwindled to a frown. I am sure he missed the innuendo, but Mr. Cox's crabby face certainly drove home the message. Off to the side of the dugout, Mrs. Haynes's mouth dropped open in disbelief. Mr. Cox was more insensitive and degrading than any Little League coach or manager she had ever seen. She looked at the eyes of the children. They must all feel awful, she thought. Is this supposed to be building confidence in these children, in my son?

Believe it or not, Little League coaches and managers inflict these kinds of abusive remarks and unrelenting expectations on their players repeatedly, every year. As a coach, you must realize how much damage you can do in the few months you have charge of your little team members—even in only a few hours a week. As a parent, you must learn to recognize unwanted and destructive behavior and do whatever is necessary to protect your children from it—even if it means rocking the boat. After all, Mom and Dad, you are ultimately responsible for who teaches and cares for your children. How much fear and self-condemnation do you want them to learn?

# *Positives and Negatives*

Mr. Cox yelled, "Get out on the field for practice." He snatched a bat out of the bag as if it were a meat cleaver, pointed it at Mark on third base, and hit a zinger that Mike Piazza would have had trouble fielding. The ball hit Mark in the chest, knocking him over. "Use your glove, not your mouth, to stop the ball!" shouted the coach. "Get up and try again, and don't let me see any crybaby crap!"

Mrs. Haynes, now thoroughly horrified, looked about for a man to take charge and sock the SOB—or at least cripple him for a day or two—but she and Mrs. Reyes, who spoke hardly any English, were the only Athletics' parents attending the game.

Parents of the opposing team, however, filled the bleachers on the other side and were doing a chorus of cheers. "Two, four, six, eight, who are the kids we appreciate!" They named each child on the team in turn, ending with, "Yes, we think you're great!" and "Go, Pirates, go!"

Mrs. Haynes came over to the Pirates' dugout. The coach was kneeling down to be at eye height with his Little Leaguers. He wore a big smile and spoke softly, yet emphatically. "You looked great out there in warm-ups. I've never seen such a talented team in all my career," he said earnestly. The kids had heard this many times before, but loved it as much now as the first time. He then reminded them that they were playing a good team and should always respect their opponents. He told them to try their best, never give up, and remember that he was always proud of them. He ended with, "Who are we?"

They shouted in unison, "Pirates!"

"Who?"

"The Pirates!"

"Let your mom and dad hear you!"

With all the gusto in their tiny lungs they bellowed, "The Pirates!"

The coach jumped and whooped, "Let's get out there and have some fun!"

The players sprang out of the dugout and ran cheering to their positions.

Mrs. Haynes walked over to look at the Pirates' lineup board. She had seen it at each game hanging at the Little Leaguers' eye level, right at the entrance to their dugout. A magnetic board etched with a baseball field, it had little magnets with each player's name stationed at his or her fielding position. To the right of the field were similar magnets with each child's name and nickname. Up first were Charging Charlie; second, King Kim; third, Rock 'Em Rachel, and so on. Each nickname engendered positive regard, marking some particular asset the child possessed.

Mrs. Haynes's sadness deepened. Why did my son get stuck with such an irresponsible, insensitive, negative-attitude, unprincipled, dumb coach, she thought, when other teams had such good, positive, caring team leaders? Coach Cox rarely had practice, and when he did, he showed up late. He never taught the children how to field; he only criticized them for missing the ball. If they did catch it, heaven help them if they did not make a good throw. When someone made a good play, his compliment was "About time you did something right," or "Like I taught you." When the Athletics were on the field, his only words of encouragement were "What are you doing? Wake up! Are you sick or do you just look that way? Get the lead out of your pants." Wesley had twice asked his mom not to put lead in the washer, as he was certain his coach saw it in his pants.

The coach had favorites, too—not that he treated them much better. Mrs. Haynes knew that the league president had constantly monitored Mr. Cox last season when he had coached in the minors, because he had a tendency not to place children in the lineup who deserved to be there. He knew it was a Little League rule that each child must be up at least once and play a minimum of two innings every game. Mr. Cox would have players change uniforms so the opposing coach would think he was actually playing all of his children.

It was the top of the first inning. The Pirates' fourth batter was up with a man on first and second, and one out. Rock 'Em Rachel strode up to the tee. The Pirate bench charged, "Let's go, Rachel, let's go!" and stomped their feet, boom, boom.

Cox stepped out and bellowed so loudly, the major Little League, three hundred years away, could hear it. "The fat girl is up. She's slow as molasses. let's get a double play."

His little Athletics giggled. Mark, on third base, chanted, "Let's go Fat Girl, let's go!"

One tiny tear welled up in Rock 'Em Rachel's eye. Her cherub grin turned into wounded-puppy pout as the other Athletics all giggled and chimed in. "Let's go Fat Girl, let's go Piggy!" For the first time, Mr. Cox smiled his approval.

The Pirate coach called time out, walked up to Rock 'Em Rachel, kissed her gently on the cap, then strode slowly toward the Athletics' bench. The bleachers, filled with nurturing Pirates' parents, gasped. The two 13-year-old umps could only cross their fingers. They did not know what to do. No rules had been broken.

The coach continued his methodical, determined journey across the field.

"Let him have it, just once—for me," Mrs. Haynes muttered softly.

Mr. Cox's snarling bulldog stance changed to the tremulous cower of a frightened poodle. Standing close to six feet and weighing 210 pounds—not much of it fat—the Pirates' coach had a somewhat intimidating stature. A hush fell over the field; the air was so taut, no one dared cough. Thunder was expected, with lightning to follow—Rock 'Em Rachel was the coach's daughter. As Mrs. Haynes bit her nails in expectation, the Pirates' coach raised his mighty right arm and placed it over Mr. Cox's shoulder in a fatherly gesture. He whispered in Cox's ear for about 30 seconds, patted him on the back, and walked away with a grin. When he got halfway back to his own dugout, he chanted, "Let's go, Rock 'Em Rachel!"

The children, at first frightened, relaxed their shoulders, and the game continued as if nothing had transpired. Mark blurted out again, "Let's go!" and was swiftly reprimanded by Mr. Cox. "Shut up and play the game."

Rock 'Em Rachel hit the ball flush; it darted through the infield to the outfield fence. Rock 'Em trotted around to third base, where she danced around Mark, who was now quiet and solemn. Rachel, however, only smiled, and waved at the cheering bleachers filled with adulating parents. One of the parents yelled, "What was that?" and the Pirates' bench jumped up: "Nice hit!" As the next Pirate trotted to first on a well-hit ball, the coach yelled out, "Who's the father or mother of that kid?" Both parents stood up and received an enthusiastic ovation from the other parents.

"What I saw," Mrs. Haynes later told me, "was the children cheering for one another, the parents all being there for their kids. Every time something occurred, good or bad, they found a way to say something positive. I'll never forgive myself for not asking more questions before letting Wesley be coached by that awful man."

Mrs. Haynes did not know it, but the Pirates' coach knew she had been at all her son's games; Wesley was on his list to be drafted the following year. He was not interested in talent—he knew that would come along if the child was encouraged. What Mrs. Haynes did know was that no matter what the score, the Pirates always won. Each child and parent came away with unconditional positive regard for themselves and everyone else on their team.

### FROM THE DESK OF DR. VINCE

*If you have a coach who is intolerable, there are a number of steps you can take as a parent. First, make sure you know all the facts and that you have not misunderstood the coach or misinterpreted the situation. Do this by discussing your concerns about the coach with other parents and assistant coaches. If your concerns appear to be valid and are shared by others, take the next step. Contact the League president to request his intervention.*

*If the response is not satisfactory, write a letter requesting your child be moved to another team.*

# 31

# ONE ROTTEN APPLE
# SPOILS THE BUNCH

*"One 'voweluable' coach is worth a thousand consonants."*

**THE YEAR AFTER WESLEY HAYNES** played for the Athletics, we lost almost 20 percent of the children from the preceding Little League season. The children had not moved out of town, been eaten by space invaders, or gone on drugs. They and their parents had just had a bad experience—usually with the coaching staff. At the heart of the problem was Mr. Cox, the win-at-all-costs coach. Umpires hated officiating his games, since he would invariably run out onto the field to disagree with a call, and other coaches—afraid of another confrontation, another argument—had nightmares the day before they were going to face his team. Cox's players had, predictably, taken on his attitude and demeanor. They would call the umpire "four eyes," or "blind as a bat." Some of the other managers decided that if they could not beat him, they would join him; soon every game involved at least one confrontation. Little League was not a game anymore, it was a hard, bitter lesson in the dog-eat-dog realities of life on the battlefield. At times, the diamond looked more like the floor of the New York Stock Exchange or Divorce Court than a hometown baseball field.

This was not just my imagination. The telltale signs spoke our clearly. Parent participation dwindled. Coaches arrived late—not just the ones facing Mr. Cox, but Cox's staff, too. I am certain he did not enjoy these confrontations any more than those who had to face him did.

# How To Find a Good Coach

Mrs. Haynes had gone to all of her son's games just to try to undo Mr. Cox's role-modeling, but she had not taken her son off the team because it was her first year, and she did not know any better. Some parents take their children out of Little League permanently before they realize they can have a choice of picking the man or woman who will become an influential part of their child's life. You do have the choice. Look for a coach who has the right A-E-I-O-U (and F):

*Attitude.* Coaches should have an attitude of positive regard and loving encouragement for all the children, parents, and umpires. This attitude is conveyed in expressions like "good play" and "nice try," especially when a child has made the proverbial error.

*Enthusiasm.* A good coach has the ability to bring out the best in children and their parents. This spirit is often catching. The children capture it and take it with them wherever they go. You see it when they cheer on their teammates who are up to bat, when they encourage their pitcher. Enthusiasm keeps children focused and is the chief ingredient in having fun. It is the "2-4-6-8", who do we appreciate," the "high five!" the welcoming smile and ready handshake.

*Integrity.* Integrity in coaching means having principles that encourage cooperation and mutual respect. It means sportsmanship—always winning, even when you lose. A coach with integrity is the type of person your child can look up to, the coach who makes you feel good about yourself and whom you want to be around. He's the coach you hope your child will grow up to be like.

*Objective.* A good coach is someone who clearly indicates why he wanted the job and what he expects the parents and children from his coaching. He will let you know that his objective is to create a positive experience for your child, one that will enhance motor skills, psychological and moral development, and future growth. Such an objective places winning games second in importance to teamwork and spirit, and reminds you why your children are in baseball. Listen to this coach and you will hear, "What is best for the children?"

*Understanding.* A good coach listens and understands the needs and expectations of each child and parent. A good coach understands his need to be reliable. A good coach gives your child adequate practice—at least once a week for T-ball, and twice a week for farm, minors, and majors. This coach is considerate and understands the need to follow through with his promises. He treats all members of his team equally; he makes you feel comfortable. His words are, "How is your child doing? How are you doing?" He gives as much praise to those who play the bench as to the "stars" on the field.

*Fundamentals.* A coach should know baseball in general and the rules of Little League in particular. Even more, though, he must know how to teach the basics of pitching, hitting and catching to little children, who may be afraid of the ball or are smaller than the bat they are trying to swing.

## *Go for the Vowels*

Which of these attributes is most important? In T-ball, farm, and minors, the coach's prior baseball know-how is a lower priority. What good is a well-trained Little Leaguer if he is not a good sport and a team player? Ty Cobb, for example, the greatest hitter of all time, was despised by many of his contemporaries. Yes, he was phenomenal—a real "winner"—but his undying love of "winning at all costs" was his only unique asset. Most who wrote about him had little to say about his honesty and integrity. A drive to win, of course, is highly regarded and encouraged in American sports: "Winning, there is nothing like it." And I agree—if you are a professional, and if your job and livelihood depend on winning. Hopefully, those who reach the pro level have been nurtured along sufficiently to become meaningful citizens who offer a wholesome example to our children after their professional sports careers end. As recent headlines attest, though, some sportspeople who are successful due to sheer talent have been trained to win regardless of what it takes. Once their career is over, unfortunately, they often continue that self-absorbed trend and wind up as gamblers or alcoholics, unable to get along or nurture others to become all that they could be. Trained to be skilled athletes who win, win, win, their own emotional growth was actually stunted. They never fully developed, either psychologically or morally. These stunted athletes are the has-beens, the flashes in the pan whom the world quickly forgets. Their mistake—and the mistake of their parents—was in developing only their talent, not their character.

Even when you know what to look for in a coach, you still have to find that person. Start by calling your league president. Little League officials hear all the complaints of parents and usually know who they would like their own children to be coach by. Give a lot of consideration to their recommendations.

Second, ask other parents who have been in the same league. You can find a list of them in the *Official Little League Guide*, published annually. Never feel you are imposing when you call a stranger about your child. Just think of the rewarding experience you may be giving him or her. Remember Reginald? He did not think twice about talking with some stranger about a car. Certainly, selecting an adult role model for your child is at least as important.

Unfortunately, the coach often picks the child rather than the other way around. You can, however, influence this decision. I have seen requests by parents who specifically asked not to have their child be coached by certain managers and have gotten their wish. This may hurt the manager's feelings, but it may also alert him that something he does needs correcting. If the choice is between getting the best for your child or protecting an adult's feelings, there really is no choice, is there?

# *Should Women Be Coaches?*

"Moms as managers will be the demise of Little League Baseball!"

"How can they ever hope to be good male identity figures!"

The truth is, moms cannot be male identity figures at all—but they can be good managers.

Some of the best managers and coaches I have seen in T-ball and farm have been women. Some of them had scant actual baseball know-how at the start, but had tons of A-E-I-O-U: positive attitude, enthusiasm, integrity, objective, and understanding. What they did not know about teaching the children how to hit and throw, they managed to learn within a remarkably short time.

Women often have reliability, wonderful objectives, and principles. They are seldom burdened with the old baggage from previous bad competitive-sports experiences, because they probably didn't play Little League as children. They have no macho image to uphold and are not threatened by the manly man's "king of the roost" hangups. They are simply more tuned into the children. I remember a perfect example of this. I was sipping hot coffee at the snack bar on a Saturday morning, when I was suddenly shaken out of my daydreams by the usual fracas that seemed to accompany any game that involved Mr. Cox and his current team, the Hawks. On this particular occasion, his face was going through a rainbow of angry colors as he threw down his hat and raced across the field to third base. "You blind bleep-bleep!" Cox screamed. "He was safe by a mile!"

Mrs. Rose, the Indians' manager, calmly walked over to the scene. Mr. Cox turned on her with fists clenched, but before he could utter another obscenity, she said, "I agree with you, Mr. Cox, but do we call it as the umpire saw it—as you have insisted on in the past—or do we do what is fair?"

For once, the Hawks' manager was stunned into silence. Mrs. Rose continued in a soothing tone. "Really, Mr. Cox, if you were my child, you would get a spanking for throwing tantrums like this. I do not even tolerate such behavior in my five-year-old. What will the children think?"

Mrs. Rose's calm, matter-of-fact honesty totally disarmed Mr. Cox—the only time I have ever see him speechless. With no ax to grind or unresolved conflicts or pride to interfere with protecting the children's best interest, she reduced what would normally have been a classic nose-to-nose confrontation into a gentle lesson in manners.

If someone were to ask me the best combination for a Little League coaching staff, I would pick a mother with a little baseball experience for manager, and two males for coaches: one a father, the other a grandfather. I would want the mother for her sensitivity, attitude, and objectives; the father for his fundamentals and knowledge of baseball; and the grandfather for his wisdom. Grandfathers can distinguish the dash from the marathon and are ready to slow down and have fun with their grandchildren.

Why do Little League presidents and vice presidents have to frantically search for coaches each season? The most common reason is the time element. People simply do not feel they have enough extra hours to make the commitment. As a doctor, I, too, had to give a lot of consideration to this problem. I have found over the years, though, that anyone can find the time to coach, if he or she is complemented by dependable, supportive parents and other coaches. Believe me, I may have lost some patients (that is, some potential patients), but my children and I will never regret the time we spent together. Although it has become a cliché, it is nevertheless true—in all my years as a physician, I have never heard one elderly patient regret that he or she did not spend more time at the office. I have heard them lament about the time they wish they had spent with their children. I, for one, will never regret the time I spent on the baseball field at Hamilton Park—nor will my children.

Sometimes the person souring the beauty of Little League is not a parent or coach—sometimes it is something much bigger, ominous, and destructive: the Ice Men.

# 32

# THE ICE MEN

*"An ice man is someone who thinks he's better than you. Ice men are a bunch of little men standing on one another's shoulders so they can look you in the eye."*

—Tommy Lasorda

**NO, I AM NOT GOING TO DISCUSS** the Neanderthal men who lived in the Ice Age, or the behemoths occasionally found frozen in glaciers. However, the Ice Men of Little League can make you feel just as cold as an ice cube, and the power they wield is often more frightening than any charging behemoth could be. The most frightening part about Ice Men is that any of us can be transformed into one—and, even worse, we often accept the designation gladly and feel honored at joining their ranks.

Vinny, six and Kaycee, three, hopped out of the van at our very first mid-season father/son-daughter Little League party, held as at the annual Fathers Softball Game.

"Wait here," I warned, watching out for other cars. "Hold my hands." I tucked my glove under my arm, looked both ways, and hurried toward the field with Vinny and Kaycee dangling from either arm.

Vinny's eyes were as wide as an owl's as they took in all the pageantry of the booths to the left and right, the knock-down-the-bottle, the ring-toss, and the other games. The scent of cooking burgers mingled with the sweet odor of chili sauce drew my attention as I looked down at my late 30s' abdominal bulge that hung precariously over my belt, as if it might fall off and plunge to the ground any second.

Over to the left, some of the moms were setting tables; to the right, a number of children dashed after one another playing tag. In the center stood several major-league coaches whom I recognized, although as a T-ball coach I had never had an opportunity to actually meet them. Vinny and Kaycee quickly ran off to play. My wife was still trying to get little Mike, just four months old, ready and would follow in a couple of minutes.

Oh, what a day for a ball game, I thought, and I took a deep breath and let the mixture of sweet aromas cross my palate again. Somewhere inside me, though, fluttered a small twinge—stomach butterflies, which I recognized from my years in competitive sports. Imagine, a Little League softball game, and I had butterflies! In my defense, I knew Vinny and Kaycee would be seeing their dad play ball against people his own age for the first time. I didn't want to disappoint them. I smiled, which gave me some small insight into how they must feel when I watch them. I spotted Tri, my T-ball co-manager. "Hey, Tri, ready for the big game?"

I could barely believe it, but I could see a little tension in Tri's eyes. "Sure, Vince," he said, somewhat tightly.

I moseyed over to the major-league coaches, and stuck out my hand. "Hi, my name is Vince." One of them, about a half-foot taller than me and dressed in jeans and a Giants' shirt and cap, gave me a half glance and continued with his conversation. I stepped back a little from the blast of cold air, and looked at the six of them standing there. The one who ignored me had his hands on his hips as if ready to give orders from the bow of a ship. Four others nodded reassuringly, and laughed haughtily. The last one folded his arms, gave me a half smile—more of a smug smirk—and looked about as if all that lay before him was his domain. His glance went right through me; my skin felt like it was rippling as goosebumps jumped through to the surface. Even the warm California sunshine could not overcome the chill I felt.

I decided my frosty reception might just have been a lukewarm entry. Not wanting to seem uninterested and too brash, I thought I should just listen. Chuck, the six-foot-two arm-folder, cast his icy glance over the playing field. "Frank, your son may just take us to the state playoffs this year." The

Giant-shirt-and-cap shook his head as Chuck continued. "If we don't win it this year, from the looks of our new prospects, we'll never do it."

"Ah," I said, spotting the perfect opening. "I'm Vince Fortanasce, new manager of the T-ball Angels, and coach of the new prospects." Since I was staring him in the face, Chuck had no way to ignore me now. For a second he returned my stare, straight into my eyes. I could see the wheels turning as he glanced at my head, then at the substantial paunch I was developing. The brief flame of combat in his eyes then went ice cold. "Hi, I hope you can develop some talent out of that little bunch." He then dismissed me with a quick turn to the others, "Let's make up a lineup," and the six of them drafted away in a group. One man, shorter than the others, trailed behind to smile and shake my hand.

"Hi," he said. "My name is Billy."

The stands were full as we dads took to the field. The Ice Men, as I learned to call them, divided up—five on one team, Billy on the other. Although Chuck called out the sides and I was picked last, I landed on his team. To my surprise, I got put in as third-base coach. "Oh well," I muttered to myself, "better than the bench."

The game proceeded somewhat differently than I had anticipated. Instead of a friendly game of softball, it was a hotly contested match, with each dad playing as if his life depended on it. There was no horsing around, no friendly chatter—only tobacco chewing, foot stamping, and grunting. Some of the older youngsters openly commented on "how pathetic" some of us dads were. Gee, these kids aren't kidding, I thought. Where did they learn to be so critical?

In the third inning, the score was 8-4, and I was still coaching third base. All of a sudden, Nathan, one of the over-the-hill Ice Men, slid all six foot five of himself into second. He immediately rolled over, clutching his hamstring. I ran over, thinking that now was my chance. Announcing my physicianhood, I took charge, briefly examined him, and helped him off the field. The next inning, Chuck begrudgingly pointed at me to take Nathan's third-base position.

As I stationed myself out there, I glanced at Vinny, Kaycee, and my wife, who was holding Michael. Somehow their smiling faces made sense, and warmed some of the terrible chill running up and down my spine.

Tri strolled to the plate. I yelled, "Hey, Tri, hit an easy one to me so I can look good."

Tri smiled and called back, "I don't know if I can get this old body to turn that far around to get it to you, Vince."

I glanced toward Chuck at shortstop as giggles came from the stands, the first sign of a healthy humor since the game's inception. He did not seem amused. "Keep your mind on the game!"

I instinctively gulped as a thread of fear crept through. Then I realized, "This is stupid." At that moment, with a man on first, the ball was drilled my way. Reflexively, I stabbed at it, pulled it in, and fired it toward second. A little high, but a perfect toss to the right fielder.

The stands moaned. My grin faded as a small black rain cloud gathered around my head. A little piercing voice announced, "Nice stop, Dad. That's getting in front of it." There with Kaycee right next to him was Vinny, his little fingers grabbing through the fence, their four eyes swelling with pride.

They're proud of me! I suddenly realized. They don't care if the throw was wide! Chuck and the other Ice Men, however, definitely did not have the same look. Their eyes were steely cold.

Moments later, to my conscious but not demonstrable glee, we were losing 8-10, and guess what—I was up, with two men on.

In the dugout the Ice Men fretted. Apparently, the rest of their team was nothing but a burden they had to carry. One Ice Man openly remarked, "The bottom of the lineup. I guess we'll have to wait until the last inning to score some runs."

Another one admonished me, "Two outs, two on . . . just get on base any way you can."

I thought, gee, if that's the case, maybe I should have brought my gun.

As I stood at home plate, I could feel Vinny's, Kaycee's, and my wife's eyes riveted on me. "Hit one for pop, Pop," Vinny yelled. Oh, the pressure! An emergency room full of head injuries sprawled all over the gurneys would be nothing compared to the pressure of that moment. I came back to reality just as the ball whipped right by me and the umpire yelled, "Strike!"

"That's it, pick the one you want, Dad!" Vinny squealed. Funny how it seemed I could hear only his voice—but not for long.

"Don't strike out, for God's sake!"

"At least go down swinging!" This last was accompanied by a blast of ice from Chuck as he led off the bag at third base. My mind went black as the next ball was delivered.

"Holy——!" Chuck slapped me on the back and shook my hand after I had trotted triumphantly across home plate. "I think we lost the ball! You're hot stuff!" I could hardly wait to hug Vinny, Kaycee, Michael and my wife. The score was not 11-10, the game was not over, and I do not even remember the final outcome. As I entered the dugout, the five Ice Men now looked me in the eye with invitation and a glad hand. "What college did you play for?"

"Seton Hall," I said, shaking hands all around.

"So which one is your kid?"

I ignored the question, choosing, instead, to leave the cold behind and make a beeline to my undying, faithful fans: my family.

As I drove home that evening, I realized I was in some way one of the boys—"Hot Stuff." Two home runs had put me there. I could not help thinking, though, about those who were not "one of the boys"—those still out in the cold. Was this what Little League was all about? Certain parents forming a circle that not only excludes other parents, but other children they think are not up to snuff? "In-crowd" parents who, in their frankly judgmental way, declare, "Yeah, you've got it—that kid doesn't"? Open prejudice based on the way people look?

Through the years I have seen even ethnic and professional Ice Men—those who, not necessarily consciously but through their actions, declare themselves to be somehow a tier above. Is this the origin of bias? Is this what we want to teach our children? Unfortunately, this middle-age pomposity does trickle down to the kids. They set up their own "in-crowd," dealing with their teammates in a similar fashion. Even more unfortunately, anyone can be pulled into this igloo arena of the self-acclaiming Ice Men.

All of us in Little League—and life—must be aware of this natural propensity to form cliques and the potential dangers in giving in to these urges. We must neither allow nor tolerate it. An essential part of leadership is setting a good example. Coaches, managers, vice presidents, and presidents must set examples of openness, goodwill and friendship to all—and tolerate nothing less.

Are you an Ice Man? Chances are you are not if your team is in last place. Chances are, you are—or have the potential to be—if you are one of the All-Star coaches or managers in the majors. To my dismay, this often becomes the domain of the Ice Men. If you are talented, or have a talented child, you are in a special, privileged position. You can exude warmth and friendship or make your staff into an exclusive polar bear club. If you are unsure where you stand, ask yourself who you shook hands with at the last game, and how much time you spent teaching the second-string players. If you cannot remember, guess what—you are part of the Ice Age, and you do not belong in modern-day Little League. All is not lost, however—you can always grow up. Start now!

# SECTION 7
## SEIZE THE DAY

**FAITH IS THE GREATEST VIRTUE** you can cultivate in your children and the greatest gift you can give to them. Never lose faith—in yourself or your children. Little League is only the first leg in the marathon of life but it is one of the few you can totally run with your child. Once that part of the journey is over, it is gone forever. Don't lose the opportunity to seize the day!

## 33

# BULL DERRINGER

*"I have seen the enemy and it is me."*

**BULL DERRINGER WAS THE NIGHTMARE OF MY YOUTH,** reincarnated to make me miserable as an adult. You know him. He is the ultimate know-it-all, the guy too good for the likes of you and me. He is clean cut and still in good shape despite the years. A clipboard always under his arm, he is flanked by two "Yes, sir" coaches.

When I first met him, he reminded me of Billy McMann, my real childhood nightmare. You knew him, too. He was not the flagrant, beat-'em up bully but the kind who left scars without ever laying a finger on his victim. He was the "better than you" bully. Somehow he was always on the winning team, always in the limelight, always one step ahead of you. He never shook hands after he beat you—he might soil his hands or his uniform. He was the only guy you knew who could slide into a base without getting dirty. He never smiled, he scoffed—with a condescending demeanor and a greater-than-thou attitude.

The only time he changed his cocky attitude was when the league president was around. Then Mr. McMean became Mr. Goody Two-Shoes. You probably remember this hypocrite also. To hear him tell it, he was the only guy on the team. He would have beaten you 100 to nothing if the other eight guys had not been around to pull him down. What made matters worse, he was probably right!

Somehow, every time I was around Billy the Kid, I felt bad. Something demonic stirred in me. I would have done anything just to see him trip over first base or strike out with the bases loaded. On the rare occasion when he did mess up, my guilt over being so envious would take some of the joy out of his mistake, but I knew I was not alone in my snickering. All the other players' faces would light up with glee, too. Billy the Kid could not have missed noticing, but it only seemed to make him even more determined to show me and everybody else how truly inferior we were. No matter how often I told myself, "I'm not going to let him get to me," he always had the perfect put down to destroy my resolve.

I remember the time I hit a home run off him, I was trotting around the bases approaching third, when I heard his voice from the mound. "Good thing you had your eyes closed, four eyes. Otherwise you would have missed it." Being a bright kid, I had a million comebacks—unfortunately, they came to me while I was lying in bed that night, stewing over his smart aleck remark. Yes, Billy had managed to make a home run into a bad dream.

Well, Billy McMann is gone now, but some years ago Bull Derringer took his place. His clothes, his swagger and his age were all different, but my gut reaction was the same. Only the commiseration of my fellow adults and my own sense of identity helped me deal more maturely with the situation his presence created. That situation, of course, was to beat the Bull at all costs.

## *The Setup*

One common phenomenon in baseball is that by midseason the children have taken on many of the adults' characteristics. If their coach bites his nails, half of them will do the same. If the manager calls the umpire a blind bum, the children will ridicule him as well. This has been proven time and time again. By midseason, therefore, all of Bull's kids were like him: neat, fit and swinging the bat like they had come out of the womb with it. And, like Derringer, they were all so sure of themselves; they were smart alecks, each and every one. Even kids I had taught had been changed into winning robots on his team, scoring runs in a methodical manner that reminded me of the cocky 1987-88 season Mets.

Early Saturday morning, my tenth season as coach, we were all to meet at the home of the league president to select our teams for the upcoming year. Having gotten up at five o'clock so I could finish rounds at the hospital and be at the meeting by eight, I was easily distracted by the permeating aroma of freshly brewed coffee and cinnamon doughnuts. I was also relatively unprepared for the meeting, except for having some rough idea of the parents I wanted on my team and a number of notes stuffed in my pocket from parents asking me to remember their kids in the draft.

Bull, of course, had been the first one there, I was later told, arriving early with his two well-groomed coaches. Each had spread out his own notebook on the table before I had even arrived. As I sat down and reached for a doughnut, I noticed that only Bull was disciplined enough not to be stuffing himself with the free goodies.

The league president, a gentlemanly and kind-spoken man, tried setting an amiable atmosphere. He explained the purpose of the draft, which was to make sure all teams would be of equal talent, so every child could feel he had a chance to compete and would feel good about himself.

We all listened intently, nodding our consent to the premise of fair play by equal and competitive teams. Within ten seconds of the draft opening, however, Bull had declared several of the president's suggestions unfair or illegal. The atmosphere quickly changed from amicable to something reminiscent of the showdown at the OK Corral. My hands perspired. My ego prodded, "Don't let Bull buffalo you. Stand up to him. Tell him off, like all the other coaches wished they could." But my mind said no. I had been elected Manager of the Year. I would keep my perspective and self-control. I would act like an adult, not a child arguing over which half of the candy bar was bigger.

I quickly cut off Bull's interjections. "I want Bull to have all my first drafts. I'll take all the players on his least-wanted list." Everyone laughed—it was like a blast of fresh air. The guns were holstered and, except for a few skirmishes, the rest of the draft was uneventful. However, I was certain one gun was only loosely in its holster, ready to be fired the moment I turned my back. He was not known as The Derringer for nothing, I reasoned. Figuring I would beat him to the draw, therefore, I made the unfortunate move of not leaving my remarks at "I'll take all the players Bull has on his least-wanted list." Before he hit the ground from that first round into the chest, I followed it with another, well-aimed shot below the belt. "And when my little, rejected kids beat you in the last game of the season, I will send them over to shake your hand." I got several real thumbs-up for that one from the other coaches. Bull merely showed me his superior, in-your-dreams smirk.

Actually, my Little League team turned out to be a good one. We handily won our first two games. Then the two undefeated teams—Bull's and mine—met. The other coaches wished me the best. "Kick his *bleep-bleep* off the field, Vince." Well, it was not even close. When the dust settled on the field, the score was Yankees 12, Orioles 6. I smile now. They had kicked our bleep-bleep off the field. Bull did not even come out to shake my hand. Not that he had it in for me, although I thought he did—he did not shake anyone's hand ever.

My little team went on to seven more losses in a row. Bull had not broken our spirit, just our train of thought. After all I had learned about attitude, about knowing one's self and keeping the game in perspective, the kids were still doing OK, but I was not. One more loss and we would be in the cellar. Right then we were just tied for it—the first time in my ten years of coaching that I had not gotten my team into first or second place. Positive attitude comes easy when you are on top!

# *The Game*

As the practices went on, for the first time, a number of players started not to show. Parental participation was also dwindling. Worst of all, my reputation as a come-from-behind coach was in jeopardy. If I continued to lose, who would buy my books? Maybe I should write a chapter, "Winning by Losing."

I feverishly looked at my schedule one Friday when I got home from the hospital. I knew I had to turn things around. I knew I could. I would be so positive, my enthusiasm would raise the players to a new level. I would give my players the "old gipper" talk. I would give my team parents the "old gipper" talk. I would give my coaching staff the "old gipper" talk—and the boot if we did not win. I knew I could do it. I had done it hundreds of times before—or at least once or twice.

During my four years in high school, my baseball team was 0 and 79. I was captain of the team my senior year. As we went into the last game of the season I swore to my teammates I would win the last one for them since we had lost the first 79 I had played in. Believe it or not, we won in the last inning of the 80th game, 8-5. I will never forget it.

Recalling that spectacular comeback, I took a look at my Little League schedule. Oh no! The Yankees! We had played them twice and to say they had beaten us was an understatement—slaughtered was more like it.

Saturday, game day, was one of those "it feels good to be alive" days. As I walked out to the field, the grass was somehow brighter and more radiant than usual, its fragrance refreshing. We were playing on the major-league field, with its manicured infield and deep red-clay dirt. Somehow it inspired me.

My players were up, too, although still smoldering about "those damn Yankees." I told the youngsters to respect their competitors, muttering only to myself, "Boy, those damn Yankees look good." I glanced around quickly— no one had heard that what I thought and what I said were not quite the same thing.

I decided to try a new tactic: no pep talk prior to the first inning. Instead of starting my first-string pitcher, I tried Conseco, who usually played third base. I saved my finest pitcher for last as a possible comeback. Maybe I could lull the Yankees into complacency and then let the guillotine fall. The back of my mind said, "Who am I kidding?"

The game began. Strangely, Bull had put in his second-string pitcher. Generally, in the minors, each team has only two pitchers. At the most, you might occasionally find a third child who can throw the ball over the plate for a strike with some frequency.

Despite my best "gipper" talk at the beginning of the second, third and fourth innings, the score was 11-5 going into the fifth and probably final inning.

I was certain the Bull would now crush any semblance of hope by put- ting in his "Ace" who rarely walked more than two or three batters a game (even the best pitchers in the minors average two to three walks per inning). But, surprise, no! The Yankees' third stringer came in.

I tried rallying my Orioles. "Who are we?" I bellowed with half-hearted effort.

"The Birds," they yelled back, equally half-heartedly.

The parents were busy discussing recipes and gazing at their watches, occasionally staring at them as if trying to will the hands to move faster. Time sure flies when you are watching your kids get beat again. The first three batters in the top of the lineup walked. Instead of cheering on their teammates as they usually did, however, the children left the dugout and took off for left field, where they could pull off each other's hats and run around as if the game were already over. This gradually deteriorated into occasional outbursts. They knew, as I did, that Bull's Yankees might snuff us out any time they wanted, simply by putting in the Ace.

In our minor league, even though only three walks were allowed, the player stayed up at bat until he got a hit or made an out. My big hitters the past six games had a total of ten hits between them—seven by one player, Big Mikey (formerly "Mighty Mike"), who I had just taken out to let one of the younger boys play as a reward for his effort.

I did not let on that I knew the outcome as I shouted once again, "Do we ever give up?"

"Never," my Birds shouted back as they briefly stopped their skirmishes on the side of the dugout.

I looked up in the stands and yelled, "Who here has a son that never gives up?" The parents momentarily looked up to acknowledge that I had interrupted their conversations, then quickly went back to talking.

Bang! A good shot down the middle, two runs in, a man on first and third and four runs to go.

I looked across at Bull, his arms folded nonchalantly, his eyes holding a steady, undaunted gaze. The next batter struck out. The following batter got up on an error, but our runner on third forgot he was on base and cheered his teammate to first instead of running himself.

The bases were loaded. My best batter was up. I knew Big Mikey was batting almost .700. I let my chest expand with hope. Let Bull put in the Ace; Mikey could hit anyone. Wait a minute—Alex was striding to the plate. I had forgotten I had taken out Big Mikey. Oh, how I hated myself. Sure, be generous, be good, do what is right and you will always wind up like this, I thought. I shut my eyes and waited—not too long, mind you—as strike three was called.

Tony was up next. Potentially our best all-around player, he had not gotten a hit in three games. Then it happened. Derringer made his move. He walked out to the mound and waved his arm. The Ace. We all knew. By this time, though, all my Birds were riveted to the game, cheering. They had even made up their own cheer, taken from the old Queen song: "We will, we will, rock you," followed by them all hitting the wooden dugout with their cleated shoes, *boom, boom.* It was ominous. Touchingly, even the parents forgot their small talk and stood to cheer in unison. The Yankees for the first time started to chant, too. I felt it. The whole thing had come down to me and the Bull. I knew it and so did he. I could almost smell a feint aroma of cinnamon and fresh-brewed coffee from the day I had laid down the gauntlet. Yes, "it" was on the line—"it" spelled *p-r-i-d-e.* Bull motioned and *he* came in. The Ace was a small player so it was not easy to pick him out of all the other spotless, professional-looking Yanks.

As the young man tossed his first warm-up ball, I realized with a start that it was not the Ace—he was still in the field. Did the Bull feel that sure of himself?

The verdict came quickly. *Blam!* Tony hit a hard drive over the center fielder to the fence. Three runs in and Tony on third. The Yankees' catcher tossed the ball back to the new pitcher. Winding up, he launched one well over the catcher's head. Tony came striding in toward home plate. When he was no more than ten feet from home, the catcher grabbed the ball and dove toward him. Tony slid into the plate. The dust flew and the crowd went wild as the ump bellowed, "He's safe!"

Pandemonium broke out—12-11, what a beautiful score! We had won. All the boys on the field began hugging one another, the parents began hugging one another and I nearly fainted. What a comeback! Suddenly, I got a sinking feeling in the pit of my stomach. I quickly glanced at my watch. We still had ten more minutes to play officially. We had to stay alive for another ten minutes, or another inning would start and all this jubilation, all my preaching about effort and how it always paid off in the end, might once again be snuffed out by the Bull. I had seen him do it a million times before—well, at least twice.

Brian, our next batter, quickly hit a grounder to first base. The inning was over with eight minutes still left in the game. My heart sank. I motioned for my players to get out on the field. The ump, too, checked his watch and acknowledged the Dodgers and Giants who were now in the bleachers waiting to take over the field for their own game. The umpire called the coaches over. "There's still more than five minutes to go. Do you want to continue, Derringer?"

Bull Derringer turned to me. Our eyes met. I refused to let him see the disappointment and uncertainty behind my façade of determination. A tiny smile began at the corners of his mouth. It looks more like a sneer, I thought. Then he said, "It's been a good game. Let's call it."

For a second, the world as I knew it came to an abrupt halt. The children leaped into the air in slow motion and seemed to hang there in dead silence as what had just happened finally registered in my obstinate, judgmental mind. Suddenly, the volume returned, the cheer of "2-4-6-8" ended and the kids headed toward one another to give their "nice game" handshakes.

But it couldn't be! Bull was leading his troops. "Nice game," he smiled. "Great comeback, Orioles." He said it over and over, until my hand and his reached out for each other. He was wearing a genuine smile; I was so numb, I couldn't muster any kind of smile.

I stammered, "My team may have won the game, but your team has by far the best coach." I thought I saw a trace of gratitude on Bull's face. He had truly won—I knew it and the ump knew it. As I sit here writing this, I want to make sure all the coaches who stayed around to offer encouragement to "beat the damn Yankees" know it too.

# *Life is Full of Curveballs*

After 45 years I thought I had it all figured out—but obviously I was mistaken. We adults must keep our minds open and recognize that it is often our own prejudiced attitudes that prevent others from being able to change. The memories and unresolved conflicts of our childhood are what cause our present and future to be just like our past—not the actual circumstances that we encounter. I learned a lesson that day that I will not soon forget. This story is completely true, not made up or consolidated from several others to make a point. Little League in Pasadena, California, reached a new high that day, thanks to the Bull. Yes, I had met the enemy—and he was truly me!

# 34

# DARLING'S DISASTER

*"Our trials are trivial when life is on the line."*

—Momma Fortanasce

**I TOSSED AND TURNED IN BED,** unable to get Don Darling and his Tigers out of my mind. I had the feeling that something was wrong, something potentially dangerous, but no one was paying attention to it, hoping it would go away by itself.

Don Darling had been managing Little League teams for eight years. Darling was a misnomer—Don was anything but. He was more like a disaster, at least to anyone who played him and his Tigers. I had heard he was a devoted coach. He got his team out to practice daily, which was good. What was bad was what he was teaching his youngsters.

All coaches try to teach their players to be assertive. Darling taught his Little Leaguers to be aggressive. The difference between assertive and aggressive is the difference between standing your own ground and knocking someone else over to take theirs. Darling's instructions demanded aggression: "When you slide into a bag, take 'em out. If they try to take home, make 'em pay." His mottoes were "Baseball is 50 percent talent and one percent guts," and "If they're afraid of you, they respect you." Don treated opposing coaches in the same manner I had heard. I was looking forward to tomorrow's game like I would root canal work.

I rubbed my eyes and grimaced. Eight-thirty a.m. Game time was 9:30 a.m. The sky was overcast when I reached the field, filled with steely gray clouds trapped against the San Gabriel Mountains. I herded my team into the dugout. Despite having gotten a rare full-night's sleep, my muscles felt tight and sore as I started running responses in my head to the inevitable confrontation with Mr. Darling. As I looked at my son and the other young faces of my team, I thought, "Isn't Little League supposed to be enjoyable? Isn't it supposed to focus on these little boys and girls?" I realized I was actually afraid—afraid of someone called—of all things—Mr. Darling; afraid of his players and their reputation for roughness.

Two days earlier, I had seen Don and his catcher, nicknamed Grizzly because of the way he mauled anyone trying to steal home. Grizzly, or Brian Birksbye, was a big kid for 11, who, it seemed, towered two feet over his opponents as they dared to approach home. Sliding into the plate with Grizzly behind it was like sliding into the mouth of a furnace, or even more, into the mouth of the giant shark in *Jaws*. The last game I saw him in, against the Yankees, Grizzly had stood in front of home plate like Goliath. As the Yankees runner turned third base to race toward home, Grizzly feigned that the ball was coming to him, and menacing bellowed, "I'm going to knock your head off with this tag." The Yank hit the brakes and dashed back to third, only to bump into his teammate running from second. The ball, in fact, was just reaching second base at the time. Fear is contagious in little people; the Yankee's panic was quickly transmitted to his teammates. The runner coming from second ran back in terror, only to be tagged out. The runner who had been heading for home plate and was now back on third got confused by the shouts of his coach to go home, and started for home again, only now to be truly wasted by Grizzly's tag. Coach Darling dashed out to congratulate his catcher, who grunted, grinned a toothless grin, and pounded his chest. The parents of the Yanks stared in disbelief. The Yanks went out to the field with their heads slung low, already beaten by the Tigers. "This is Little League baseball?" I thought again. This is how we teach sportsmanship? How would I handle Darling and his monsters? In T-ball, it had been easy. Now, with ten-, 11-, and 12-year-olds, the game had taken on a new life. The children were more defiant, less easily controlled by intervention. Eleven marks the age of transition for many boys and girls, when parental influence begins to slip; when they get to 13, it does a complete nosedive. At the same time, their friends and idols—rock stars and the like—become all-important in the teenagers' eyes. Actually, it would not be so bad if the parents' influence simply slipped and flopped, but as soon as they become teenagers, our once adoring children begin to openly defy and occasionally berate the very people they used to call Mommy and Daddy. Why? Well, that is another book. I am going to call it My Father's Revenge.

## I Tried—Oh, How I Tried

Unless the coaches are in unison—unless there is a consistent example—children this age will be defiant, especially if led by an adult. Darling had only one thought: Win, even if you have to use force. I had heard him say it a dozen times. "These kids got to use the talents God gave them. If they are big, well, the big fish eat the little ones." Yes, yes, that is what a parent on his team told me. "The big fish eat the little ones." What was most startling about Darling was his stature: five-two and, at best, 120 pounds soaking wet. The psychiatrist in me came out. It was the "little man," or Napoleon Bonaparte syndrome (or, as one mother called it, PMS—Puny Male Syndrome). Darling was acting out his own wish to be a big man by intimidating others through his Little Leaguers, because all his life he had felt small. Now he was unconsciously getting even—you could see it in his eyes and in his elation whenever Brian "Grizzly" Birksbye struck terror in the opposing players as they approached home plate.

I got to the ball field with time to spare. My team warmed up while their parents climbed into the stands, looking as if they were climbing into a dentist's chair. I could read the concern on some of the parents' faces as they eyed Grizzly and then their little sons and daughters. The concern had washed away any hint of sparkle. In place of encouraging cheers, the moms and dads shouted warnings to be careful. Three parents came up to me and asked if I could do something to keep the game from getting out of hand.

Actually I already had. My father had often told me, "Problems happen. What's important is how you deal with them." I had dealt with this one by calling Jack, the league president, the night before and explaining my dilemma. Well aware of the situation with Darling, he was more than happy with my solution. He joined the ump and me as we approached Don Darling, who was clutching his lineup board on the sidelines and yelling instructions to his Tigers. Don looked up to find us all converging on him.

I let the umpire start. He cleared his throat. "Look, there will be no intimidation permitted while I ump. Anyone who threatens or intimidates another player will be promptly thrown out of the game." Jack then added his own admonishments. Surprisingly, Darling's face did not show a single telltale reaction. He only smiled and said, "Certainly." As Jack and the ump left, I extended my hand in friendship to Don—and he unveiled the acrid rebuttal that had been hidden behind his friendly façade. "Chicken to play with the Tigers, Vince? You've been in T-ball too long. You look like a big guy, but you're really a wimp. I thought they called your son 'Mighty'. I wonder where he got that name from—certainly not from you."

Me, a wimp? Me! Suddenly I was shoved back through a time warp 35 years to the schoolyard and Penne, the most ornery, redheaded, freckle-faced, half-pint bully in the school. He had pushed me in front of my buddies, and in front of Grace, my secret sweetheart. "You're a chicken, Fatso," he had sneered in the demeaning voice only a bully can pull off.

"Oh, your mommy won't let you fight. You wimp. You chicken." I can still hear his nasally voice saying it over and over again. "You wimp. You wimp. You wimp." Oh, how I hated that word!

My little buddies had been disgusted with me; they gazed downward or off into space—anywhere away from me. All I could see of Gracie was her back as she walked away. I had been a head taller than Penne and twice as heavy—just as I was with Don Darling.

No, I told myself, I will not make the same mistake twice. That wimp image had haunted me ever since that fateful playground scene. As a young man, I had worked out this conflict by lifting weights, learning karate, and, finally, becoming a bouncer in college. It had not been enough just to be the bouncer at the Chop House, the most popular college bar; I had to get a job bouncing at the toughest bar in town, where no college student with any brains would go. I ended up having a fight every night but did not quit until one of my fellow bouncers got shot to death. That must have awakened me, I guess. Now Darling was stirring up this sleeping giant again, but this time, I was no longer a kid. I was an adult, a respected medical professional, by God.

# *When You Get to the End of Your Rope, Tie a Knot and Hang On*

My anger grew to an internal fury, but all I said was, "Get ready, Don, for a good game." Then, of course, I shook his hand hard enough to crunch his bones and make him wince in pain.

As I turned and walked away, I lectured myself: "Oh, Vince, don't let it get to you." My better judgment, though, told me I had done the right thing. Of course, knowing that did nothing to help loosen my tightly welded jaw or lower my skyrocketing blood pressure. My fists were clenched so tight I could have crushed a piece of coal into a diamond. "Well," I consoled myself, "at least I didn't say my mother wouldn't let me fight."

I returned to the dugout, gathering up my team for a rousing "gipper" talk. "Fellas, the Tigers have a bad reputation and a bad attitude. Today we are going to teach those bullies a lesson. The meaner they are, the nicer we'll be. When they see their threats don't scare, they'll stop using them. Then we'll show them that one good sportsman is worth a team full of bullies." I must have struck a chord in them, because when I gave them the cheer, "Who are we?" they answered with amazing gusto immediately,

"The Cardinals!"

"Who are we?"

"Cardinals!"

"Who?"

"Cardinals!"

"Okay, get out there and paint 'em red."

Renato, one of my coaches, came over and slapped me on the back. "Great talk, Vince. 'Kill 'em with kindness.' I like that." Why is it our friends can see right through us?

I did not enjoy the type of game we played. Don had his players sliding into every bag with rubber cleats high. They taunted the Cardinals, but all my Birds held steady. Darling and his coaching staff continually egged their team on, calling to them, "Come on, be aggressive! Take 'em out! Drive it through 'em!" By the bottom of the sixth inning, the score was 3-3. My little guys were getting worn down by the Tiger jeers. Even worse, the team parents were getting ten sneers to every cheer they yelled. I took my team aside before they got up for the last inning.

"Okay, guys, they've given us their best, and the score is tied. Now let's show them what real baseball is all about."

I looked into the stands. The moms and dads were chewing their nails, probably praying for rain so they could just take their kids out of danger.

Two outs, a man on second and third. I was coaching third, where my runner, Luke Nakayama, stood. The Tigers' catcher, Grizzly, pointed at Luke. He did not have to speak a word—his sneer and menacing snarl said it all. Luke gulped and his chin began to quiver. Luke was a dutiful, disciplined little boy with a loving family; his parents were at all his games. Honor and discipline were the mainstays of his heritage. I placed my hand on his shoulder and firmly told him not to be afraid of Grizzly. The umpire was in control. What slipped out of my mouth then I have regretted ever since. "Stand up to them, Luke. Be a man, or you'll regret it for the rest of your life." God, I cannot believe I said that. Thirty-five years later, knowing everything I did about psychiatry, I was still reliving my childhood.

Luke looked at me, then at Grizzly. He closed his eyes into slits, stuck his jaw out in defiance, and tightened his fists until his knuckles whitened. I could hear his parents say something in Japanese in the background. I did not know exactly what it was, but Luke's face became even more determined.

The pitcher threw a fast ball right down the center of the plate. Kaycee smacked the ball dead center, hitting it into the hole between short and second base. The shortstop dove, deflecting the ball toward second with his glove. The second baseman picked it up and shot it toward Grizzly, who was covering—and blocking—home plate. Luke Nakayama, all three feet of him, slid right under Grizzly, but not in time to avoid getting Grizzly's gloved fist in the throat. Through the cheers and shouts and groans and cries, the ump bellowed, "You're safe!"

We all jumped off the bench in frenzy, hugging and shouting. Over the din, Grizzly cried out in terror, "He's choking. He's choking!" Luke lay face up, clutching his throat. As we all rushed toward him, his lips began to turn blue, his eyes went up into his sockets, and his body became rigid and began to shake.

# Nothing Like a Good Dose of Reality

Luke was limp by the time I got to him. The rest of the 50 adults and 25 youngsters stood motionless, stunned, not knowing what to do. As I kneeled by his side, my thousands of hours of medical training kicked in. I knew I had less than three minutes to do something, or little Luke, whom I had urged to "be a man," would be permanently brain damaged or dead. I checked his pulse by sliding my finger alongside his tiny neck. His carotid bounded loudly. I then placed my ear over his mouth, but could feel no breath. Luke was not breathing! "Call the paramedics," I shouted. I tried mouth-to-mouth resuscitation repeatedly—unsuccessfully!

"Does anyone have a sharp knife?" Luke needed a tracheotomy, a hole through the front of his neck right below his Adam's apple, so he could breathe. I would have to be careful to avoid the thyroid gland full of blood vessels, or he would bleed to death.

The last tracheotomy I had performed had been in an emergency situation just after my internship as an emergency room doctor in Shirley, Long Island. That had been over 23 years ago.

It had now been more than a minute since the Little Leaguer had gone down. I had only another 120 seconds to do something or it might be too late. I called for a straw, to be used as a tube to be placed in the trachea—if, that is, I could find it, and get it open with a knife. I quickly picked Luke up, turned him upside down, and slapped him firmly between the shoulder blades five times. Nothing came out. I then thrust my fist just below his rib cage several times. Someone—it was Darling—held out a Swiss army knife, open to the razor-edged cutting blade. As I completed the third thrust, Luke suddenly let out a spew of air, along with a wad of pink gum. His little shoulders heaved as his grayish-blue body turned first white, then pink. He opened his eyes, and his mother and father suddenly came back to life. Sobbing feverishly, they hugged their baby, while the crowd went crazy, cheering and screaming with relief.

I slumped back on my heels, exhausted, relieved, shaken, I do not know what else. Looking up, I found Don standing with the handle of the knife still extended toward me. His eyes were glassy, his face still registering disbelief, horror, and guilt. Grizzly was sobbing in his dad's arms, "I didn't mean it, I didn't mean it." How ridiculous our conflicts seemed in that moment.

I stood up to meet Don's still stunned gaze. I was going to say, "Don, these are only children. We have to protect them so they can grow up to be men and women. This is just a game—something to play, something to bring happiness and adventure so they can look back with fond memories, and, hopefully, with experience they can use." But I did not speak a word. Don was obviously traumatized; his body language made it clear there was no lecture, no words of remonstration I would use that he was not already rebuking himself with. The true meaning of what we were doing out on the field had suddenly become so apparent to us all. Life is precious. Life is to be savored, not devoured. These were children, on a Little League baseball field, not soldiers on a battlefield. From that day forward, the Tigers were never feared again—their coach had realized the true meaning of the game.

## *It's Baseball, Not Football*

"I'm never going to allow my child to be subjected to this dangerous sport called Little League." If that is what you are now thinking, think again. In my and my fellow physicians' experience, Little League is the safest of all sports. It has one-20th the injuries incurred by football, and one-tenth the ones incurred by soccer. Still, we adults must recognize what dangers do exist and make certain they are minimized. The biggest danger, and the one most important to confront, is any aggressive behavior that can harm the children physically and psychologically. We want our children to be assertive, not bullies. We want them to stand up for what is right and fair, not push for the extra advantage or win through intimidation and humiliation. If I have learned nothing else from my experiences on the ball field, I have learned that our children will adhere to whatever standards they see us follow—for good or evil. Whether we know it or not, we are always setting an example.

Every Little League parent and coach must know the fundamental safety rules of baseball, and insist on compliance:

**No player should chew gum while playing**, as Luke did. Gum chewing is as dangerous for a major leaguer as it is for a Little Leaguer—it is, in fact, dangerous in any situation in which a person is engaged in physical activity, such as baseball, jogging, or even bike riding. If the gum is not lodged firmly between the teeth, it can be easily inspired into the windpipe any time a jolt, a yell, or even the anticipation of something exciting causes a forcible inward breath.

**Little League coaches and managers must learn life-support techniques**, not only for children, but even for the parents and grandparents who attend the games.

**No child should be allowed to swing a bat without supervision.** Unattended bat swinging actually causes most of the more serious injuries in children's baseball. Collect all the bats, even those the children bring to the game, or give each child's bat to the parent to hold when it is not his turn at the plate. No child should be permitted to carry the bat home with him unless it is placed in his game bag. Many children get hurt in the parking lot when a child, dreaming of hitting a home run, swings the bat inadvertently into the nearby head of another child.

### AL AND AL'S COACHING CORNER

*Coaches must recognize the real purpose of Little League is to give children a positive experience that encourages them to keep trying, and to work toward gaining those important ingredients they will need as adults—effort, consistency, discipline, and empathy. They, as well as the team parents and managers, need to realize that the Little League diamond is not a field for working out adult unresolved conflicts, setting right childhood mishaps, or proving macho worth. The Little League field is for children to have fun.*

# 35

# COACHING THE LAST-PLACE TEAM

*"It's not over till it's over."*

—Yogi Berra

**I NEVER INTENDED TO WRITE THIS CHAPTER.** I never had a losing team. Then, in my 11th season, I did—and I learned the real difference between being positive when you are winning and being positive when you are at the bottom of the heap.

The sun was setting. The third baseman, Saji, had beads of perspiration dripping from his furrowed little forehead. His jersey was so drenched it could not hold any more perspiration. The catcher, Andrew, gave the sign to Brent out on the pitcher's mound. Rearing back, Brent launched another strike-zone throw to the plate. The crack of the bat on the ball resonated in my empty skull cavity as my eyes tracked yet another shot through the short-stop's legs, past the left fielder, and all the way to the outfield fence. One run, two runs, three runs. I screamed, "Third, third, third," as the ball was thrown past the second baseman, got bobbled by the pitcher, and was finally hurled into the stands just as the fourth run crossed the plate.

Ecstasy for the Giants—they jumped all over, giving each other high fives, low fives, and inside-out fives.

In contrast, my team's small shoulders were slumping, their eyes drooping and cast to the ground. The score was into double figures already, with only one man out in the first inning. Custer's Last Stand was near-victory compared with this massacre. At least Custer did not have any survivors to remind him of what had happened.

I glanced at my team parents. One mother's fist was clinched in anguish; another was absentmindedly wringing her hands as if she were washing them of this inning. Mama Maria's rosary was thoroughly worn out. Only grimaces, not grins, showed on their faces as another screaming line drive darted through our Orioles, who kept to their positions even though each hit brought their chins a little closer to the ground.

Toward the end of the third inning, the ultimate insult was cast in our faces. The Giants' coach smugly called out, "Jimmy, we have to complete three innings, or the game will be incomplete." Jimmy deliberately hit a dribbler to first, then proudly trotted to the base like a rooster crossing the chicken coop.

Twenty-seven to two. My enthusiasm was paper thin. What could I do, pray for rain? Even better, maybe a small earthquake would erupt—nothing dangerous, just enough to call the game. Hey, it had worked in the World Series when the Athletics played the Giants. As the game plummeted to a close, I tried to round up my Birds.

"Two, four, six, eight, who do we appreciate? Giants! Giants!" echoed across the field, but I was the only Oriole hearing it. My team parents and children had all evaporated rather than walked off the field. I stared at the vacant diamond, the distant chatter of the boisterous victors moving away toward their cars. Taking a deep breath, I lugged the field bag off to my own van. Alone, so alone! Contentment breeds success, I had always preached. Hogwash!

This had been the 12th defeat in the past 14 games of the season; we had won our first two times out. The Giants were the only team near enough in the standings to be seen with us on the same page. One more loss, and our team name might drop off the end of the weekly Little League newsletter. I lay awake in bed that night long enough for my wife to notice. "What's wrong, worried about a patient? Someone threatening to sue you?"

"It's much worse than any of that," I moaned. "I'm a loser. I can't help my little team. You had to be there, it was terrible."

"I was there," she reminded me. "You know, they really aren't as bad as they look." I groaned.

"Well, I know what I could do," I said to myself. "I'll show them what I've been writing really works!"

Have you ever just finished telling your buddies how you kicked the heck out of the local bully, only to turn around and find him standing behind you? Now your fantasy is facing reality as the blood drains out of your face. That week, I called all the parents personally: "Hello, Mr. McGinnis, this is Sean's coach. What did you say? 'When is your child going to win?' That's what I'm calling about. Winning and losing are only a matter of attitude. Did you know that learning how to lose can actually be more important than winning? Let me explain."

Mr. McGinnis listened intently, or maybe just fell asleep. I hoped what I told him would make a difference, as his son, Sean, had the bad habit of saying what everyone else was thinking—especially when I was trying to make them forget it.

Besides all the phone calls, I went to great lengths to make that week's practices especially inspiring. I must have bellowed "nice play," "nice hit," and especially "nice try" a thousand times. I even made new signs to put up in preparing for our weekend game, which was against the devastating Dodgers, of all teams. Their uniforms seemed especially bright that day, the sunlight gleaming off them as if they were polished armor. They all looked as if they had grown a foot in the past two weeks, compared with my Birds.

"Everybody in the dugout," I called. I had gone over my speech several times as I drove to the field. The Gettysburg Address was mere humdrum compared with this inspirational monologue. I started with reality. "Well, team, we've had a tough time. But tough is what we're all about, isn't it?" I raised my voice two or three octaves, my usual cue for my tots to bellow, "Right, Coach!"

And they enthusiastically did—sort of.

"The Dodgers are a good, tough team, but we are . . . "

"Better," they obediently chimed.

I then launched into my absolutely most inspiring gipper talk. It even got my own adrenaline pumping. As I ended, each little face gleamed. Pausing, I could see a raised hand out of the corner of my eye. "Yes, Sean?"

With a high-pitched sneer he said, "Who are you kiddin', Coach, they're gonna kill us again." Eleven little heads nodded in unison. Abraham Lincoln had his John Wilkes Booth—I had my Sean Edward McGinnis.

# *Losing is Only an Attitude*

The score was 6-7 going into the next-to-last inning—the first time in eight games the other team had fewer runs earned than a marathon has miles. For once, the official scorekeeper had not gotten bewildered trying to figure out how to show double figures in one inning on the scoreboard out in right field. Did you know that the numbers for those little boxes only go from one to nine? If a team scores ten runs or more in one inning, it cannot be put up. No one had ever needed to think of that eventuality, until my Birds flew to the Little League field.

Despite McGinnis shocking us all back into reality, my call to the parents had worked. The stands thundered with enthusiasm. Mama Maria's rosaries were left at home under orders (though she informed me she had said several prior to the game). Wringing hands and clenched fists were changed into applause and chants: "Let's go, Orioles, let's go! Boom! Boom!" Their stomps on the dilapidated wooden stands resounded across the field. The incessant chorus was as daunting as it was enchanting. At the end of the second inning, the umpire warned me, "The opposing coach says you're intimidating his kids."

I looked up in dismay. "I didn't mean anything negative toward his children. I was only urging my little guys on."

The umpire winked. "I know, and I told him that myself. Keep it up, and you might just beat this rowdy bunch."

Okay—we were down by one run and up to bat. Ball four—I had never heard such sweet words. Andrew, our fastest runner, trotted to first. Strike three, a number I had never before realized I could detest so severely. I knew winning was not the reason for playing the game—I had pounded that into the parents' heads all week. We were there to see the children grow, to show unconditional love to all the players, even if they lost.

"I know losing is never fatal," I prayed. "But, Lord, winning once in a while instills confidence and repetition of positive behavior, too." Andrew streaked to second, safe by a mile.

James was up next. I gave him a pep talk, and reminded him to swing only at those balls that were between his knees and chest. James, all three feet of him, had the habit of thinking he was six feet tall, like his dad. Even with the bat extended over his head, he could not make five feet. Henry, the Dodgers' pitcher, went into his windup and lofted one six feet high; James went amnesiac and swung. Strike one!

"Nice swing," I croaked out with as much enthusiasm as possible. "Remember now to swing at one over the plate."

The next pitch bounced into the dirt. Using a golf swing, James shot the ball past the pitcher. Unfortunately, it was cut off by the shortstop, but what James lacked in pitching selection, he made up for in speed.

Runners on first and third, one out. Brian, the bottom of the bottom of our lineup, strode to the plate. Measuring out his distance with the bat, he stood three feet from the plate—a small precaution, he had previously told me, in case of a wild pitch. The Orioles' parents were in a frenzy. "Let's go, Brian, let's go! Boom! Boom!"

Brian was 0 and 21 for the year but had walked several times. Mama Maria started praying. Andrew inched off third by four or five yards, despite my pleading with him to get closer to the base so he would not be picked off. James darted for second as the first ball was pitched. Clang!—a sound so previously nauseating now resounded like the clash of cymbals as an inside pitch sped off Brian's bat over the outstretched hand of the first baseman. One run, 7-7. Around came James as the right fielder gathered up the ball and started his throw to home. The reverberation from both sides of the stands was deafening. The ball slammed into the catcher's mitt just as James slid into home. A momentary hush, then, "Safe!" The crowd exploded.

All the Orioles sprang from the bench to whoop around Brian. His gleaming smile could have lit up a moonless desert night for a week. This is what Little League is all about, I thought happily. This is what makes all the time, aggravation, and work worthwhile.

Something had happened that evening—to the team, and to the parents. The players had never had much talent, but that game, they found something that transcended any inadequacy in throwing, batting, or fielding: they found heart, just like the "Damn Yankees" song said they "gotta have." Heart gave them hope and opened them to the concept of "try and you will succeed." Yes, it was true: each and every one of those Little Leaguers was a winner no matter what the score—8-7, or 100-7!

*"Remember: failure is success if you learn from it."*

—Mike Scioscia
**Angels manager**

# 36

# The Team That "Got It"

*"Life is a marathon, not a series of 50-yard dashes."*

**MY 11TH SEASON CAME TO A CLOSE** with a record 16 losses, four wins, and one tie. The last five games were more rewarding than any I have ever coached. After our win from the Dodgers, I tried to maintain the positive attitude that had lit up my Birds, as they had been nicknamed in the league (as in "For the…" the joke went).

We lost our next game in the last inning to the Expos, a formidable team, but, I told myself, it had only been a warm-up for the following, more important encounter with the Giants, who were only one game ahead of the last-place team—us! The beating they had given us earlier would have been long forgotten but for their coach's bad habit of constantly reminding them about "that great win against the Birds—twenty-seven to two." We played them in the second to last game of the season.

## One for the Books

To warm up, my little Birds were having fun playing the games I taught them, which, in actuality, were designed to sharpen their fundamental baseball skills. Winning seemed far from their minds. They were just there to have fun. Finally, ten minutes late, as usual, the umpire called, "Ball in!"

I rounded up my team, stood especially tall before them, and placed my hands on my hips. "Well, fellas, this is a good team we are playing. No matter how many runs they score, will we give up?"

"No way, Coach."

"Who are we?"

"Orioles, Orioles!  Orioles!"

"Well, then, let's go out there and have a great time!" I did not voice my subconscious thought, Let's win.

Suddenly, as always, McGinnis raised his hand. "Let's beat these guys, they said we stink!  Larry, their pitcher, told me yesterday in the schoolyard we're for the birds."

I immediately went back to the lineup and scratched in McGinnis to start the game. Nothing like a little positive incentive for constructive criticism, I thought.

It was a long and exciting game. It was the bottom of the fourth, and definitely last, inning. Our right attitude, adulatory parents, and recent win/near-win streak had paid off. As the sun sat over the horizon, the score was 3-15. That's right—all we had to do was hold them scoreless, rack up 13 runs ourselves, and we had the game locked up!

Sean McGinnis, the closest thing I have ever seen to a leprechaun, was up first. I had kept him in the whole game. I even had him catching the last inning—something he had pleaded for all year. The Giants had been unmerciful, with Larry, their pitcher, laughing and ridiculing my Birds the most. McGinnis had tried with all his heart to hit Larry's pitches, but he could succeed only in striking out.

As Sean stood just outside the batter's box, I placed my arm over his slumped shoulder. "Do we ever give up?" I whispered in his ear.

"I don't know," he said, shaking his head no.

"Imagine hitting a line drive right over Larry's freckled head. Remember, Sean, he expects you to swing at his first pitch, so wait till the third one." Sean walked up to the plate. Ball one. Ball two. On the third pitch, Sean reared back to swing, and the ball hit him in the arm. Gritting his teeth and straining to keep back his tears, he held his hand over his tiny biceps and rubbed. No way was his friend Larry going to see him cry. Sean trotted to first, staring at the pitcher, but he did not stop there. As soon as he rounded first, he immediately took off for second.

"No!" I yelled, but Larry was so stunned at this brazen act, his throw went over the second baseman's head—and Sean was on third.

No outs, man on third, and 12 runs to tie, 13 to win. Improbable? Yes. Impossible? No. What happened next must surely go down in the annals of Little League history. For once, the Birds were the ones who caused the score-keeper trouble with placing double digits on the scoreboard. Maybe all my motivational techniques had caught up to them—or maybe they had been inspired by Sean's boldness. Whatever the reason, they just kept hitting the ball and pulling in the runs.

Second and third, two outs, 11 runs. Mighty Mike, my most reliable hitter, was up—and he was ready. The Giants' stands were silent. Larry had long ago been taken out as the game extended into the second half of the hour. The opposing coach was loudly complaining, "My players can't see."

The ump only laughed. "Seems the batters aren't having any problems."

The Giants' pitcher went into his windup and threw. The ball was two feet too high, and a foot outside, but that did not stop Mikey—he hammered it down the right-field line. One run across! The game was tied. I could not hear my own shouts over the noise from the stands as hefty Mike lumbered around first base. The Giants' first base coach ran out toward right field, barking, "Throw it to home, throw it to home!"

It was the fastest relay I have ever seen. The right fielder paid no attention whatsoever to his imploring coach and threw the ball to second. Mikey, counting his chickens before they had hatched, was skipping around to second, totally unaware of the throw. The ump bellowed, You're out!" just one beat before the 13th run cross over the plate, and two seconds before the sun set. The parents on both sides were wildly jubilant. Victory was snatched form the jaws of defeat—but for whom? It was the ultimate Little League victory—both sides had won.

Since it was too dark to play another inning, the ump declared the game over. As I meandered off the field, I was overwhelmed by the wonder of it all. Had I been wrong about their talent? No, I had been around for too long to have been mistaken about that. Then why had it happened to set my last-place team on a winning streak? The only answer I could come up with was that the parents had finally begun to believe in their children, which sparked the players' belief in themselves. What else could explain it?

In the last game of the season, the Birds were up against the Twins, who needed this win to make the playoffs for the league championship. I can only sum it up as a 17-8 slaughter. The Orioles made 19 hits in five innings, scoring a total of 29 runs in six innings—which was about as many as they had previously scored all season. Why?

I have talked of focus, timing and encouragement. Despite all my platitudes, one coach once told me, "You can say what you want, but if your team doesn't win, your kids will walk away losers." When my team was two and 12, that statement haunted me. Baseball is only a small part of my life. I work a minimum of 12 hours daily with patients whose lives occasionally hang on my decisions. I lecture physicians, and I am involved with bioethics of medicine. Little League baseball, however, is a focal point in my life—a testing ground for ultimate truth and success. I may touch many people's lives in medicine, but I still feel a void. Millions of little lives are affected yearly in Little League—unfortunately, for many, that effect is negative. I have yet to speak to a parent whose child has not had several bad experiences in Little League. I believe this can be changed. The "Bad News Bears" image so many Americans identify Little League with can be changed to the Good News Cubs—or Padres, or Birds, or Dodgers.

# *The Recipe of Encouragement*

Before I "got it," my 11th season team was two and 12. One of those wins was a forfeit, the other a 6-5 surprise. The other teams were maturing, and the children who already had potential were rapidly gaining confidence as their skills improved and their teams won. I had given it some thought. Confidence comes from skills and winning, but does one need both, or just one of the two? And which comes first? With my schedule at work, I knew I could not possibly increase the number of practices. My co-coach, a deeply dedicated father and friend, was born in Brazil and knew a lot about soccer but little about baseball. I wrote down my problem: "How can I improve their skills and, at the same time, reinforce their efforts with positive feed-back, since it is unlikely I can give them the reinforcement of winning a game?"

I thought about the concept of reflected self-image: a child assesses him-self on how his parents or an adult surrogate, in this case the coach, regards his performance. Well, I could certainly reflect a positive image to the chil-dren, and see to it that the other coaches and parents did, too. Creating a pos-itive environment where the children could grow at their own rate was anoth-er thing.

How could I increase what seemed to be the all-important ingredient—their confidence? No matter how easily I attempted to pitch during practice, some children missed that ball more often than not, while others did fairly well. They all did OK playing the field in practice but faltered during the actual game. After long reflection, I decided I needed to drastically change the practices. One thing my Birds could do was fly—that is, run. I institut-ed three new things: practice forms that would show them they could suc-ceed, constant reinforcement of that concept, and training sessions that were more fun than drills.

If you have been at standard Little League practices, you know that everybody takes their positions while the coach hits the ball to the infielders. They throw it around to first base, then practice double plays. All the while the coach yells, "Bend your knees, keep your glove down, keep your eye on the ball." Meanwhile, you can catch the outfielders feeling like second-rate citizens and falling asleep. Obviously, all this had to change.

I started with batting. I taught them bunting and pepper. In ten minutes, they had caught on, and I could place one batter against three fielders. The fielders lobbed the ball from ten feet away to the batter, who bunted. All the players learned quickly and had a high rate of success. I played especially with the least-talented children, giving them the extra help they needed. In these little groups, I could also get more parents involved. Parents become amaz-ingly understanding when they are part of the coaching staff. One rule, though: never let a parent coach his or her own child at practice.

Next, I divided my Birds into three groups of four equally talented play-ers. We played "catcher up." One child would throw fly balls, and the other three would try to catch them. Three catches, and you could throw the ball.

In two practices, I accomplished more with many of my players than I had in the entire previous seven weeks.

We then went to infield practice, but with a twist. I had the usual out-fielders put on helmets and act as runners. This gave the infielders the chance to practice under game conditions. At the same time, the usually less talent-ed children, who played outfield, learned the strategies of running, leading off, and sliding. Finally, at the end of the practice, we had our base-running race. Each child kept track of his own times, both to first base and around all the bags. The parents cheered them on.

With a little "creative timing," each child improved over each practice. Some of them really improved. Those who had formerly felt clumsy were most affected by this, as they tried harder than ever to beat their own previ-ous best.

By the third practice, a miracle had occurred. Everyone arrived on time to practice, and, even better, though the sessions started going beyond the allowed hour, no one complained of being tired anymore. As an added reward for their great efforts, I would take them to McDonald's for a burger. The traditional practice was gone. Each child had been grouped with other children who had similar talent, so they could all enjoy themselves and suc-ceed. As they succeeded, they tried harder. Practice became fun, a game. Even the coaches and parents had fun seeing the children so happy, which made our enthusiasm at the games real, and carried the spirit right back to the chil-dren.

The team that did not have it, got it. No, we did not have the raw talent of the other teams, but what we had now was something more important. The children were having fun and were not afraid of losing. Their parents were proud of them, and they were proud of themselves. The true ingredi-ents of a Little League team had been sown: camaraderie, fun, discipline, contentment, and increasing effort. Put them all together, and they grow confidence.

# I Grew Up

As I look at Little League in retrospect, I think of my now 20-year-old son, Vinny—the "Bionic Man" at six. Little League was only a small, albeit important part of his development. When I first entered the game I would dash to the field. Each pitch, each ball hit to him, had me sitting at the edge of my chair. I was overwhelmed with emotion at each little event. This often made me place incredible expectations on my son, and agonize over things I now see as utterly trivial. I am sure I was only hurting him as he read my disappointed and angry facial expressions. I see things so much clearer now. Little League is just one of the miles of the marathon of life. The most important part of it is making sure our children have a wonderful experience that teaches them to try, and to be content with their effort and themselves.

We, as parents, must put Little League in the right perspective and not get lost in the moment. We must remember that we teach our children through our actions and facial expressions. We must demonstrate behavior and advice to our children that encourages repeated effort, knowing that effort will eventually bring discipline. We must give the encouragement that breeds contentment. Little League can and should be exhilarating and fun. For me, it has been a 12-year trek through one of the most beautiful parks in the world, where jewels have sparkled and lit up my life like no other diamond ever could.

Yes, Little League is alive and well in Pasadena, California. The number of children participating has grown by 40 percent since my fourth year in the league. People are learning that the family that plays together, grows together. The great American Pastime is no longer an endangered species. As you close this book, call your child and take him, or her, to a ball game. My wish is for you to know the same pleasure I enjoy whenever my daughter, Kaycee, says, "Dad, every time I pass a baseball field, I just feel good all over!"

Ah, baseball! I love it!

# Al and Al's Guide to Practice

**LITTLE LEAGUE CAN BE FUN,** instructive and a building block for each child's path to success. (As Dr. Fortanasce has said, success in Little League is equipping your child with the tools to deal with the problems life will throw at them). In Little League those problems are small, but after all, that is how we all begin: by first taking care of ourselves and then later in life taking responsibility for our jobs and our families. Yes, it all begins at practice.

Little League practice is not just to learn the rules and skills of baseball but also is an opportunity to learn life lessons. It's at practice that your children get the chance to learn the secrets of success. It's a cliché, but practice really does make perfect, and it's practice that makes the difference when, as Mike Scioscia puts it, "the bases are loaded and the Series is on the line." Your child may never be in the World Series, but in life, no matter what path he chooses, he'll face equally challenging situations. How he deals with them will depend on what you teach him.

## *Sorry Sam*

Sam was a good guy. He agreed to be a coach for the right reasons—the kids. But Sam knew about as much about coaching Little League as he did about rocket science. Not much.

This was the Birds' sixth practice and it was pretty much like all the others. Sam arrived late as did half the team. It's not that Sam was lazy but just disorganized. Well, maybe he could be called lazy, because he never took the time to plan anything out. Worse still, when he and the kids finally showed up, he was alone. His coaches had important stuff to do, like taking the car to the shop, doing the laundry, that sort of important stuff. Those who did turn up were never utilized well.

Sam's teams were noted for their turnover of players as by midseason many of the kids got bored and decided that Little League was just not much fun. Those who stayed tended to run wild, taunting one another. Sam didn't insist on much and he didn't want to discourage any more kids by yelling at them. We've found that many parents and coaches adopt the same attitude.

As the Official Coaches of Little League, we have discovered that the way to avoid Sorry Sam's dilemma is by following one simple rule: make it fun!

# *The Importance of Practice and How to Make it Fun!*

How do you make practice successful? Our years of experience have taught us that there's only one answer to that question: you make it fun. That doesn't mean you let the children run wild without any discipline. No, it takes planning and the cooperation of parents and assistant coaches to make practice both fun and beneficial.

# *Remember K-I-D-S*

Coaches, K-I-D-S stands for the four principles parents must learn to enforce:

K—Keep on time.

I—Indicate clearly what you want: say it, do it, repeat it.

D—Discipline: be firm and kind to kids and parents.

S—Smile a lot.

Good practice plans can be more effective if a team has one or two assistant coaches. In this way, each coach can work with a smaller group of players when teaching a skill or executing a drill. Assistants can be the most valuable resource for coaches when used properly. Coaches should work closely with them in organizing the practice and listen to their opinions and evaluations of the team. There is a real need for carefully written plans for a practice. There may be times when you cannot prepare a well-planned written practice but jotting down a few points you would like to cover would be of great benefit. We all realize the difficulty of a volunteer finding the time to do this, but a written guideline organizes thoughts and times for an efficient practice.

Every practice should follow these important guidelines:
1. Is planned and 90 minutes maximum.
2. Begins with exercise and warm-up.
3. Teaches one or two skills.
4. Includes throwing and catching drills.
5. Reviews the last practice and teaches a new skill.
6. Includes five or six drills or activities.
7. Includes a game-type component.
8. Should end with a "test," either verbal or by demonstration of the skill taught.

Practice is where most athletes spend most of their time in a sport and where the results of a team are developed. How a team practices will usually determine how a team will perform in a game situation. Practices will also allow the coach an opportunity to develop each player and the team to full potential. It is the most important part of the game and a must for players to experience success personally and as a team.

In preparing practice session plans, take into account the time available, the number of players present and the equipment you have available other than baseballs and softballs (such as batting cage, screens, tees, etc.). Being well organized before and during the practice makes it easier to concentrate on a coach's primary responsibility—teaching.

Coaches must do their very best to be enthusiastic and let all players know that you are excited about having them on your team. Let them know it makes you feel special to be part of their lives as well. Coaches should always give positive feedback to each player at every practice. Developing proper baseball/softball skills is a very slow process, and there is absolutely no room for any discouragement. Positive feedback to players will in turn help them to understand and improve their performance of skills, techniques and drills. NEVER PRACTICE MISTAKES. Repetition of the proper technique will lead to athletic success and life success.

Discipline is a concern for most coaches. Practices should not only be organized but should be run as efficiently as possible. This will happen only with the proper discipline by coaches and players alike. Some expectations for both the coach and players alike could include:

- Always be on time and advise your coach of late arrivals or absences.
- Wear proper clothing for practice.
- Listen when coaches or fellow players are talking.
- Do your best at all times.
- Hustle on and off the field.
- Respect one another.
- Stress safety at all times.

How does fun fit in with a practice session? You can only enjoy Little League if you love the game, and you can only love the game if you are having fun! Why would you want to play if you aren't having fun? As a player, it isn't something you have to do . . . you choose to play this game. And as a coach, having fun should be the first and most important goal for yourself and the players. Fun becomes part of a practice when there are a lot of activities for children to burn up the energy they have stored up during the day. This will work very well with short lines, active drills and including coaches in player competitions whenever possible. Safety is a very important aspect that must be kept in mind at all times. A proper warm-up, the use of proper equipment at practice, clear instructions, first-aid kits, proper use of available space and good common sense are essential to ensure the safety of everyone involved in the practice.

As a coach, please take advantage of the numerous resources available to you. There are hundreds of books, videos and teaching aids that will help you in all areas of the game, especially on how to run a practice. We highly recommend this book, *Life Lessons From Little League: Revisited.* Attending coaching clinics offered not only by Al and Al but by many high school and local college coaches would be extremely valuable. These clinics will not only give you the up-to-date information on training techniques by the official presenters but also the sharing of ideas with other coaches whom you meet at the clinic. There are many thousands of parent volunteers working as coaches with our children and many come to the sport with no coaching background and limited knowledge of the game. What they do have is a strong desire to help the kids. Clinics should be the answer. The motivation and commitment are in place. Make sure that your kids get off on the right foot by arming yourself with the right learning tools to create a solid foundation for successful and meaningful practices. Remember, it is all about the KIDS and only you can make it happen!

# APPENDIX B

# BEING A LITTLE LEAGUE UMPIRE

*By Mike Legg and Tim Ward, Former Umpires of Little League*

**LIKE PARENTS AND COACHES,** umpires are role models. Everything a coach, parent or umpire does and says communicates a message to the players—and that message should always be the same: Fun and Sportsmanship are always more important than the result. Umpires are responsible for ensuring that players are provided with a fair, fun, safe and positive environment in which to play.

## *The 10 Keys to Being an Umpire*

1. Remember: the game is for the Little Leaguers, not the parents or coaches or you.
2. Know and carry your rule book.
3. Enforce the Little League rules of fair play.
4. Listen to coaches' and children's concerns.
5. Have the proper uniform and equipment.
6. Stay calm, especially when others are not.
7. Insist on good sportsmanship.
8. Always be fair and impartial.
9. Remember the spirit of Little League and its motto.
10. Make sure the children have fun.

### *1. Always remember that the game is for the Little Leaguers*

Player safety and fair play come first. Emphasize enjoyment and good sportsmanship before, during and after the game, during all of your interactions with players. Support players' endeavors with positive encouragement. Commiserate with a player if he makes a mistake, congratulate a player if he makes a good play. But make sure your comments are spread equally between the two teams.

Umpires need to ensure that players have the correct equipment and make sure a player does not wear anything dangerous to either himself or others.

Good umpires develop positive feelings of self-worth in the children and in themselves.

### *2. Know and carry your rule book.*

- Know and properly apply the rules of the game.
- Understand and follow all age-specific rules and regulations.
- Stay updated on rule changes and interpretations, equipment improvements, etc.

Attend Little League umpire training courses and meetings.

### *3. Enforce the Little League rules of fair play*

Recognize and compliment sporting behavior on the part of players, coaches and parents. Stress that foul or abusive language will not be tolerated under any circumstances.

### *4. Listen to coaches' and children's concerns*

Never publicly criticize a coach, parent or child. Listen to their concerns and try to explain your decision making if they are confused. If everyone at the ballpark pulls together, the kids will benefit by enjoying a positive, consistent environment.

### *5. Have the proper uniform and equipment*

Wear the proper uniform and keep it in good condition. Like a policeman or nurse, it's harder to achieve the respect you deserve if no one can distinguish you.

### 6. Stay calm, especially when others are not

Maintain control when confronted with emotional reactions from players, coaches and parents. Demonstrate respect for players, coaches, spectators and fellow officials.

Exhibit self-control and self-discipline at all times and recognize the effect your behavior has on players, coaches and spectators. An umpire's role is a difficult one, at times unappreciated by those who like to blame all their own failings on you. Stay in control by blocking out comments from the bleachers and remaining focused on the game. Keep a sense humor as well. If a coach is screaming abuse at you, appreciate what an idiot he's making of himself and don't be afraid to politely but firmly asked him to stop.

### 7. Insist on good sportsmanship

Ensure that players, coaches and parents show positive respect for the rules and your authority. Acknowledge acts of sportsmanship with a kind word to players, coaches and parents of both teams. If players are continually criticizing each other, urge them to work together as a team rather than against each other. If a coach is being negative or abusive towards his players, ask him to stop.

### 8. Always be fair and impartial

Avoid conflicts of interest. If the coach of one team is your neighbor, or the other coach backed into you in the parking lot, don't let your predisposition towards the team cloud your judgment. Decisions based on personal bias are dishonest and unacceptable.

Good umpires always provide honest decisions and positive encouragement while ensuring that the rules are enforced in a fair and unbiased manner.

### 9. Remember the spirit of Little League and its motto

"I will do my best and strive to win, but win or lose I will try my best."

### 10. Make sure the children have fun

You can do this by applying common sense.

The purpose of Little League rules is to provide a framework to promote the game's spirit—that it is fun, fair, and safe. This means the rules are there to facilitate play, not inhibit it. As an umpire you have the decision-making power over a game. But when making a decision ask yourself:

- Is it safe?
- Is it fair?
- Does it promote fun?
- The most important of these is FUN.

# *Why Become an Umpire?*

Without a judge there is no court. Without an umpire, there is no baseball. The central reasons for becoming a Little League umpire are no different than the reasons for becoming a player or a coach. Become an umpire:

1. To have fun.
2. To help teach kids the rules and the spirit of the game.
3. To develop children's character, sportsmanship and sense of self-esteem.

For a love of kids and the game of baseball.

Unfortunately, good umpires are rarely remembered. They umpire so fairly and efficiently that players, coaches and parents hardly notice they're there. They don't make many mistakes (at least no glaringly obvious ones) and everyone's attention remains on the players and the game rather than the man with the rule book. It's the bad umpires who always grab the headlines and stick in the memory.

Tom Boyle says, "Remember that umpires have feelings, too." After a close game I saw a young umpire not much older than 17 sink into the seat of his car. I went over to see what was the problem. I recognized him as "Five error" Tony. Almost in tears, he explained how after calling 150 pitches and 50 plays correctly he missed one call and everyone hated him.

Have mercy on umps. They are human and they try their hardest for the love of the game.

# APPENDIX C

# THE HISTORY OF BASEBALL

**BASEBALL IS BELIEVED TO HAVE BEEN FOUNDED** in England in the 1600s. Originally, the game had three bases, and the idea was to hit the ball with the bat. Each base was actually a stake driving into the ground, some three feet high. Fielders put their base runners out by hitting them as they dashed to the base with the thrown ball. This was known as "plugging the runner."

English settlers brought this bat-and-ball game with them to America. By the 1700s, it had begun its evolution into One Old Cat, Two Old Cat, and then, simply, Town Ball. One Old Cat used only one base and required three players: a pitcher, a catcher, and a batter. As the game become more sophisticated, two more bases were added, along with additional players.

A *Little Pretty Pocket Book*, first published in 1744, gives us an example of early baseball, and clearly states its purpose—enjoyment.

"the ball once struck off
away flies the boy
to the next destined point,
and then home with joy."

As you might imagine, the stakes or posts banged into the ground were neither fun to run into, nor very practical. They were soon replaced with flat stones—and it does not take too much imagination to picture the injuries those, too, could inflict. Finally, sacks filled with sand became the precursors to today's bases.

Logic (and, I am certain, many a large welt) caused plugging the player to be changed into tagging the runner. Originally, all runners had to be tagged out. Eventually, due to frequent collisions at the bases—especially first—that rule was finally changed. The new rule said that a defensive player only had to touch the bag to score the out if a player was running from one base to another. To be fair, the rules said, the player who had just hit the ball could run past the bag on first base without being penalized or tagged out as he returned to the base. Even before the rules of the game were formally written, these and other common-sense safety rules evolved over the course of time.

Abner Doubleday, legend has it, created the contemporary game of baseball in Cooperstown, a small village in New York. Cooperstown now houses the Baseball Hall of Fame. A general in the U.S. Army, Doubleday is believed to have popularized the game in central New York. Although he may not have been the one who actually invented baseball, he is definitely responsible for its widespread popularity.

Alexander J. Cartwright, founder of the Knickerbocker Base Ball Club of New York, apparently wrote down the first set of rules for the game. He established the distance of 90 feet between bases, the standard of nine positions on the field, and the difference between fair and foul territory.

On June 19, 1846, the Knickerbocker Club played the New York Nine at Elysian Field in Hoboken, New Jersey, in what is historically considered the first official baseball game. During the Civil War (1861 to 1865), New England Union soldiers spread their love of the game throughout the states. In 1876, William Hulbert, owner of the Chicago White Stockings, formed the National League. Its first league game, between Boston and Philadelphia, was played on April 26, 1876, with more than three thousand in attendance. In 1901, the American League was born, setting the stage for the World Series to evolve.

Baseball continued to spread in popularity through the newspapers and, finally, the radio. The first radio broadcast of a game took place on August 25, 1921, when station KDKA in Pittsburgh transmitted a play-by-play account of the contest between the Pirate and the Philadelphia Phillies. On August 26, 1939, baseball first appeared on television over station W2XBS.

The first baseball gloves did not make their appearance until 1875. Originally, the players played bare-handed and use bats borrowed form cricket. Cricket "bats" are actually short, flat-sided poles. Round bats were introduced to baseball in 1862. At first, when they were made of white ash, the best bat wood was found in the forests of Pennsylvania and northern New York. However, due to the concern over bats breaking or splintering and causing injury, aluminum bats made their appearance in the late 1960s and early 1970s. At one time, more than 10 million wooden bats were made a year. With the lower cost of aluminum bats today, only a million or less wooden ones are now made per year. Aluminum bats are still not used in the majors, though, because they would cause big changes in the game, and possibly wipe out many hitting records.

Uniforms were first introduced by the New York Knickbockers in approximately 1851. They included long, dark-blue trousers, webbed belts, white shirts, and straw hats. At first the uniforms were very baggy, but, in a style pioneered by Willie Mays in the early 1960s, they have since become more close-fitting. The Pittsburgh Pirates wore the first batting helmets on September 15, 1952, using them not only at bat, but in the field as well. After a few years, the Pirates decided their players needed to wear the helmets only on trips to the plate.

The early helmets had no earflaps. Earflaps were actually developed for Little League play, and copied later by the major leagues. I remember well the first year helmets were introduced to Little League on Long Island—1953—because it was the year I began to pitch. Luckily for three players, our helmets had earflaps. I still question the policy of not having T-ballers wear helmets on the field.

# *A Part of History*

Helmets always remind me of Andrew. We were playing an evening game, the third game of the season, and not many parents had shown up, for one reason or another. Andrew was up at the plate with his helmet on. He hit the ball off the tee and dashed toward first. He grinned as the first-base coach told him to head toward second. The right fielder picked up the ball, ran after Andrew as he turned first, and threw it at his back, hitting instead the back of Andrew's head. He must have gotten confused and thought we still "plugged" our runners, rather than tagged them out. Luckily, Andrew was wearing his helmet. After the play, the umpire gently admonished the right fielder, who truly had not recognized his error. The inning was soon over, and the Blue Jays were up to bat.

Andrew, who was then in his first year of little League, ran out with all his teammates, to play left field. The Blue Jays put a man on first and second. One of their bigger players smashed a line drive into the outfield. Little Andrew dashed headlong toward the ball with his arms extended, only to catch it squarely on his forehead. His legs flew out from under him, and he handed on his back. I dashed for left field. Our shortstop, Mary, however, alert as usual, caught the ball on the bounce off Andrew's head, turned and tagged the base runner out as he rounded second and third. When I arrived at Andrew's side, he was just picking up his helmet. He had forgotten to take it off to play the field! I looked at his head—not a mark. The helmet had protected him.

For the rest of the year, I had all the outfielders wear helmets until I was certain they could catch the ball safely. Perhaps the Pirates were correct by having their players use the helmets out in the field. While it may be awkward for the infielders, it is an added safety measure for those children with poor catching skills. I feel coaches should have the prerogative to use and be supplied with any equipment that will protect their Little Leaguers.

Andrew was actually lucky twice: first, that he had his helmet on to protect him from possible injury and a potentially bad experience that might have made him ball-shy (and robbed us of our eventual star catcher); and second, that the dugout Mom had not shown up that day. She probably would have reminded him to take off his helmet and put on his hat!

# THE HISTORY OF LITTLE LEAGUE

## *1939*

**IN EUROPE,** Hitler's armies marched into Czechoslovakia, marking the start of World War II. In America, the Great Depression tapered to an end, bringing forth a new sense of vitality, strength, and optimism to every fiber of American society. In Hollywood, *Gone With the Wind* and *The Wizard of Oz* exploded onto the silver screen, delighting moviegoers across the country. In Cooperstown, New York, the Baseball Hall of Fame opened, compensating only somewhat for Lou Gehrig's "Farewell to Baseball" speech.

Another momentous even occurred that year, one that would have far-reaching effects for millions of children and adults. It did not make the front page or the radio newscasts, but like a small seedling peeking its head up through the hard ground, it changed the face of America, eventually becoming more important, in a positive sense, than any of the other remarkable happenings of the same year.

In 1939, Little League baseball was born.

Two teams of boys—sponsored by local companies and wearing baggy uniforms—played the first Little League baseball game on June 6, 1939, in the small rural town of Williamsport, Pennsylvania. Carl Stoltz is said to have originated the idea, so his nephews Harold "Major" Gehron (age eight) and Jimmy Gehron (age six) would have a chance to play organized ball. Necessity (once again) being the mother of invention, Soltz recalled his own disappointment when, as a child, he could not play baseball because the older boys dominated the field, leaving the smaller ones with nothing to do but sit on the sidelines and watch. He decided that some day he would start a league specifically for younger boys, so they could compete against each other.

The first Little League consisted of 30 boys on three teams sponsored by Lundy Lumber, Lycoming Dairy, and Jumbo Pretzel Co. By 1989, that number had grown to 2.5 million children, and more than 7,500 programs.

Initially, the rules governing Little League baseball were the same as the adult major leagues'. The field was soon scaled down, however, to a more reasonable size for the players, with a homeplate-to-pitcher's mound distance of 46 feet. To make Little League safer and more competitive, Dr. Creighton Hale studied the game, and intervened to move the mound back two feet. In 1959, he invented the Radial-ribbed batting helmet used even today.

With our men returning home from the battlefields of WWII, Little League quickly spread across the country. In the first Little League World Series, played in 1946 in Williamsport, Pennsylvania, the Maynard Midgets beat Lock Haven, 16-7. Soon, Little League burst outside the U.S. boundaries, with Quebec entering the first foreign team to play the World Series. Little League was introduced to the Orient via South Korea in 1951 and spread with enthusiasm through the Pacific Rim. In 1957, a non-U.S. team won the Little League World Series for the first time, when a young boy name Angel Macias threw a perfect game against La Mesa from California, giving the Monterey, Mexico, team a 4-0 win.

In 1962, Japan sent the first Asian team to the Little League World Series, and five years later, West Tokyo won the title, starting a dominance that would continue until 1982, when, during those 15 years, Asian teams would win the World Series pennant 13 times.

Today, Little League is truly a world sport, with more than 52 countries offering programs. Not only has it helped bring the peoples of the planet a little closer, it has become socially innovative. In 1974, due to the changing social climate, girl teams were introduced to Little League via softball. In the same year, T-ball allowed six- to eight-year-olds to learn the basics of the game in a safe, noncompetitive manner.

America has always had a romance with baseball, and a soft spot in its heart for children, so President Dwight D. Eisenhower's declaration that the second week in June be known as National Little League Week was applauded across the nation. In 1964, the U.S. Congress granted Little League baseball a federal charter, making it the only sport ever to be given such an honor, even to this day. What a fitting tribute to a sport that indeed embodies the American spirit of equality and fair play for all!

# Celebrate the Heroes of Baseball
## in These Other Releases from Sports Publishing!